D1594890

# EMETT

*a step-by-step guide to*
Emotional Maturity Established Through Torah

# EMETT

MIRIAM ADAHAN

F E L D H E I M   P U B L I S H E R S
*Jerusalem  /  New York*

First published 1987
Corrected edition 1999

ISBN 0-87306-410-0

Feldheim Publishers, POB 35002 / Jerusalem, Israel

Feldheim Publishers, 200 Airport Executive Park, Nanuet, NY  10954


www.feldheim.com


*Printed in Israel*

To the memory of my father,
Sol Dann, *z.l.*
who taught me that to lead a meaningful life,
one must have meaningful goals and be willing to fight for them,
and to my mother,
Anne Dann Luborsky
whose love and *joie de vivre* has
always been an inspiration.

In memory of my father and in honor of my mother,
I pledge the proceeds of this book
to charity for the poor in Eretz Yisrael.

# Acknowledgments

I wish to express my profound sense of gratitude to Rabbi Zelig Pliskin, author of *Gateway to Happiness*, for serving as special advisor to EMETT. His broad Torah knowledge, innovative counseling experience, skillful editing, and empathic understanding combined together to greatly enhance this manuscript in numerous ways. EMETT can be viewed as a practical methodology to integrate into one's everyday life the concepts found in his classic works, *Gateway to Happiness* and *Love Your Neighbor*.

There are also many people, too many to mention here, who helped me develop my ideas and assisted in the preparation of this book. I want to thank my sister, Rivka Rothstein, who first gave me encouragement to put out the initial EMETT manual. Also my sister, Judith Karbal, who gave of her time and creative talents to contribute to this book. My brother, Moshe Dann, painstakingly went through previous editions and helped refine my style. Likewise, my friend Susan Weiss. I am very grateful to Rabbi Leo Levi and his wife, Miriam, for their help. Also to Rabbis Elimelech Silberberg, Manos Friedman, and Chaim Citron, who laid the proper foundation for the Torah attitude put forth in this book. I want to thank my daughter, Dalya, who babysat her three younger brothers and uncomplainingly kept our home in order so that I would have time to type. And great appreciation to my husband, Carmeli, without whose support I would not have been able to write this book. I also want to say a special thanks to Avraham Karbal who, with great warmth and wisdom, introduced me to the treasure of *Pirkey Avoth* almost thirty years ago and who has remained an inspiration and a friend. And last, I want to thank the thousands of people who have attended EMETT meetings since we began this method. With courage and determination, they have brought great love and joy into many Jewish homes, have brought light into darkness, and have inspired me with their examples.

Lastly, I owe a debt of thanks to the Recovery Inc. Organization which has given me permission to use their four-step example as the basis for the EMETT method. Several terms used in this method are taken from their book, *Mental Health Through Will Training*, by Dr. Abraham Low.

Miriam Adahan

בע"ה
כסלו תשמ"ה

*Emunah* and *bitachon* breed  peace of mind and are a prerequisite for a happy life. Depression and resentment prevent us from experiencing our *emunah* and *bitachon*. It is a great act of *chesed* to help people attain higher levels of *emunah* and *bitachon*. Mrs. Miriam Adahan has devoted much time and effort into helping people strengthen themselves and view life events as learning experiences. May the Almighty bless her in her efforts to help others, and may she have much success in assisting people to live according to Torah principles in all areas of their lives.

> Rabbi Chaim P. Sheinberg
> Yeshivath Torah Or
> Kiryat Mattersdorf
> Jerusalem, Israel

בע"ה
אייר תשמ"ה

In the humble estimate of the undersigned, Miriam Adahan's work — EMETT — together with her program of implementation of its contents, are a major breakthrough in making available wide and profound Torah teaching to help people overcome tension, anxiety, and conflict, and to help them find healing and refinement of character and soul through the wellsprings of Torah guidance. In an age which is so outer directed, but so much in need of inner guidance for the refinement of our divinely endowed souls, the author and her work deserve unreserved commendation.

> Rabbi Nachman Bulman
> Kiryat Nachliel, Migdal HaEmek
> Israel

# Foreword

Each person chooses daily the quality of his life. You choose your thoughts and behaviors. If your choices are elevated thoughts and behaviors, which include Torah study, trust in the Almighty, love, kindness, and good deeds, you will live an elevated life. If you choose hostile, aggressive, depressing and self-pitying thoughts, and unconstructive behaviors, your life will be full of pain and contention.

The path of Torah is a path of life: compassion, mercy, love, happiness and joy. To travel this path one must integrate and internalize the beautiful Torah concepts which create the elevated and transcendent human being. It is easy to give lip service to high ideals. But only if one puts them into practice will they constantly affect his life. In my counseling experience, I have met many people who could quote the right concepts but they had difficulties in applying them in their own lives. EMETT classes have already proven highly effective in helping those attending to internalize Torah ideals pertaining to emotions and interpersonal relations. With the publication of EMETT, many new classes will be formed and this will give added strength to all those attending.

The four step methodology of EMETT is a wonderful tool for becoming more aware of your initial response to events and for giving you the inner resources to deal with these events in a Torah-consistent manner. Be patient and little by little the method will help you make major improvements.

A word of caution is necessary. The level of any class will depend greatly on the individuality and expertise of the leader and the personalities of those attending a specific group. The classes will be most effective if those attending have compatible goals. Much care should always be taken not to speak *lashon hara*.

I feel confident that the EMETT handbook and classes will help many people to reach higher levels of happiness and loving-kindness in their lives. These traits have a snowballing effect; when you improve yourself, you naturally influence others in your environment in positive ways.

Rabbi Zelig Pliskin

# Contents

# Introduction

This book is an outgrowth of a series of classes which I began in Berkeley, California in 1978. The title of the course was EMETT, which stands for Emotional Maturity Established Through Torah. My goal was to help the women of our small Orthodox community integrate the lofty ideals of Torah into the most minute aspects of daily life and also to foster better communication with each other and our family members. The combination of Torah plus my years of experience in counseling seemed perfect for the development of a nonpsychoanalytic, disciplined method to achieve greater insight and self-mastery. The EMETT method allowed the members to become more emotionally open and honest without excessive self-preoccupation on the one hand while allowing expression of selfhood on the other. From that pilot group came the principles which we felt would help others achieve greater spiritual refinement.

Everything you find in this book is meant to be taken in a total Torah context. If you have doubts as to how best to apply the method to your particular problem, please see a Torah authority. There are no new principles mentioned here. Everything is based on Torah. I have simply tried to facilitate the integration process by bringing examples of how others applied Torah ethics in their daily lives. As with any method, some of the principles can be wrongly used. For example, an attitude of indifference may be adopted when action is needed. Recognize that while this book may seem to provide quick answers, life is never simple. If you are able to integrate the principles only five or ten percent of the time during the first month, you are doing very well. Have patience while the process of change begins to work. Use this book as a guide, but do not hesitate to seek help if you are in the midst of a major crisis or conflict.

Reading this book is like reading an exercise manual. It is important to diligently practice the disciplines. In particular, it takes great effort to discipline your mind to think only those thoughts which will increase your *emunah* and *bitachon* and strengthen your faith in yourself so that you can face loss and frustration with dignity, creativity, and loving-kindness. It is suggested that you read the book first to get a general overview of the EMETT methodology and terminology. Then go back and take the time necessary to internalize and integrate the concepts in your daily life. Don't expect instant success in your biggest problem areas. Self-leadership is a lifelong process and you will always be finding new applications of the principles and new difficulties which call for creative problem solving and insights into your own areas of weakness and unawareness.

# WELCOME LETTER TO NEW MEMBERS

EMETT stands for Emotional Maturity Established Through Torah. It also means "truth" in Hebrew. This name expresses our goal of involving ourselves in an ongoing process of ever greater self-awareness and understanding of each other. We focus on the improvement of our *middoth*, for "All service to Hashem is dependent on mending one's character traits" (*Even Shleimah*, p.17). During our weekly sessions, we review and practice the disciplines necessary to achieve greater inner peace, tolerance, faith, compassion and positivism.

## WHAT OCCURS AT AN EMETT MEETING?

The meetings are structured as follows:

1. Members read from the EMETT book for approximately 15 minutes.
2. Four or five members give examples of how they used EMETT principles when confronted with a stressful event. Following each example, the other members offer "Highlights" — additional insights and endorsements. (Approximately 45 minutes).
3. Question and comment period. (15 minutes).
4. P.E.P. (Positive Experiential Programming). This is an optional relaxation and visualization period.

## WHAT SHOULD A NEWCOMER KNOW?

First, be aware that you cannot understand EMETT from just one meeting. The methodology and language may be unfamiliar, and even confusing to you at first. We suggest that you attend four or five meetings before deciding if you can benefit from EMETT. In addition,

1. New members do not give examples until they have

attended at least two meetings and read a good portion of the EMETT book.

2. No food, smoking, or distracting handicrafts.
3. No discussion of religious or secular transgressions. No discussion of physical or mental abuse or danger. Counseling is recommended for those involved in such serious situations, or those facing major life changes or ongoing difficulties.
4. Refer to the person giving the example as "he" or "she," in order to maximize the latter's ability to listen to the comments and concentrate with objectivity.
5. No advice-giving, moralizing, diagnosing, or criticizing are allowed during meetings.
6. All members of EMETT, including the leaders, are in the group to focus on their own character improvement and to offer encouragement and support to others. If expert advice is necessary, please seek it outside the group.

## WHY IS EMETT SUCCESSFUL?

One of the main reasons for EMETT's success is due to the fact that it is not emotionally suppressive, yet at the same time it keeps members from becoming overly immersed in negative emotional states. Members are free to express their innermost feelings without fear of others being critical. The safe, supportive atmosphere encourages members to be honest. When other members express understanding and respect, the example-giver becomes more self-accepting and aware of his or her inner strengths and hidden potential for growth.

Second, we focus on our successes in dealing with minor stressful events. This builds confidence in our ability to cope with far greater stresses in a positive manner.

Third, EMETT teaches members to look at all events as opportunities for greater self-awareness and refinement. This discipline greatly reduces the degree of anxiety, anger and discouragement which many people experience when faced with frustration and loss.

## WHAT IS THE SPECIAL EMETT LANGUAGE?

EMETT members use a language which is aimed at bringing greater inner calm, *emunah* and *bitachon*, and joy into their lives. The major terms with which you will become familiar are:

TEMPER: Temper is a false perception of present danger, or a fearful, exaggerated prediction of future loss. There are two types of temper: the anxious-retreating temper and the hostile-aggressive temper. To be "in temper" means to be out of touch with reality. Temper prevents us from thinking and acting constructively.

NORMAL RANGE (or "average") means that the situation or people involved are essentially normal, and can be dealt with calmly and objectively. It is the opposite of "exceptional."

TRIVIALITY refers to an event which is essentially harmless, though perhaps annoying or painful. This means that there is no danger to one's physical or mental well-being, and does not involve a major life change (death, divorce, etc.), or transgression of religious or secular law. We want to avoid great emotional involvement in trivialities so that we can devote ourselves to priorities: i.e., Torah and mitzvoth.

ENDORSEMENTS: These are supportive statements which encourage a person's perseverance in Torah ideals.

SECURE THOUGHTS: These are thoughts which encourage a calm, positive approach to stressful events, as opposed to insecure thoughts which promote anxiety, resentment, and self-pity. A disciplined mind, positive goals, and a loving attitude toward self and others help mental health.

# 1.

## Torah Principles:
## The Foundation of EMETT Classes

I have set before thee the blessing and the curse; choose life.

(*Devarim* 30:19)

There are many instances in the Torah which point out the inherent power of free choice given to us all. It is this power which gives us superiority over the animal kingdom and enables us to grow in awareness and understanding. However, there are times when we do not utilize this great gift. Instead of responding logically and constructively to various situations, we react automatically, as if we had no choice in the matter.

For example, you might think to yourself, "Whenever a family member fails to cooperate with my requests for help, I feel unloved and unloving. I often yell angrily or seethe in silent resentment." Or, you may think, "Whenever someone criticizes me, I feel like a total failure and brood about it for hours." You might think that such responses are "natural" and unavoidable and that you cannot help but react as you did. Yet this implies that you are more like a marionette than a free-willed human being.

When you give people, places, and things the power to pull you into a state of negativity, then you have at that moment given away your independence and your power of choice. The degree to which you have given up your power to choose is the degree to which you feel enslaved by forces which you imagine are beyond your control. In order to break these automatic habit patterns, it is necessary to identify them and to work at developing the intellectual and emotional honesty which is necessary for growth. The goal of EMETT is to help you achieve this greater awareness and to teach you a means of maintaining a sense of positivity, *emunah* and *bitachon* even in the midst of distress or loss.

19

The following Torah principles form the foundation of this methodology:*

1. "...freedom of choice is given..." (*Avoth* 3:19).
   Developing ever-increasing freedom of choice in thought, speech, and deed. Overcoming conditioned responses of negativity.
2. "Serve God with joy..." (*Tehillim* 100:2).
   "The Divine Presence does not rest upon a man when he is depressed and worried, nor when he is boisterous, but only when he is possessed of the quiet joyfulness that flows from God's commandments" (*Pesachim* 117a).
3. "Whatever the Almighty does He does for the good" (*Berachoth* 60b; *Orach Chayim* 230:5).
   "A man is obligated to bless Him for the misfortunes which occur just as he blesses Him for the good" (*Berachoth* 9:5).
   Finding the *brachah,* the ultimate good in all that happens to us, however hidden it may seem at the moment.
4. "Love thy neighbor as thyself" (*Vayikra* 19:18).
   Developing love for others. Avoiding bearing a grudge, vengeance, resentment, and hostility.
5. "Judge all men charitably" (*Avoth* 1:6).
   Judging others favorably, no matter how hurt we may feel.
6. "...what does God require of you but to act justly, to love *chesed* and to walk humbly with your God" (*Michah* 6:8).
   Developing a love for acts of loving-kindness.
7. "Do His will as if it were thy will..." (*Avoth* 2:4).
   Giving up our self-preoccupation and selfish desires in order to carry out His will with diligence and determination.
8. "No man bruises a finger down below without it being decreed first in heaven" *(Chullin* 7a)
   Recognizing the *hashgachah* (personal hand of God) in all events.

When things are going smoothly, you may have little difficulty putting these ideals into practice. However, when you are distressed, you may try to deny responsibility for your behavior and blame people, places, and things for your gloomy mood or angry outbursts. It is all too easy to justify bad habits by saying, "I was coerced by a force beyond my control," when that force was merely the selfish desire for comfort or the egotistical desire for domination. It is convenient to say, "I just couldn't control myself," or "It's not my fault. I was provoked." However, this contradicts a fundamental Jewish principle:

_____
* An elaboration of these principles can be found in *Gateway to Happiness.*

Every man is endowed with a free will. If he desires to bend himself toward the good path and be just, it is within the power of his hand to reach out for it....Every man is capable of being as righteous as Moshe...or as wicked as Yeroboam, wise or foolish, merciful or cruel, philanthropist or miser, and so on in all his other tendencies....He alone, of his own free will, with the consent of his mind, bends to any path he may desire to follow.

(*Mishneh Torah, Hilchoth Teshuvah*, V:1-2)

The Rambam's statement is our most important guide in the creative process of self-improvement. When we fail, it is often because we do not have the conscious awareness of the resources necessary to overcome negative thoughts and harmful impulses. This book will help you develop those resources. Then EMETT classes offer the opportunity for constant practice of the disciplines necessary to keep our thoughts and actions in harmony with Torah principles, so that we are able to "turn away from evil and do good " (*Tehillim* 34:15).

## AVOID LASHON HARA IN EMETT CLASSES

Torah sources stress the great importance of avoiding *lashon hara*, speaking evil of others. The Talmud (*Yoma* 9b; *Gittin* 57b, Rashi) specifies *lashon hara* as the cause of the exile of the Jewish people from Eretz Yisrael. EMETT classes provide no exception to this rule. EMETT helps members cope in a confident, creative, and tolerant manner with the most stressful events in their lives. Often, pain, frustration, and disappointment result from people in your immediate environment. You may live, study, or work with people who are impolite, selfish, immature, unaware, bigoted, stingy, or cruel. You can increase your ability to deal with such individuals assertively or with detachment by speaking about such painful situations without divulging the identity of the person. We must not mention anything which would cause other members to think negatively about someone else. This is true even of young children, unless we are mentioning problems within the normal range and commonly associated with the children of their age such as difficulty getting them to bed or getting them dressed. The group leader must stop any hint of *lashon hara* (see *Guard Your Tongue*, by Rabbi Zelig Pliskin, based on the Chafetz Chaim).

However, there are ways to speak about the problem while avoiding the sin:

1. Talk about the situation without mentioning the person:
   "Someone in our building has refused to pay for an expense which all the other tenants agreed to pay."
   "A person I know is very domineering. I just don't know how to be assertive in his presence."

"I did a number of favors for a certain relative and did not receive so much as a 'thank you.' "

2. The leader should encourage members to write a four-step example anonymously. The leader can read this out loud to the group after which members can offer comments. Whether it's a matter of noisy or nosy neighbors, sloppy mates, critical relatives, or an emotionally disturbed in-law, this is one way to gain some relief and insight into how to cope with the problem. Write out the four steps in their entirety. This will encourage other members to do so.

3. Ask a theoretical question as to whether or not certain behavior falls within the normal range, taking care that others should not realize the identity of the person.

4. Find other outlets for your pain. Talk to a Rav or a therapist about your problems.

# 2.

# EMETT: A Method
# for Achieving Self-Leadership

Only as the soul knows itself can it know its Creator.

(Abraham Ibn Ezra)

Each of us is a complex combination of feelings, beliefs, conditioned responses, and inherent personality traits. The more you understand your unique combination of traits, the more capable you will be of harmonizing this complexity so that you can meet the ever changing demands of everyday life in a constructive manner. You do not want to be driven by whim and impulse, nor be swayed by negativity from within your own mind or from external sources. You want to develop the courage to do acts of *chesed* even though they require giving up personal comfort. You want the strength to protect yourself and others from harm even though that may require doing something you fear to do or incurring the disapproval or anger of others. To lead a life of Torah study and mitzvah fulfillment requires continuous acts of self-leadership. Any stressful event can be used as an excuse to lose self-control and to sink into self-pity and resentment, or be seen as an opportunity for self-refinement. The choice is yours.

The goal of EMETT is to help you remember your highest priorities of Torah observance at the very moments when you are most likely to forget them. Such self-leadership will occur more frequently as you study this book. In particular, you will find yourself focusing on two crucial questions each time you face a conflict or crisis:

1. What mitzvah can I perform in the midst of this pain? For example:

   "Instead of yelling at a family member for not being ready on time, I can perform the mitzvoth of remaining silent, of giving the benefit of the doubt, of not harboring vengeful thoughts or bearing a grudge. I can express my feelings respectfully, without hostility, for the sake of *shalom bayith*. While waiting, I can study Torah."

"Instead of brooding gloomily about the money we lost on that business venture, I can perform the mitzvoth of compassion for my husband, of bearing the burden with him, and acceptance of suffering with love and being happy with our portion in life."

2. What particular *middah* can I strengthen at this moment? (Examples of *middoth* are patience, respect, acceptance, gentleness, cheerfulness, industriousness, orderliness, humility, perseverance, resourcefulness, self-discipline, silence, truthfulness, etc.)

"When a friend informed me about a new purchase she had made, I felt a stab of jealousy. Then I thought of how I could use this event to work on the *middoth* of cheerfulness, gratefulness, and humility. My self-pity gave way to a feeling of inner harmony and real happiness for her pleasure."

"When I made that stupid remark, I could feel my self-esteem plummet to zero. But instead of brooding about the event, I thought how this incident would help me be more patient with others when they make mistakes and how I could work on the *middah* of humility by avoiding perfectionism."

"When one of my children said something disrespectful, I felt anger burning within me and wanted to humiliate him in return. But I saw this as an opportunity to practice compassion, to remain silent for a few seconds while the anger subsided, and to use my resourcefulness to find ways of helping him to want to be more respectful instead of creating further resentment by hitting him or making a hostile remark back."

This is not a one-time process. Rather, you will find that as you ask yourself these questions hundreds of times, they will become integrated into your thinking and you will notice that what used to seem like automatic, uncontrollable, negative response patterns will gradually become more and more under your control. And this will happen spontaneously the more you put EMETT tools into practice.

As a child, when you didn't get what you wanted, you often responded with aggression and anger, or by sulking in self-pity. These childhood habit patterns continue into adulthood unless you find other resources to cope with frustration and hurt. Maturity demands that you develop a variety of tactics which will maintain your sense of dignity as well as allow you to treat others in a respectful manner, even if you are in pain. The four-step process explained next is designed to help you bypass the negativity which often accompanies a painful event, or to overcome that negativity as quickly as possible.

EMETT will not make your life stress-free or painless. This is not possible. Nor is it helpful to deny the pain you may be experiencing over various disappointments in your life. What EMETT can do, however, is to help you to cope with pain and stress in a positive manner so that you are freed to reach whatever potential you are capable of reaching at any given moment.

A word of caution: do not push yourself excessively. This is an endless journey. Do not be ashamed that you have imperfections. We all do. Rather, be happy that you have had the courage and honesty to face them and that you have the desire to be part of this exciting process of self-refinement.

## THE EMETT PROCESS

On the next few pages you will find the unique EMETT process for overcoming self-pity, discouragement, depression, and hostility. Do not expect to understand it on the first reading. You will need to read the entire book more than once to understand how and why this method works. It may seem easy on paper, but it isn't in practice, especially when the bills seem unusually high, when people disappoint you, or you are ill and waiting for the results of the medical tests. Yet this is our *avodah* (spiritual work) in this world — to elevate the mundane, to bring Godliness into every aspect of our lives. Jewish history is full of stories of great men and women who practiced Torah principles under the most brutal conditions. Such strength of character is not dependent on luck. It is something which each of us can acquire with patient self-discipline and the awareness of the techniques and resources necessary to meet frustration and loss with the proper Torah attitude.

This book can provide the tools. You then have to make the effort. And that effort cannot be a one-time phenomenon. Like a garden which must be tended daily lest the weeds overtake the flowers or a body which must be exercised in order to keep it from becoming stiff or flabby, these spiritual tools must be used continuously throughout the day in order for you to retain a spirit of tolerance, loving-kindness, and joy in the service of Hashem.

✶　✶　✶

## OUTLINE OF EMETT PROCESS

STEP ONE   The Event: Briefly describe the incident in which you chose to respond with non-constructive behavior (thought, speech, and/or deed). Focus on what is related universally to the other members and on identifying your negative habit pattern when faced with frustration or loss.

STEP TWO   The Temperamental Working-up Process:
   a. Describe your insecure thoughts about present losses or possible future loss or harm to yourself or others.
   Describe your condemnations of yourself and others.
   What do you want that you are not getting from yourself, others, and/or life?
   b. What were your harmful impulses, both active and passive?
   c. What were your upsetting physical sensations?
   d. What were your upsetting emotions?

STEP THREE   Overcoming Temper: Mention a few of the tools you used to bring yourself out of temper (a state of negativity composed mainly of gloomy predictions about the future and condemnations of self and others). Some key ideas are: priorities, choices, trivialities, normal range, distressing not dangerous, compassion, forgiveness, detachment, divert attention, acceptance, lower standards, realism, 1-10 scale, etc.
   What positive muscular acts did you take? (Remember, any act of self-restraint can promote self-respect and inner strength.)

STEP FOUR   Endorsements: What can you endorse for in this example? Mention the positive thoughts and actions you took to overcome "temper."
   Optional: How might you have acted in a similar situation before EMETT training? What *middoth* did you strengthen as a result of the way you handled this event?
   Optional: Close your eyes. Imagine the event and watch yourself responding according to your negative habit pattern. Now, see yourself handling the event with EMETT tools, with flexibility, patience, perseverance, faith, and self-confidence.

## THE EMETT PROCESS

The EMETT process involves giving a brief description of an event during which you chose a negative response, either in thought, speech, and/or action. In order to maximize insight and objectivity, you should choose a relatively minor event. If the situation is more complex, choose just one aspect of it, so that you and the group do not become overwhelmed. In class, we do not discuss issues involving transgressions of religious or secular law, or events which are causing or may cause damage to your own or another's mental or physical health.

STEP ONE: Briefly describe the incident during which you responded with non-constructive behavior. Take two or three minutes to give essential details, such as time, place, and people involved. Make sure that the latter does not involve *lashon hara*. As you talk, focus on what is universal about the event, to make it relevant to the listener and to lessen the storytelling. (The important thing is to identify your individual negative response pattern to events of this type, rather than to relate the particulars of this situation.)

STEP TWO: The Temperamental Working-Up Process
  a. (1) *Insecure thoughts*: "What is your worst possible fear concerning how this event may harm you or someone else in the present?" (The loss can be minor or major in any of the following areas: physical pain or discomfort, material loss, emotional pain from humiliation, rejection or failure, loss of mental capacity or a spiritual loss, some other defect or disaster, or loss of fulfillment in some area.)
    (2) *Condemnations*: "What words would describe your condemnation of yourself or others?" (E.g., "failure," "inadequate," "selfish," "thoughtless," "stupid," "crazy," "brat," "lazy," "immature," "mean."*)
    (3) *Unfulfilled demands*: "What did you want that you were not getting?" (E.g., approval, communication, competency, control, cooperation, health, love, normality, perfection, privacy, respect, sensitivity, stability, wealth, wisdom, absence of problems.)

  b. *Harmful Impulse*: State your harmful impulse, even if you did not give in to it. (Note that some items can be positive or negative, depending on the circumstances.)

---

*All lists on these pages are partial. Add your own items when needed.

(1) *Active*: E.g., argue, complain, criticize, damage property, defend, hit, leave, lie, overeat, speak with hostility, grimace, yell.

(2) *Passive*: E.g., oversleep, "process" (brood, condemn mentally), sulk in self-pity ("poor me"), undereat, withdraw in hostility, denial or apathy, procrastinate.

c. *Describe Your Upsetting Physical Sensations* (E.g., dry mouth, fatigue, heart palpitations, pressure in head, racing thoughts, stomach churning, teeth clenching, tightness in back or face.)

d. *Upsetting Emotions*:

(1) Anxious-retreating temper:

| | | | |
|---|---|---|---|
| afraid | feelings of | left out | sad |
| alone | unreality | "lowered feelings" | |
| ashamed | frustrated | misunderstood | stifled |
| attacked | guilt-ridden | neglected | trapped |
| betrayed | helpless | numb | unappreciated |
| conflicted | hopeless | overwhelmed | "unfaired against" |
| disappointed | humiliated | panicky/ | (by man or God) |
| discouraged | hurt | desperate | unfulfilled |
| disoriented | inadequate | patronized | victimized |
| empty/useless | jealous | unloved | weak/vulnerable |

(2) Hostile-aggressive temper:

| | | | |
|---|---|---|---|
| angry | burdened | disrespectful | manipulated |
| aggravated | cold/unfeeling | exploited/used | punitive |
| annoyed | contemptuous | impatient | resentful |
| bitter | disgusted | irritated | vengeful |

STEP THREE: Self-leadership, *emunah*, and *bitachon*.

Mention the thoughts and actions which overcame temper. For example:

a. *Tools to Acquire Secure, Strengthening Thoughts*: (1) *hashgachah pratith* (*hashlamah*, acceptance), (2) priorities (*ratzon Hashem, shalom bayith*, self-esteem) as opposed to trivialities, (3) choice of attitude (work it up or down), (4) find the good: "it's a *nisayon* — a learning experience, a test, an opportunity for growth." "Focus on the joy of the mitzvah." (5) normal range — averageness, (6) compassion: Judge *"le-chaf zechuth"*; practice forgiveness, "He's doing the best he can with the tools he has"; depersonalize — no *davka*, no deliberate intention to hurt, (7) seek peace, not power: avoid empty ego victories, (8) practice detachment: either divert attention or gain objectivity with the "mental helicopter," (9) is there an issue of right and wrong? (10) bear the discomfort: "It's distressing, not dangerous," function with discomfort; time heals; comfort will come; comfort is a want, not a need, (11) total view, (12) part acts, (13) don't compete or compare to your disadvantage, (14) cultivate the spirit of gratefulness, (15) know that you don't know, (16) "It's temporary," (17) calmness, love, and confidence generate calmness, love, and confidence, (18) humor, (19) have the courage to make a mistake, (20) realism vs. romanticism (e.g. lower standards if necessary), (21) drop the judgment of superiority or inferiority.

b. *Positive Actions*: What mitzvoth did you perform (e.g., studied Torah, prayed, performed acts of *chesed*, etc.) or positive muscular acts (PMA's) did you take to help you overcome temper? (The latter might be: remained silent, walked away, did the thing you feared to do, wore the mask, shared your feelings, acted assertively but without hostility, listened, exercised, spoke softly, hugged the child, did the task without grumbling, etc.) Remember, every act of self-restraint increases self-respect, as long as it is done non-compulsively.

STEP FOUR: Endorsements.

Celebrate the growth. "The smallest victory that you win [over the *yetzer hara*] regard as important so that it may be to you a step to a greater victory" (*Duties of the Heart*, vol. 2, p. 23). Endorse for effort, not success. Possible points to consider:

a. What would you have done in a similar situation before EMETT training? What negative habit pattern did you break in this example?
b. How did your change of attitude lead to a reduction of temper? For example, you may have avoided (1) erroneous beliefs, conclusions, and assumptions, (2) unrealistic ("romantic") demands and expectations of yourself and others, (3) exceptionality, (4) exaggeration of discomfort (awfulizing) and excessive emotionalism, (5) gloomy extrapolation into the future, (6) excessive responsibility, or (7) evasion of responsibility (withdrawal, denial, procrastination, passivity).
c. What *middoth* did you strengthen as a result of this event? (E.g., acceptance, cheerfulness, compassion, courage, decisiveness, diligence, *emunah*, flexibility, gentleness, humility, industriousness, love, orderliness and cleanliness, patience, perseverance, positivity, resilience, respect for others, resourcefulness and creativity, self-discipline, silence, truthfulness.)

THE HIGHLIGHTING PERIOD: After the member has given the example, he or she remains silent while the other members offer "highlights." These are of the following:

a.  Reinforcing the improvement by mentioning the positive thoughts and actions already shared by the member. E.g., "She should endorse herself for mentioning her feelings without temper." "I liked the fact that he helped, even though he would rather not have done so."

b.  Mentioning the EMETT tools which were implied in the example but which the example-giver may not have been aware of using. E.g., "He had the courage to make a mistake since he had no idea at the outset how things would turn out." "She wore the mask because she knew it wouldn't help matters if she told him how she felt at that moment."

c.  Mentioning possible "self-sabotage." E.g., "She said that her example is exceptional, when in reality many of us experience the same thing." "He said he had a 'killer headache,' which was temperamental language."

### SAMPLE A

*Step One:* I borrowed something from a friend and then accidently broke it. That's when I started to work myself up.

*Step Two:* I had the insecure thought that I would be rejected by this friend. I also thought that I'm unreliable. I started to lose trust in myself, to make a blanket condemnation of myself as inadequate. My impulse was not to tell my friend, to withdraw from the whole issue and not deal with it. I had very distressing sensations when it happened: stomach tightness and pressure in my head. My feelings were of anxiety, helplessness, humiliation, and slight panic at the moment it happened.

*Step Three:* I told myself that my priority in life is to do *ratzon Hashem* and for that I must keep my spirits up. I recognized right away that I had a choice of attitude. This certainly is an average experience which happens to a lot of people and my response to it was within the normal range. The total view of myself was that generally I am a very trustworthy and responsible person. I dropped my unrealistic desire for perfection.

Then I did the thing I feared to do most, which was to call the person and tell him exactly what happened. His response gave me another example on which to work, but I'll save that for another time. I also offered to pay, which he accepted.

*Step Four:* The pattern which I broke in this example was that I usually brood for quite a while whenever I do something wrong, as if what I did was so terrible. In the past I definitely tended to over-emotionalize these situations and to extrapolate into the future, thinking that I'll always mess things up and people will always reject me for one reason or another. I stopped those thoughts by recognizing my tendency to put myself down. I worked on the *middoth* of truthfulness, diligence, humility, acceptance, and resilience.

[Following this the group offered "highlights." This gave added encouragement and insight into the sample, using EMETT language such as the sample giver's ability to focus on solutions, not feelings, the recognition of trivialities and the "normal range" behavior involved, and particularly his determination to do the thing he feared to do.]

## SAMPLE B

*Step One*: I asked someone to help me rearrange the chairs in the shul after a *simchah,* but he ran off after mumbling some excuse. That's when I got into temper.

*Step Two*: I had a lot of condemnations of him and the other people who didn't care enough to stay around and help. I was condemning them as irresponsible and self-centered. My unfulfilled desire was for cooperation and unselfishness from everyone. My insecure thought was only that I'd have to do it myself. My impulse was to stew in resentment and a "poor me" attitude. My active impulse was to push the chairs around with a lot more noise than necessary and grumble to the one other person who did stay to help. I felt alone, betrayed, disappointed, devalued, frustrated, humiliated, powerless, self-pitying, unappreciated and unloving. I also felt angry, hostile, bitter, burdened, contemptuous, disgusted, used, vengeful, and disrespected.

*Step Three*: *Baruch Hashem,* I was able to cut into the temper with EMETT tools and divert my attention after quite a struggle with my *yetzer hara.* I saw this as a learning experience and the opportunity to do a lot of mitzvoth, particularly to find mitigating circumstances, take away the *davka,* give the benefit of the doubt, and turn the whole thing into a big triviality. I practiced gratefulness: for the one person who did stay and for my being healthy and strong and able to do this work. I functioned with discomfort until my mask of calmness began to work to produce real calm.

*Step Four*: I'm really working to break this pattern of condemning people who don't act as I want them to. I don't have to hurt others just because I feel hurt. I avoided excessive drama about this situation and worked on the *middoth* of acceptance, cheerfulness, compassion, diligence, humility, positivity, self-discipline, and silence because I avoided all grumbling and *lashon hara.*

### THE "FAILURE" EXAMPLE

*Step One:* I had worked very hard getting everything ready for Shabbath. I asked one of my children to bring me the candles and he said, "I'm too wiped out." That's when I got into temper.

*Step Two:* I let him have it. I didn't control myself. I yelled at him that he thought he was wiped out? Well, I worked so hard...and on and on... I was really nasty to him. I lit candles with a lot of bitterness. My insecure thought was that we would never have a peaceful family life and that I was an inadequate mother. I kept thinking that I would never get control over my angry outbursts and that I had already damaged my children emotionally because of my nasty temper. I was afraid I'd lost all the improvement I'd gained since coming to EMETT classes.

*Step Three:* (a) Then I caught myself in my downward spiral. The truth is that the total view is positive. I've been doing so much better since I came to EMETT and this was the first time I had exploded so angrily in a long time. I used to hit them whenever I was upset with their misbehavior or lack of cooperation, and I have almost completely stopped, with the result that I am in much closer communication with them and they are generally helpful. I have to remember that it's going to take time to undo the damage I've done. I have to endorse for the small gains and for my effort even if I'm not always successful.

*Step Three*: (b) I did a lot of positive muscular acts. I told my son I had made a mistake. At first he pulled away angrily and made a face, but I got him to play a game of checkers with me and after that we were able to talk about what had happened. We reversed roles and replayed the scene when I had asked him for help and he gained insight into my feelings.

*Step Four:* Before EMETT, I would have looked for excuses to stop working on myself. If I had lost control like this, I would have thought, "See, I can't change, so I might as well just go back to being like I was before." I'm dropping my excessive emotionalism about my mistakes and strengthening all of the *middoth* in the list, especially patience, respect for others and diligence.

### THE "NON-TEMPER" EXAMPLE

*Step One:* We've been looking for a new apartment and found exactly what we wanted. It was even cheaper than we had expected and in the perfect location. My husband told the couple that he wanted one day to think it over. The next morning I went back to sign the papers and the lady told me that another couple had taken it the night before! Oy. It was quite a startle. But I went right to Step 3.

*Step Three:* The feeling of disappointment rose and fell as I recognized this as our *hashgachah pratith*. The big thing was that I avoided all anger at my husband. He is cautious and it wasn't his fault. I took the secure thought that we would find something else, maybe something even better. I kept thinking, "I can think thoughts that will bring me tranquility or thoughts which will bring me inner turbulence." I chose the former. I also thought of the mitzvah of being happy for other people's good fortune.

*Step Four:* My past negative response pattern would have been to brood about this for days and certainly to attack my husband, even in front of the children. I always thought that if I was hurt, I had the right to hurt back. I would have walked around with a "poor-me" attitude for days.

(Although the majority of examples should be of the type mentioned in Samples 1 and 2, the leader can, at times, allow "failures" or "non-temper" examples.)

## CHOOSING AN EXAMPLE

Try to choose an example over which you had a strong emotional charge but which, in retrospect, was a relatively minor event. We do this for a number of reasons, chief of which are:

1. If you choose a major, heartbreaking event or serious mental or physical illness, you are likely to feel overwhelmed emotionally and to not have the objectivity to gain insight into what you need to learn from the event. You may want only to have others listen to your pain and share it with you, rather than focusing on the major goal of EMETT, which is the breaking of negative response patterns.
2. The group tends to be overwhelmed as well. It is almost impossible to stay within the fifteen-minute time limit allotted for each example, if the example involves great pain. Thus, other members are deprived of the opportunity to express themselves with their own examples. Also, other members may feel silly when they give a more trivial example after a major one.
3. You will tend to feel discouraged because it is hardest to apply EMETT to such events. The achievement of disciplines such as forgiveness, courage, and accepting pain with love take more time with more painful situations. If you are not successful, you may think that EMETT is ineffective in general and you may not want to continue using the EMETT tools. We want you to feel strengthened from giving an example, not weakened.

Remember, by practicing EMETT on a relatively minor event, you are automatically affecting every aspect of your personality. Your response to any event is only one link in the entire chain of temper. Break it at its weakest point and you have scored a major victory. Also, EMETT is like a spiritual exercise program. If you try to do too much at once, you won't feel successful. Another way of looking at it is to think of EMETT as a desensitization process. If you were terrified of snakes, you wouldn't try to desensitize yourself with a boa constrictor during the first session. You would start with a plastic model from the toy store. So, don't start with your own particular "boa constrictors." Start with something small in that general area.

For example, if you have a certain relative who has been a torment for the past thirty years, do not give that example in group. Instead, give a lighter example about your reaction to other people who produce a similar, though less painful, response. If you have a lot of self-pity over a major painful event in your life, talk about the self-pity you experienced when something less painful didn't go your way. If you tend to explode when you don't get your way with a family member, talk about how you responded when a clerk or other stranger didn't meet your expectations. In this way, you will slowly build up your ability to deal with more difficult events.

Remember, most EMETT leaders are not trained professionals and that EMETT is not meant to be a substitute for therapy. If there is any mental or physical abuse in your life, seek outside help immediately. In the meantime, use EMETT to help yourself learn to be more assertive, to stand up for yourself and maintain your self-respect, and to overcome your anxious-retreating or hostile-aggresive temper whenever possible (see pp. 36–37).

It may be frustrating for you not to talk about the most dramatic, exceptional problems of your life in class. However, if you want to make the most progress, remember that you must start with the small success so that you will be encouraged to go further. Failure to focus on the "workable examples" may be a way of avoiding the responsibility for character development by keeping yourself in a state of discouragement over the major ones.

## DETAILED EXPLANATION OF THE FOUR STEPS

### STEP 1: DESCRIBING THE INCIDENT

Give a brief description of the stressful event to which you reacted with a harmful impulse. The event can be from one of two sources:

a. *Your inner environment*: (e.g. headaches, other physical aches and pains, an emotional "down," fearful thoughts of possible future problems, condemnations of people who aren't acting as you'd like, ruminations about past painful events.)

b. *Your outer environment*:

(1) People (e.g. insults, broken promises, snubs, inefficiency, carelessness, etc.)

(2) Things (breakdowns, losses, mechanical disorders, bad weather, etc.)

When giving this step, focus on your particular automatic, spontaneous response pattern rather than the details of the example. You want to include enough details to make it relevant and interesting to the listener, yet avoid storytelling. The group leader will help you briefly summarize this step in two or three minutes if you are having difficulty doing so. The important thing is to:

a. Identify your negative response pattern and

b. Identify the universal aspect which is relevant to the other members.

| EVENT | NEGATIVE RESPONSE PATTERN |
|---|---|
| "Last week, I got snubbed by someone I thought was a good friend." | "I immediately felt rejected and devalued, and I wanted to withdraw from the whole event." |
| "Again, I noticed a personality trait in one of my children that I don't like." | "I got very angry and wanted to force her to change immediately." |
| "This morning I broke something and ..." | "I started condemning myself." |
| "My wife told me she needed thousands of dollars in dental work." | "I felt humiliated and depressed because I feel like a failure for not having more money." |

While a few more details can be given when necessary, stick to the minimum. The leader can mention something like, "I'm sure we can all identify with this example of a social snub/ getting angry when we see imperfections in others/ making mistakes/ feeling discouraged because of financial pressures. Let's go now into Step 2 to understand the temperamental response."

You might not always have a temperamental response to an event:

"I heard my kids squabbling. I didn't want it to escalate, so I separated them and got each one to choose something constructive to do by himself."

"I woke up feeling a little 'down' but immediately recognized this as temporary and got ready for work, knowing that the mood would pass if I didn't pay any attention to it."

This kind of response is far different from the temperamental one:

"I heard the kids squabbling and exploded at them. I can't stand it any more! It's driving me crazy. I feel like a total failure."

"I woke up feeling 'down' and started snapping at everyone to leave me alone."

The purpose of EMETT is to help you identify and overcome your negative response patterns. If you did not have any negativity of thought, speech, or behavior, choose another incident in which you remember having a harmful impulse to yell, hit, brood, condemn, etc. It's a good idea to take a fresh example from the night before or earlier in the day.

## STEP 2: THE TEMPERAMENTAL RESPONSE

While most people think of the word "temper" as synonymous with anger, EMETT's definition is closer to that of *Webster's New Collegiate Dictionary* (1973 ed.) which is, "A state of feeling or frame of mind at a particular time dominated by a single strong emotion." More specifically, temper is a state of unnecessary or exaggerated emotional pain caused mainly by condemnations of oneself or others, plus irrational demands and unrealistic fears concerning possible future danger or loss. You know you are "in temper" when you experience various distressing feeling states such as self-pity, discouragement, hostility, or jealousy. When you are in temper, you are out of touch with reality. Almost anything — from a sink full of dirty dishes to the sudden appearance of an unexpected guest — can put you into temper unless you diligently practice the disciplines necessary to maintain inner harmony. There are two types of temper:

*The anxious-retreating temper*. This is a state of mind which makes you feel inadequate and discouraged. It makes you want to retreat from people and obligations. It stems from the conviction that you must have everything you want in life and that you must always do well, that to be lacking means to be inferior, and to be inferior means to be unworthy of love, respect, and happiness. In this state of mind, you experience feelings of shame and anxiety. You lack trust in your ability to cope adequately with the normal pressures of life. This attitude can make you submissive or apathetic in the face of danger or abuse. You feel powerless and discouraged. The fear of disapproval and discomfort can also cause you to deny problems which need prompt attention because you fear having to face the disapproval of others who might discover that you are imperfect. On the other hand, it can cause you to exaggerate and dramatize minor aches and pains and grumble about ordinary, mundane chores in order to show the world that you are weak and inadequate and therefore incapable of carrying out your responsibilities (see p. 77).

*The hostile-aggressive temper.* In this state of mind, you feel that you have the right to hurt others because you feel you have been hurt by them. This temper tricks you into thinking that it is best to use force to get what you want, when in most cases, it would be more constructive to talk calmly or walk away. You know you are in the hostile temper when you have even a spark of self-righteous superiority, vengefulness, or desire to dominate others beyond what is called for in that situation. The hostile temper can be as subtle as a condemnatory thought of another ("My goodness! She's so slow! I can't stand it!") or as strong as a violent attack on the person's body or possessions.

Whenever you are in temper, you are responding inappropriately by either overreacting or underreacting. Yet it is not always enough to simply spot that you are in temper. You also need to understand *why* in order to begin changing deeply ingrained habit patterns. The next section will teach you how to examine your beliefs so that you can understand why you act the way you do and then make necessary changes.

### FOUR ASPECTS OF THE TEMPERAMENTAL RESPONSE

When you get into temper over an event, you respond in four ways: insecure thoughts, harmful impulses, unpleasant sensations, and distressing feelings. The "firing order" may be different depending on the event: i.e., you may experience harmful impulses first, such as to throttle someone or to sulk in self-pity; or you may experience the feelings foremost, such as feeling insulted or enraged. At other times, you may first experience a churning sensation in your stomach and only afterwards be aware of your thoughts and feelings. Whatever the particular order for that event, it is important to be in touch with all four aspects of your tempermental response as this is your internal "feedback system" alerting you to the fact that you are in temper. You can remember it by the acronym TISF: thoughts, impulses, sensations, and feelings.

*Insecure Thoughts.* The most difficult, yet the most important work in terms of overcoming temper is to uncover and challenge your insecure beliefs, many of which you may not even be aware of having. What makes this step so all-important is that it is the thoughts which actually produce the particular degree of negative emotional charge which you experience in response to an upsetting event. Obviously, you experience a far different degree of charge if you think an event is going to cause you minor discomfort which will be of very short duration, than if you think that the event will cause you far greater pain and be long-lasting or permanent. For example, you can notice a child misbehaving and think either:

A: "He's just going through a difficult time. When he has eaten a good meal or had a good sleep, he'll be just fine."  Or,

B: "I've had it! I'm sure that he's going to grow up to be a very problematic person!"

You will react far differently depending on your thoughts at the moment. Let's take another example, such as a slight toothache. Think of your response:

A: "It's probably a minor filling which won't cost much money."  Or,

B: "Feels like a major infection in the gums requiring thousands of dollars in payment, hours in the dentist's chair, and terrible pain."

You cannot reduce your emotional "charge" over an incident if you are thinking insecurely until you first get in touch with your thoughts and examine them to see if they are realistic or not. Obviously, if you have a child who really is exceptionally difficult or you are in need of extensive, painful dental work for which you do not have the funds, you are going to feel greater anxiety. However, whether the situation is minor or serious, you do not want to be immobilized by self-pity or anger. You need a clear head in order to figure out how best to solve the problem. This is why it is essential to be aware of your attitude toward the event since any unnecessary negativity or emotionalism can block proper action.

The hardest part about getting in touch with your insecure thoughts is that they are sometimes so fleeting that you barely realize that you have had them. Yet a micro-second thought of, "I'm about to collapse," or "I'm a failure," can produce a long list of harmful impulses and distressing emotions which can last for days or longer. You cannot eliminate those negative impulses or feelings until you begin to work on those attitudes.

Insecure thoughts come at various levels—low, medium, and high:

| EVENT | LOW LEVEL | MEDIUM LEVEL | HIGH LEVEL |
|-------|-----------|--------------|------------|
| sleepless night | minor fatigue | difficulty functioning, minor loss of vigilance | loss of control (leading to damage or injury) mental illness |
| an insult | short-lasting hurt feelings | loss of an unimportant relationship | loss of a very significant relationship |

| EVENT | LOW LEVEL | MEDIUM LEVEL | HIGH LEVEL |
|-------|-----------|--------------|------------|
| illness | minor discomfort | bearable pain | unbearable pain, loss of job, major handicap |
| disappointment | short-term lowered feelings | bearable loss | major loss |

High level insecure thoughts lead to images of death, disaster, divorce or some other permanent handicap. You might immediately be aware of these if someone fails to come home on time or is abusive. Other insecure thoughts are more subtle and are implied in statements such as: "I'm unlucky." "I can't cope." "The situation is hopeless." "I don't deserve this." "I can't stand it!" "I can't go on like this!" "This is awful!" The implication of such statements is that something awful occurred or is about to occur. Other insecure thoughts have to do with possible emotional pain:

> "I'll just die of embarrassment/humiliation/rejection/grief."
> "If I don't get what I want, I'll be miserable."
> "I have to have what I want or I'll lose control and hurt myself or someone else."

Whether it's a full night's sleep or financial security that you want at the moment, the fact that you're not getting what you want often produces insecure thoughts. An insecure thought is a thought that makes you feel bad: it makes you angry, self-pitying, depressed, etc. And you must first uncover those thoughts in order to understand why you are in those negative emotional states.

To help you get in touch with your insecure thoughts, you or the EMETT leader can ask the following questions:

> "What is the worst possible thing you feel will happen if this event continues?"
> "What do you feel you are missing out on by being in this situation at present?"
> "How do you feel you have been **damaged** by having gone through that event in the past?"

The answers may be as follows:

> physical pain: "I'll have to work extra hard." "My body will suffer."
> emotional pain: "I am being rejected, ridiculed, ostracized, humiliated, manipulated."

mental pain: "I'm unfulfilled, unstimulated, and bored." "My mind will get rusty."
material loss: "I'll be impoverished." "Something I cherish will break, get lost, or otherwise be damaged."

The same can be applied to others: E.g., "Those I care about will suffer loss of respect, bodily harm, or other hardship."

There are three main sources of insecure thoughts:

1. *Insecure Interpretations of Present Events:*

| EVENT | INSECURE INTERPRETATION |
| --- | --- |
| "She didn't clean up." | "It's *davka* to get me angry." |
| "He hasn't called for ages." | "He doesn't care." |
| "The house is a mess." | "I'm a failure as a homemaker." |
| "The kids are fighting." | "I'm a failure as a parent." "It's *davka* to get me upset." |
| "I made a stupid mistake." | "I'm stupid." |
| "Someone criticized me." | "It's true. I'm not a worthwhile person." |
| "She nags me to help all the time." | "She's lazy and is trying to take advantage of me." |

2. *Insecure Predictions of Possible Future Losses:*

| EVENT | INSECURE PREDICTION |
| --- | --- |
| "She left the house a mess." | "She'll be a terrible wife when she grows up." |
| "He's very aggressive." | "I'll never be able to reason with him." |
| "I didn't get enough sleep." | "I won't make it through the day." |
| "He didn't eat." | "He'll be grouchy the rest of the day." |
| "I don't feel well." | "I'll always be sickly. It will only get worse." "I'll be permanently sick." |
| "I'm not very efficient." | "I'll always be a loser. I'll never feel good about myself." |
| "I'm not happy at the moment." | "I'll never be happy." |
| "Things aren't going well." | "It's bound to get worse as time goes on." |

"The children aren't cooperating."

"It's going to be wild! Disasters will inevitably happen and I'll be to blame." "I'll collapse."

"The mechanic cheated me."

"People will always make a fool out of me."

3. *Insecure Conclusions from the Past*:

| EVENT | INSECURE CONCLUSION |
|---|---|
| "My mother had a terrible old age." | "When I get old, I'll be helpless and a burden on everyone." |
| "No one ever really cared about me." | "No one can ever care about me." |
| "I was always shy as a child." | "I'll never be able to make friends." |
| "I have never been very disciplined." | "I'll never have control." |
| "I've always been a complainer." | "I'll never learn to be grateful." |
| "I was over-protected as a child and now I hate to work hard." | "I'll always try to get out of having to work hard and as a result I'll never accomplish anything worthwhile in life." |
| "She can't say, 'No.' " | "People will always take advantage of her." |
| "I've made so many mistakes." | "I can't trust myself anymore." |
| "He had a stomachache last week and didn't want to go to school and he has another one today." | "He'll be a lifelong hypochondriac. "He'll use illness to get attention." |
| "My daughter lost something again." | "She'll never be reliable." |
| "I spent the whole week trying to control my screaming habit and still haven't been completely successful." | "I'll never be able to change." |

*Why Is It Necessary to Reveal Insecure Thoughts?* This step is important for many reasons, foremost of which is that once you have exposed your insecure thoughts, it is far easier to determine whether they are realistic or not. Very often, when people are experiencing discomfort or when they fear discomfort in the future, they have a strong feeling of danger. They don't know why they feel threatened, but it seems somehow dangerous not to have things be the way they want. The source is rooted in childhood. Little children often attach danger to minor discomforts such as being embarrassed or not getting some trivial item that someone else has. Also, some people are more naturally inclined toward insecure thinking because of childhood traumas, such as the death of an important person, divorce, high level of strife in the home, or serious illness. For such people, death and disaster were a part of their daily lives. These patterns can continue into adulthood so that even a minor upsetting event such as a pile of dirty dishes or a mildly ill child can push the inner "panic button." The process of EMETT helps people think more securely by substituting calming thoughts for anger- or anxiety-producing thoughts.

It is usually useless to tell yourself or another person who is having high level insecure thoughts to "calm down" or "take it easy." Insecure thoughts automatically produce negative emotional charges and distressing physical sensations, and make it much more difficult to control harmful impulses. Only after the insecure thoughts have been challenged and eliminated can you calm down. Don't be upset if you can't get in touch with your most insecure thoughts right away. This takes time. If you are having a strong emotional reaction to an event, however minor, it means you are having medium or high level insecure thoughts. Look for them.

*Take your Insecure Thoughts to their Final Destination.* If you have a strong emotional charge, keep taking your insecure thoughts to their "final destination" by asking, "And then what will happen?" For example:

> "I'm afraid to take on that project. What's my worst possible fear? That I won't succeed. And then what? That I'll feel humiliated. And then what? That people won't like me. Then what? I can't handle that."

> "Sick kids have kept me up for nights. What's my worst fear? That I'll barely drag myself around tomorrow. Then what? I'll scream at them and hit. Then what? That they'll be damaged for life. They won't love me. I'll feel like a failure."

> "My husband wants me to take his parents into our home for me to take care of since they're old and can't take care of themselves. My worst fear: that I won't have a life of my own, that I'll collapse from overwork, that I'll be tied to the house and never get out. I'm ashamed that I'm thinking these thoughts. My insecure thought is that I'm not a good person for not being totally willing to do this mitzvah and that no one will look after me when I'm old because I feel like this. I'm afraid this will cause a lot of tension in the family."

> "My son didn't do his homework. My fear is that he'll get scolded in school tomorrow and will be in a lot of pain and I'll feel badly for him.

That's all. He's basically a responsible child, so I don't have insecure thoughts about his future. Now I can calm down."

If you are not aware of any insecure thoughts, go directly to "condemnations" or "unfulfilled desires" and you will discover them there in statements such as, "She's always going to be cold and grouchy," or "I'll never have the kind of relationship I want."

*Condemnations.* In this step, acknowledge whatever condemnatory thoughts you had about yourself or others. Some key words which may have popped up into your mind when you were going through the event are likely to have been: "pest," "kvetch," "slob," "lazy," "pompous," "cold," "bully," etc. The most temper-producing condemnation of all is the blanket condemnation of total failure or inadequacy on the part of yourself or others:

"She didn't even return my phone call. What an inconsiderate person!"

"I couldn't control the kids. I'm totally inadequate."

"He didn't offer to help. What a cold, uncaring, mean, selfish person!"

"Look at how she treats her younger siblings. What a bossy brat!"

Condemnations often imply insecure thoughts:

"He's so uncommunicative. What if something is really wrong and he just turns cold and doesn't care? It could be disastrous."

"My daughter is such a slob. Who would want to marry her? Maybe no one! And then she'll be miserable and me too."

"I'm so inadequate. My children will really suffer."

"She's such an approval-seeker that you never get an honest answer because she always tells you what she thinks you want to hear instead of the truth. It's a totally frustrating relationship. It might lead to terrible problems."

"I'm such an idiot when it comes to finances. People will always take advantage of me. I'll never be able to hold things together financially."

In Step 2, you are not concerned with whether or not your insecure thoughts, condemnations, or unfulfilled desires are reasonable and realistic or irrational and exaggerated. Rather, you are simply expressing what went on in your mind during the time you were in temper. It's important for you to acknowledge your temperamental response fully, whether or not it makes sense from an objective point of view. This helps you become more honest with yourself and insightful about what changes need to be made in both attitude and behavior.

*Unfulfilled Demands.* We all have desires about how we want ourselves, others, and life to be. Obviously, these desires cannot all be satisfied. The greater the gap between what we want as opposed to what we have, the greater the degree of temper, i.e., anger and anxiety. In order to narrow that gap and become more realistic about what can be fulfilled and what cannot, it is important to first identify the demand. They usually fall into three general categories:

- power (over our bodies, over others, over life, to make things go smoothly, etc.)
- pleasure (physical comfort, positive emotions, enjoyable and uplifting mental stimulation, play, variety and excitement, relaxation, health and wealth, etc.)
- prestige (approval, respect, cooperation, honor, etc.)

At this point in the example, simply state your unfulfilled desire without being concerned as to whether it can be classified as realistic or not. Often, just by stating it, you will become more aware of your need to accept what is unalterable or your need to increase your *hishtadluth* (determined perseverance toward change):

"My mother is very sick and I'm exhausted from taking care of my family and running back and forth to the hospital. What I want is for no one to ever get sick!"

"I want to have a stress-free life and no demands on me so that I can sit and study without worrying about what's going on at home."

"I just want one good night's rest."

The reason that "unfulfilled desires" is placed in the same section as "insecure thoughts" is that your insecure thought may be simply that you won't get what you want. And perhaps by not getting what you want, you or those you love might suffer harm. For example:

"I'll lose control, and everything will fall apart and someone will get hurt."

"I'll be physically uncomfortable and won't be able to stand it."

An unfulfilled desire also can be in the realm of emotions. For example, many people feel lonely because they cannot share their thoughts and feelings with those closest to them. It is common not to share the same perception of reality with one's spouse, to feel differently about child-rearing, the optimal degree of orderliness necessary in the home, and financial matters. This leads to the emotional pain of feeling misunderstood, unloved, unappreciated and alone. The "unfulfilled desire" may be for greater communication and emotional intimacy. The desire for a "shared reality" may be as unattainable as the desire for a million dollars.

Simply being aware of the desire is important in terms of identifying the source of your pain. The next step is to let go of what you cannot have or to try to get what you want. This same principle applies for all desires, whether for financial security, physical health, or personality changes in yourself and others. Only when you are out of temper can you put the words of Rabbi Mordechai of Lekhivitz into practice:

> If things do not go the way you wish them to be, you should then wish them to be the way they are in reality.
>
> *(Mi-gedoley Ha-Torah Ve-ha-chasiduth,* vol. 20, p. 107)

*Harmful Impulses.* All people have harmful impulses at times, both of aggression and indifference. When someone wakes you up from your Shabbath nap prematurely, you may want to throttle that individual. When an appliance breaks down, you may want to kick it. You may sometimes want to withdraw into bed or inactivity for days or find excuses not to meet important obligations. Thankfully, most people overcome their harmful impulses and respond constructively. However, when you are aware of a harmful impulse, either active or passive, it is important to be in touch with it even if you did not act on it. Thought leads to speech and speech to action. So the mere thought of harming yourself or another might some day lead to action, since you have planted that seed in your mind. By identifying your destructive patterns, you can understand what is leading you to have these impulses, and thereby be able to restrain them more easily.

It will sometimes happen that you have an almost automatic impulse to harm as your immediate reaction to an event, even before you have insecure thoughts or distressing feelings. For example, if you were hit often as a child, your automatic impulse may be to hit your own children. Or, it may be the opposite: you may be overly indulgent out of fear that if you don't give people everything they want, they might hurt you in some way. Thus, while no conscious thought may be connected to the present impulse, it may help you to go back into your own personal history to discover what might have produced these present habits.

| EVENT | POSSIBLE HARMFUL IMPULSE |
|---|---|
| "When I think people are doing something *davka,* | I get very angry at them." |
| "When I am in discomfort, | I adopt a 'poor me' attitude and sulk." |
| "When I don't get proper respect, | I get angry." |
| "When I feel powerless, | I explode." |
| "When the house is a mess, | I feel inadequate and start screaming." |

| EVENT | POSSIBLE HARMFUL IMPULSE |
|---|---|
| "When I am disappointed, | I overeat." |
| "When I make a mistake, | I brood for hours, then get hostile." |
| "When I notice an imperfection in someone else, | I spend at least a few minutes condemning him mentally." |
| "When I notice an imperfection in one of my children, | I blame myself and think it's permanent and then get very angry." |
| "When a family member wastes money, | I have to give him a lecture, make him feel really bad, and punish him in some way." |
| "When anyone asks me to do anything, | I feel I must do it immediately." |
| "When someone disapproves of me, | I get nervous and compulsive about winning the person's approval." |
| "When a child or my wife asks for help, | I refuse because I'm afraid that if I give an inch, they'll take a mile." |
| "When I see my daughter-in-law pampering her children (or treating them harshly), | I want to dominate her and force her to take my advice." |

When mentioning your harmful impulse, recognize that it might not be harmful under different circumstances. Sometimes it *is* the best thing to go to bed and get some rest. At other times, that would be an evasion of responsibility. Sometimes it is best to speak up and talk back. Other times, it's best to be silent and walk away. At this stage, you are mentioning what was negative for *you* at the time. If you are generally a confrontational, argumentative person, it might be a harmful impulse to always give in to that habit even if in the same situation a more passive person might find it harmful to avoid confrontation and argument. You need to work on your own *middoth* and do what is best for your own growth. That is why you will sometimes find that what is harmful for you is not so for another. Anything you do obsessively or compulsively — from cleaning the house to being stingy — stems from insecure thoughts and bad habits. By recognizing these patterns, you can more easily begin to break them.

At times you may not know if an impulse is harmful or not:

"Am I going needlessly to the doctor for this minor pain or is it good to be cautious?"

"Does this child really need my attention right now, or am I giving in too often?"

"Is this an act of sincere self-sacrifice or is it masochism?"

"Am I being kind or a push-over?"

"Am I being protectively assertive or overly aggressive?"

"Am I being meticulous or petty-minded and compulsive?"

These are questions which each member must answer for himself. Do not allow others to make that decision for you. When in doubt, think of what your past habit pattern has been and practice going against it at times. For example, if you always have to have everything in order, practice letting go a bit in order to spend time giving to others. If you are generally passive and unassertive, practice standing up for yourself. Doing the opposite of your past habit pattern may not seem "natural" at first, but it will help you gain insight into the source of your fears and bring you greater inner harmony.

When describing your impulses in class, it is important to recognize that in overcoming your bad habits, you may have to be satisfied with small increments at first. For example, if your past habit was to hit your children when they are uncooperative, then one step up may be to just yell. One step up from that may be to yell for a shorter period, or to delay it for a few minutes. If your past habit pattern is to fall apart whenever the house is a mess, then one step up might be to tolerate small messes without exploding, yet not fault yourself for reverting to your old habit pattern when there is greater disorganization and chaos. If you are hypersensitive to criticism, you might find yourself brooding in painful self-pity for two hours instead of two days. This is why a harmful impulse for one may not be so for another.

*Distressing physical sensations*. It is important to identify where you feel symptoms when you are in temper. Temper often manifests itself in physical symptoms. These inner tip-offs will alert you to the fact that you are perhaps subconsciously upset about something.

> *Example*: I went to the dentist with a terrible toothache. I had the insecure thought that it was really something serious. But he said that the pain was only the result of grinding my teeth at night. He asked what was going on in my life which was upsetting me. At first I denied that there was anything. It took me a while to realize that there was something going on that I was reluctant to face.

> *Example*: I tend to overwork myself and then collapse. Now I realize that just before my breaking point, I get lower back pain. If I spot that pain before it gets strong, I can take a few minutes out to relax.

On the other hand, you may be feeling jittery, "blue," or fatigued not because of temper but because of lack of vitamins, hormonal swings, weather sensitivity or a host of other factors. If the physical symptom is not relieved with EMETT tools, consult a qualified expert and do not rely on self-diagnosis.

*State your upsetting emotions.* This is your opportunity to describe how you felt about the event. Don't worry about how you think you should have felt or should be feeling. Do not deny your feelings, as they are important indicators of your state of mind at any given moment. Having an upsetting emotion is a little like having a flat tire. It is not useful to say, "I'm going to pretend that it's not there and keep on driving." The fact is that something is wrong. Don't suppress your pain. Only after you have acknowledged the problem are you able to do something about it. Be honest:

> *Example*: "I felt resentful when she didn't call to find out how I was after the operation. As a matter of fact, now that I look at this list, I also felt left out, unloved, betrayed, disappointed, hurt, and vengeful."

> *Example*: "When I saw that he hadn't done what I had asked, I felt helpless and even a little hopeless about our relationship. I was jealous of people with better relationships, had lowered feelings, felt 'unfaired against' and victimized. And then I got vengeful. I wanted to give him the silent treatment for a few days."

Feelings of fear and anxiety usually underlie hostility and anger. List your emotions from whichever was strongest at first and then go to the other ones. Many of the emotions on the list are combinations of feelings plus thoughts. Obviously the thought, "This child is trying to exploit and manipulate me," is going to produce far different emotions than the thought, "This child has an emotional need right now for reassurance and communication." However, at this point in the four step method, simply state how you felt. When you get to Step 3, you will then become aware of how certain negative thinking patterns automatically produce various unpleasant emotions.

## STEP THREE: OVERCOMING TEMPER

Mention the major tools which helped you overcome your temper. Look over the list to help you remember which ones were most powerful at that particular time. For example,

> "I recognized that it is our *hashgachah pratith* right now to have this added expense and that my response to the financial burden is definitely within normal range. The important thing was that I focused on my goal in life which is to do *ratzon Hashem*. I didn't take out my frustration on others. I took the total view of my life, which is that things are generally positive and I usually cope well. I recognized that the feelings of

discouragement and helplessness were temporary and that I could go on and function with this discomfort and do what had to be done even though I had uncomfortable feelings."

"I gave her the benefit of the doubt. I showed compassion even though I was burning inside at the moment. I took away her intention to hurt me and recognized that she herself is in pain right now and simply took it out on me. I thought of the phrase, 'calmness generates calmness,' which is exactly what happened. I wore the mask of calmness until I did actually feel better. It was definitely distressing, but not dangerous."

Mention the mitzvoth and positive muscular acts which you did at the time:

"I studied Torah and my anger subsided."

"I didn't return an insult with an insult."

"I didn't cry." Or "I cried and then I felt better."

"I went outside and took a brisk walk until I calmed down."

"I decided to bake a cake and go over there and ask for forgiveness."

"I turned on a tape of Chasidic music and diverted my attention while I did the dishes."

"I decided to put my mental health first and not be compulsive about the housework."

"I looked in the mirror and suddenly felt so old. I decided right away to perform the mitzvoth of gratefulness to Hashem and loving-kindness to others in order to divert my attention from gloomy thoughts."

Mention the habit pattern which you broke in this example:

"It used to be that when I was hurt, I would sulk in self-pity. This time I diverted my attention and went on with my life."

"I used to think that if I was feeling a little blue, I had to give in to it. This time, I got myself going by putting forth energy."

"I thought that you had to scream at kids when they did something wrong. This time, I wrote it down in a notebook and at night, when everything was quiet, talked about it."

Mention the thought patterns which you avoided:

"I didn't emotionalize the mess. I didn't jump to the erroneous conclusion that because the house isn't neat that means I'm inadequate. And I avoided extrapolating into the future and thinking that it's always going to be like this."

Mention the *middoth* which you strengthened as a result of the event. Even if you did not achieve total success in your example, just the awareness of the need for change and for self-improvement is endorsable. You can always find at least one *middah* which you displayed during your example. Look for it! It will lift your spirits and encourage you to grow.

## THE INITIAL RESPONSE VS. THE WORKING-UP PROCESS

It is important to distinguish between the initial response to an event as opposed to the temperamental working-up process. The initial response is composed of whatever thoughts, impulses, sensations, and feelings erupted spontaneously, over which you had no control — a "flash" lasting only a few seconds:

> "I instinctively jumped back when I saw that big dog running toward me."
> "The blood drained from my face when I heard the news."
> "I was startled when I looked at the clock and saw how late it was."
> "I stiffened when he told me how much it would cost."

Any shock, disappointment, loss, or frustration will spark an initial response. Your task is to avoid working it up into a temperamental explosion or implosion, which is what would happen if you let your imagination go wild with insecure thoughts, became engrossed in condemnations, or gave in to the impulse to hurt yourself or others. If you can catch yourself at the moment of startle, before there is any negativity or panic, you can often bypass temper and go right to Step 3, focusing on constructive solutions or "turning chilly" to situations over which you have no influence.

To a large extent, we are not responsible for the harmful thoughts and impulses which arise in us at times. Therefore, we need not feel guilty for them. (See *Shi'urey Da'ath,* vol. 3, p. 67.) However, we are responsible for entertaining those thoughts or giving in to the impulses. Any initial response can be worked up or down. The more quickly you become aware of your initial response, the more quickly you can work it down by avoiding fearful predictions and unnecessary judgmentalness which keep temper alive. Of course, this does not apply if there is real danger or the possibility of major loss, when it is appropriate to feel anxiety.

In the beginning of EMETT training, you will still indulge in your old habits — criticizing, complaining, sulking, or withdrawing. However, the awareness of your ability to control yourself will often result in a less intense or shorter temperamental reaction. You may yell, but not as loud or as long as you wanted to initially. You may brood resentfully about some incident, but only for five minutes instead of five days. In time, your response pattern will change in proportion to the extent to which you practice EMETT tools.

Eventually, situations which used to spark a strong negative reaction will produce only a slight response or none at all.

Your initial response may change from day to day, depending on how much stress you are experiencing at the moment. Other initial responses are deeply ingrained, having to do with social conditioning or inborn sensitivities. These may or may not be open to change.

> *Example*: I tried to overcome my extreme sensitivity to noise, but without success. However, I now control my hostile outbursts toward those who make noise and take preventive measures by wearing ear-plugs to sleep and avoiding noisy events when possible.

> *Example*: A neighborhood bully had been terrorizing the children on the block. My initial response was to be mean to him like everyone else. But I overcame it. I invited him into our home each day, spent time talking to him, and bought him some inexpensive gifts. Gradually he improved. For a while, my initial response was still negative, since he was often quite unpleasant to be around, but I worked it down for his sake and for the sake of society at large. I knew that only by showing him love would he be able to be loving.

> *Example*: I asked my husband if he would like to visit my relatives and he said, "No." Then I told him, "That was your initial response. Now, will you consider it for a minute and let me know again." And he said, "Well, you said it so nicely, I think I'll go with you."

> *Example*: When I saw that the neighbor had used my parking space again, I was filled with rage. I told myself that that was my initial response and that I needed to work it down before going to talk to him.

As you can see, there is a big difference between:

a.  the immediate sensory response, startle, or discomfort,
b.  the realistic pain, loss, or discomfort involved in the event,
c.  the temperamental working-up process, with a resistance to or denial of reality,
d.  a full acceptance of the realities of the situation.

At times, you may be able to go from "a" to "d," with no pain whatsoever.

> "I was criticized, but realized the person was tired and didn't really mean it."

Or, you may go from "a" to "b" and then to "d."

> "I was criticized. My feelings were hurt. But I quickly gave her the

benefit of the doubt, realizing that she's been under so much pressure lately."

Or, you may go through the entire process:

"I was criticized. My feelings were hurt. I started condemning her for being so insensitive and mean. I felt devalued, hostile, and angry. I wanted to say something mean back but controlled myself. Finally, I realized that she didn't mean any harm. She really thinks she has my best interests at heart. I told her to try to be more tactful."

### RECOGNIZE YOUR DEEPLY INGRAINED HABIT PATTERNS AS INITIAL RESPONSES

The hardest habits to change are those which you consider almost a part of your very nature. It will take much patient effort to undo these:

*Example*: I used to tell people that I had a Ph.D. in self-pity. Once I recognized the problem, I could catch myself in that pattern every time I didn't get what I wanted. I would drum it into my head night and day that the only way to overcome this bad habit was through constantly cultivating a spirit of gratefulness and seeing something positive in all that happened to me. I even kept a "Happiness Notebook," in which I wrote down the good things that happened each day to stop my grouchiness and pull me out of my lowered feeling states.

# 3.

## General EMETT Principles

### DISCIPLINE YOUR MIND: THINK , DON'T PROCESS

Inner peace and self-refinement can only be achieved through the continuous practice of many specific mental disciplines. All these disciplines involve making choices — in particular, to think positively, with *emunah* and *bitachon*, or negatively, with self-pity and resentment. In order to begin the process of disciplining the mind, it is important to remember that you have the choice as to what to let into your brain and what to keep out. It has been estimated that the average person thinks about ten thousand thoughts a day, many of which go in and out without any conscious, intelligent discrimination and supervision. Just as we are scrupulous in the observance of laws of *kashruth* and what we put into our mouths, so too must we be careful to keep our thoughts kosher, to monitor our mental processes.

One of the most destructive habits in which we all engage at times is what we call "processing." This is insecure, negative brooding which inevitably leads to temper. When you "process" thoughts, your mind may be racing madly like a ticker-tape machine or crawling along slowly, gloomily reviewing past failures, present difficulties and possible future predicaments. Processing makes you feel helpless, hopeless, and hostile. Constructive thinking, on the other hand, helps you face your problems realistically, with confidence and objectivity. Learn to recognize when you are processing, as opposed to thinking. Processing can take many forms:

"I was standing there washing the dishes and wondering if my children would think negatively about me when they grow up."

"I was waiting in line, brooding about many of the failures and mistakes of the past."

"When I saw that my son forgot his lunch, I processed for hours whether it would be over-indulgence to bring it to him or cruelty not to. I eat myself up either way."

"I'm just eating myself up thinking about that relative who snubbed me at that wedding the other night."

"I could just kick myself for not getting that item when it was on sale. I think about it all the time — how stupid I was for procrastinating."

"It's been thirty years and I still can't forgive him for not helping me out when I asked for money."

"It just eats me up that we don't do more together as a family."

"I eat myself up thinking about what might happen if..."

"I keep going over and over all the things that were wrong with my childhood."

Just as you do not allow destructive people into your home, so too must you be disciplined not to allow destructive thoughts into your mind. Instead of processing:

1. Get in the habit of asking yourself, "Is this thought I'm thinking right now going to make things better?" "Is it helping me to work things out or making me more discouraged?"
2. Be forgiving of those who may have hurt you in the past. Let go. It's gone. It is of no use to carry around those old resentments.
3. Make lists, organizational charts, reward and incentive systems, chore schedules, and set periods for family conferences in order to work things out in a calm and respectful atmosphere instead of brooding about why things aren't going more smoothly.
4. Engage in physical activity: vigorous physical activity often stops the brain from dwelling on negative thoughts.
5. Recognize your particular areas of processing (e.g., old age, money, appearance, etc.) and stop yourself assertively with a firm command to divert your mind toward constructive solutions.
6. Don't review the past with shame and blame or preview the future with anxiety. Learn from the past and prepare for the future.
7. Change your attitude so that you learn to see every situation as having potential for growth. Don't deceive yourself into thinking that a bad situation is acceptable when you have power to lead a happier life. However, when you have no choice of action, look for the good.
8. Take action: consult a Rav, go to a lawyer, exercise your body more, talk to experts about the problem, change jobs, take a vacation, make your life more interesting with classes and projects so you have less time to process.

9. Don't think, "It's awful," when you really mean, "It's uncomfortable."
10. If you are experiencing negativity, use it as a learning experience, to learn more about what puts you into a temper and how to avoid it next time.

One of the positive results which this discipline will give you is greater self-control and objectivity. Instead of reacting impulsively and compulsively to stressful events, you will find yourself saying, "Wait, let me see what's going on here before I make my usual condemnations or react with hostility and discouragement."

> *Example*: When my daughter told me she wanted to wear her Shabbath shoes to school, I caught myself processing, "Why does she always have to argue about everything? What's going to be with this child? How can I go on with these constant conflicts?" I broke into my processing and became objective. I said to myself, "Wait, she simply doesn't want to wear her old shoes. I can understand that. Let me figure out a solution which will get her to save those good shoes for Shabbath alone."

> *Example*: When I saw that there was no mayonnaise in the fridge, I was about to talk gruffly to my wife about her failure to keep staple food items stocked at all times as I like. Then I thought, "Wait, is the mayonnaise more important than *shalom bayith*?" "How can I get family members to write used-up items on the shopping list so that this doesn't happen?"

> *Example*: I had a difficult childhood — a lot of yelling and hitting and general strife and chaos. I used to spend a great deal of time processing how terrible things were in the past, how unhappy I was in the present, and how awful things were bound to be in the future. It was only with a great deal of discipline and a strong will that I trained myself to avoid dwelling on the past or the future and instead to think, "How can I make this moment meaningful? What mitzvah can I do, what thought can I think, which will bring me or someone else greater happiness?"

There are times when you will have to use the greatest of efforts to stop processing an event. Over and over you will have to tell yourself, "I make the firm decision definitely NOT to think about

"...the time I lost all that money."
"...the time she hurt my feelings."

Rabbi Salanter said, "According to the Torah, we should only think about other people when we want to help them in some way" *(Chayei Ha-mussar,* vol. 1, p. 107). That means you avoid "processing" about other people's personalities or motivations unless it leads to greater understanding and compassion and to help them in some way.

## LET THE MUSCLES TEACH THE BRAIN: POSITIVE ACTIONS OVERCOME TEMPER

> One should practice again and again the actions prompted by the proper attitudes...and these dispositions will then become firmly fixed in his soul.
>
> *(Hilchoth Dei'oth,* I:7, p. 48a )

The above principle is extremely important for us all. Whenever you feel lethargic, gloomy, or unloving, you can overcome negativity by doing something positive. Calmness generates calmness. A loving act toward someone makes you feel more loving. Confidence generates greater confidence. Perform some positive act even if it seems forced or insincere at the outset and you will eventually lessen the gap between where you are and where you would like to be. A positive muscular act can override the mind's negativity, proving that you are not as helpless, fearful, or inadequate as you thought you were a few minutes before. Whisper when you are angry; give someone to whom you are feeling hostile a small gift; force yourself to take a brisk walk when you are suffering from temperamental fatigue; do something which requires self-discipline when you feel low; breathe calmly when you are tense, etc., for

> Minds are shaped by deeds.
>
> *(Sefer Ha-chinuch,* precept 16)

Temper dies a natural death when you force yourself to make positive muscular acts (PMAs). PMAs can conquer negativity when the mind is in a downward spiral. If you tell yourself, "I can't look for a job until I have more self-esteem," you will become less confident because doing the thing you fear to do is what builds confidence. If you wait for the confidence to come first, you will only sink further into apathy and feelings of inferiority. Likewise, you might say, "When she acts more loving, then I'll be nicer to her." Don't wait. Show compassion and appreciation and you will awaken love.

> A person comes to love the one to whom he gives....When demands begin, love departs...make demands upon each other, your happiness is at an end.
>
> *(Strive for Truth!,* pp. 130-132)

When you feel anxious or endangered and know that the fear is not based on a present reality, do something which requires calm controlled movements, such as breathing slowly or singing an uplifting song. The muscles will teach the brain that there is no danger. The more you feel out of control, the more anxious you will be. Therefore, *any* act of control will lessen anxiety, even if you are involved in an event over which you actually have little or no power, such as an unexpected delay, illness, or irritating situation. The best cure for many types of depression is disciplined activity.

> Just as zeal can result from enthusiasm, so enthusiasm can create zeal. As a result of the willed quickening of his movements, there will arise in him an inner joy....If, however, he is sluggish in the movements of his limbs, the movement of his spirit will die and be extinguished.
>
> *(The Path of the Just, p. 89)*

There was once a famous general who seemed to be the epitome of self-confidence. Only after his death was it revealed in his memoirs that he waged an inner battle as fierce as the outer ones he fought. He wrote that when he would experience anxiety, he would tell himself, "Tremble fool, but walk on!" So too must we often "walk on," overcoming shyness, inertia, anxiety, and uncertainty. By "doing the difficult," the difficult will seem less formidable. A determined muscular effort to do something positive when the mind is filled with negativity will overcome that negativity. You may have a *yetzer* (self-centered passion) to avoid putting forth the effort to do an act of *chesed* or to restrain the impulse to criticize. Somehow, you manage to overcome laziness, fear of rejection, and selfish egotism. You restrain yourself and act in accordance with God's will. It is only after you have done what is right that you feel the inner glow of strength which comes from overcoming your baser desires. The muscles teach the brain that you have the power to control yourself, that you are not as weak or incompetent as you thought, and that you are capable of growth.

Any act of self-discipline will promote self-esteem and will be self-strengthening as long as it is done from conscious choice, and not from compulsion (i.e., neurotic need to punish) or from blind habit.

> *Example*: We made *aliyah* six months ago. It hasn't been easy and we were getting discouraged at the bureaucratic red tape and cramped quarters. We sat around and complained, making each other feel worse with all our indecisiveness and feelings of inadequacy. Finally, I decided to make some firm decisions and take the consequences, whatever they would be. By acting with firm determination, which was partly bluff at first, we felt imbued with greater enthusiasm and confidence.

> *Example*: My doctor told me that my feelings of despondency would be greatly reduced if I would exercise vigorously three times a week for half an hour. I've always hated to exercise. It took an incredible act of will power to get myself out of my house and to the exercise class. However,

once there, I felt invigorated and more clear-headed and joyful. When I move my muscles in a healthy manner, my brain gets the message that I'm not in as bad shape as I thought.

*Example*: I had a nasty run-in with a neighbor. The last thing I wanted to do was go over and make peace. But I did it anyway. It was a real effort for me to push my feet forward and talk calmly, even though I felt cowardly inside. Even though the neighbor responded with hostility, I felt that I had won an inner victory.

*Example*: My old habit is to keep quiet if something bothers me. I've never believed in sharing my feelings with others. But recently something hurt me very much. I decided to break an old pattern and talk about how I felt. I was embarrassed at first. I thought I would be looked down on for admitting how resentful, angry, and disappointed I felt toward someone who had always thought I was such a "together" person. But afterwards I felt more real, more human, and I was able to feel the warmth of human contact which I had denied myself when I was so emotionally suppressed.

*Example*: My response is to cry a lot and give in to hostility whenever I feel depressed or overwhelmed. But when I started to get lowered feelings last week, I decided that I was going to smile a lot and avoid the temptation to make everyone suffer along with me. I kept my inner distress to myself and was extra nice to everyone, even though it felt insincere at times. The result was that I began to feel stronger and to regain my self-respect. The "down" was over more quickly than usual.

## AVOID TEMPERAMENTAL LANGUAGE: IT LEADS TO TEMPERAMENTAL ACTIONS

Your words have a tremendous influence on your thoughts and actions. Imagine, for example, what would happen to a teacher if he thought before entering the classroom, "I just can't control these wild kids. They're not responsive to anything I say. I die every time I think about going in there. What a catastrophe." Think of the effect such thoughts would have on his performance. The same is true for you. You free yourself from the tyranny of temper only as you learn to recognize and avoid all thoughts which promote insecurity and discouragement. Avoid the sloppy use of emotionally-charged words. Discipline yourself to use a spoken and unspoken language of security and faith. Especially avoid the following:

1. Words which promote *excessive emotionalism*: "A *killer* headache." "I just wanted to *die* of embarrassment." "What a *catastrophe* when the

caterer forgot the cake." "Look at this living room — it's a *disaster* area!" "How *tragic* that you missed the lecture." "I'm about to go *crazy*!"

2. *Exaggerations*: Words like "always" and "never" are rarely true. Does your mate "never" help? Does the child "always" argue with everything you say? Do you "never" feel happy? Such words keep you worked up in anger and anxiety. Even the words "very" or "oy" can be exaggerations which spell the difference between calm problem-solving and inner turbulence. Is the child doing "very" poorly or is he actually doing an average job which needs temporary special attention? Are you really going to "throttle" the kid, or do you want to say that you are very very frustrated at that moment?

3. *Extrapolation*: Words which keep you worked up about possible future disasters should be avoided.

> "I don't give my child attention because if I give an inch, she'll take a mile."
> "My boys are 2, 4, and 6. When I think of the appetites they have now, I shudder to think of what our food bills will be when they're teenagers."
> "I'm only thirty-seven and have a slight case of arthritis. I get depressed thinking about how crippled and helpless I'll be when I'm eighty."
> "When the doctor told me that I had given birth to a girl, my first thought was how are we going to pay for another wedding!"
> "Look what a mess her room is! No one will want to marry her!"

It is useful to think of future plans in order to formulate constructive activities for improvement. But if thinking about the future gets you worked up, divert your attention.

4. *Exceptionality*: Avoid words like "crazy" or "severely handicapped" unless they are true. Avoid words that make you or those around you think that their present behavior is outside the normal range, unless it really is.

5. *Emergencyizing*: Don't make yourself or those around you anxious about doing something "right this second" unless it's true that it must be done right now.

6. *Evasion of responsibility*: Don't say "I can't" when the truth is that you don't care to. Don't say, "I have no strength, time or energy to do it," unless that's true.

There are times when temperamental language is more frequent. One is when you may be suffering from what can be termed "lowered feeling tones." Like the musical scale, feelings also have different "tones" — enthusiasm, excitement, anticipation as opposed to dullness, boredom, and apathy. When you are having lowered feeling tones, life may look grey and you may feel listless. Do not attach danger or permanence to lowered feelings. It is normal and natural to have highs and lows. Let them come and go without attaching excessive drama to either. You have a choice to think :

| | | |
|---|---|---|
| "I'm feeling terribly depressed." | vs. | "I'm having temporary lowered feeling tones." |
| "I'm totally shattered." | vs. | "I'm very disappointed." |
| "I'm about to collapse." | vs. | "I'm very tired." |
| "I can't stand this!" | vs. | "This is distressing, but bearable." |
| "What a brat! She's so spoiled!" | vs. | "That's challenging behavior. We have a problem which calls for a solution." |
| | | "She's a normal kid who just doesn't like frustration." |

Be careful with your words. They have a great effect on your ability to cope. The same goes for your voice. An excessively dramatic voice can upset you and others. One mother said that she spent two years developing the pleasant, soft tone which she uses when working with handicapped children. It took her that long to overcome her previous harshness. Your voice and your language may seem to be so much a part of you that it seems they can't be improved. Yet this is an excellent place to start working on yourself. Like all bad habits, the more you give in to them, the more permissible they seem. Our Sages tell us,

> When a man transgresses and repeats his transgression, he deludes himself into believing that what he has done is permissible.
>
> (*Yoma* 86b)

While temperamental language is not a transgression in itself, it tends to make you think insecurely which, in turn, makes it harder for you to control your harmful impulses. (I'll never have what I want, so why should I put forth any effort to get it?")


## ACKNOWLEDGE APPROPRIATE PAIN

It is very important to distinguish between pain over a real loss and temperamental pain, which we bring on ourselves with our condemnations, unrealistic expectations, and demands. Real pain needs to be validated, and often expressed:

"I felt so hurt when I saw that father yelling at and shaming that child in public."

"I feel so much anguish for the Jews who are suffering in Russia and those living under other totalitarian regimes."

"I feel lonely now that my children have left home."

"I asked a family member to help me with something and he said, 'No,' very gruffly and walked away. It was like a slap in the face. I felt so hurt."

"A certain family member gives me the silent treatment whenever he is upset with me. It's very painful."

"We suffered a great loss recently. I still feel a lot of grief."

You don't pretend not to have a toothache when the pain is a constant reminder that something is wrong. The same is true for an emotional pain. If changing your attitude does not make you feel better, then you need to talk to a compassionate person who can give you understanding and direction, or who can simply empathize with you.

*Example*: I have three small children and a good husband. I kept telling myself that I should be happy. But it didn't work. I finally talked about the problem to someone who helped me understand that I have certain creative needs that were not being satisfied, and that when I found an outlet, I would feel better.

*Example*: After my husband died, I kept telling myself that I should get busy with projects to divert my attention from my grief. But I could hardly get out of bed in the morning. I was so filled with sorrow. Finally, I found a woman counselor who also happened to be a widow. She gave me the opportunity to express my sadness as much as I wanted. She also helped me feel that I could go on, despite the great pain which is always there.

## FIND OUT WHAT TEMPER GIVES YOU: THEN GET IT IN A HEALTHY WAY

The greatest service of God lies in the purification of motive.

*(Strive for Truth!, p. 99)*

People behave the way they do because their actions are somehow rewarding in the present or because they were rewarding in the past and became automatic, conditioned responses after a period of time. We all have an innate drive to satisfy various emotional needs. If they are not satisfied in a positive way, a person will seek satisfaction in non-constructive behavior. He uses temper to get the illusion of love, prestige, power, and pleasure. But it is not real, and therefore never satisfies his deepest needs.

| NEED | HEALTHY SATISFACTION | UNHEALTHY SATISFACTION |
|------|----------------------|------------------------|
| love, trust, attention, emotional intimacy | unconditional acceptance, being cherished, having the time to talk to others about one's thoughts and feelings | demanding attention through illness, excessive drama, tantrums, etc. or being excessively "good," passive, dependent, and non-assertive in order to win approval |
| power, autonomy, self-respect, competency, usefulness, productivity | developing self-mastery and understanding of the world, being successful at life tasks which build self-confidence and encourage initiative and creativity | getting power over others by attacking, being defiant, rebellious or criticizing, bullying, stifling others' independence and initiative through manipulation and fear |
| security, order, discipline, structure | having a non-chaotic home life with discipline and order | adopting one's own rituals to "magically" keep oneself from being hurt, excessive rigidity, compulsivity (e.g. neatness) disciplined to the point of masochism and self-denial |
| relaxation, variety | having time to let go of restraints without being out-of-control, engaging in non-goal-oriented play | withdrawal into self-absorption, strange fantasies, inability to form close contact, no emotional intimacy |

The task of a mature adult is to keep from going to the extreme in any area and to find a balance between them all. Unlike children who have limited resources and awareness to accomplish this task, you need not be locked into negative behavior in order to have those needs met. If you find yourself engaging in obsessive or non-constructive behavior, ask yourself the following questions in order to determine what is missing from your life and how you can fill that need in a positive way:

1. What am I getting out of this behavior? How is it useful to me to be sad/weak/hypercritical/a doormat/compulsively neat, etc.?
2. What message am I trying to get across to people by acting this way? What am I trying to get people to give me by acting this way?
3. If I stopped acting like this, what might I lose? What might people not see about me that I want them to see?
4. What positive actions could I perform in order to bring me closer to my goals, improve my *middoth* and fulfill these needs without hurting myself or others?

## AVOID UNREALISTIC, "ROMANTIC" DEMANDS

Insisting that your demands and desires be fulfilled keeps you in a state of tension. We all have reasonable desires for security, cooperation, honesty, politeness, respect, and so on. But what happens when we don't get it? The notion that "I *must* have what I want, or something terrible will happen," causes you to be upset when you don't meet your own impossible standards or to be angry at others when they fail to do so. The demands can be temporary (a moment's rest, a decent meal, or a simple "thank you" from someone for whom we've done a favor), or long-range (for love, prestige, or wisdom). Either way, the frustration of those demands will keep you in temper unless you recognize that not getting everything you want in life is not usually "awful," but rather inconvenient, uncomfortable, or unpleasant.

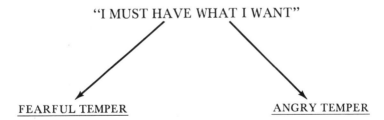

"I MUST HAVE WHAT I WANT"

FEARFUL TEMPER

ANGRY TEMPER

GUILT
("If I'm not perfect, I'm not worthwhile.")

RAGE
("I can't stand not having what I want!")

DEPRESSION
("I'll never have what I want in life; therefore, I'll never be happy.")

IMPATIENCE
("I can't wait to get it! I must have it NOW!")

| FEARFUL TEMPER | ANGRY TEMPER |
|---|---|
| **BITTERNESS, SELF-PITY**<br>("Nothing good ever happens to me. Nobody even cares.") | **HATRED**<br>("I hate them for not giving me what I want.") |
| **FEELINGS OF INFERIORITY**<br>("If I were more worthwhile, I'd have achieved what I wanted.") | **GUILT-MANIPULATION**<br>("They're driving me crazy! This will be the death of me! Look at the pain they are causing me by not giving me what I want. I'm going to make them feel bad.") |
| **ANXIETY**<br>("Oy, what if I never get it?!!") | |
| **VICTIMIZATION**<br>("They could give it to me if they wanted. I'm helpless to get myself out of this bind.") | **NAGGING, COMPLAINING, WHINING**<br>("I'm going to nag till I get it.") |
| **BLAME**<br>("It's all their fault that I'm unhappy.") | **EXCESSIVE USE OF FORCE**<br>("I'm going to MAKE them give me what I want. They only listen when I yell!") |
| **JEALOUSY**<br>("They have what I want! It eats me up!") | |
| **SHAME**<br>("I'm so ashamed that I don't have what others have.") | **JUDGMENTALNESS: FEELINGS OF SUPERIORITY**<br>("They're bad, inferior, inadequate people for doing this!") |
| **DISCOURAGEMENT, HOPELESSNESS, DESPAIR**<br>("I'll never have what I want, so why should I put forth any effort to get it?") | **JUSTIFICATION OF ABUSE**<br>("They *deserve* to be punished! This will teach them a lesson!") |

It is healthy to get in the habit of examining your demands objectively: the romantic, irrational, unreasonable ones should be eliminated. Reasonable desires should be dealt with reasonably, not with the excessive emotionalism or sense of emergency which demands imply.

## RECOGNIZE TRIVIALITIES: FREE YOURSELF FROM PETTY-MINDEDNESS

An interesting story is told about the Gaon Rav Ephraim Zalman Margolis (1762-1828). One of his most precious material possessions in his elegant home was a mirror of extraordinary beauty. One day, a servant girl slipped, fell right into the mirror and smashed it. To his wife, the Rebbetzin Margolis, the loss of this mirror came as a shock and she could not hold back her tears. Her husband, on the other hand, viewed the scene calmly. "Doesn't this great loss affect you at all?" she asked. "I'll answer your question on some other occasion," replied the Gaon quietly. It seemed that the moment he considered opportune to answer her question was a long time in coming. Each time she asked, the Rabbi changed the subject.

A full year passed. The matter seemed completely forgotton when suddenly one day the Rabbi asked his wife, "Tell me, what do you say now to the loss of that mirror last year?" "Oh that? *'Meilah, a kaporah.'* I've long since dismissed it from my memory," she answered calmly. "Ah, now the time has come to give you my answer," retorted Rabbi Margolis. "A year ago, when you stood so angry, so deeply hurt at the loss of that old piece of silvered glass, I pictured to myself how I would feel about it a year later. What you just said, I said to myself that day, and thereby spared myself unnecessary pain."

*(My Soul Thirsts*, p. 48)

New members to EMETT are sometimes bothered by the fact that they are asked to relegate the majority of the daily events in their lives to the category of "triviality." "How can you tell me that those unwashed dishes are a triviality?" "How can you tell me that that social snub is a triviality?" "That lost jacket sure doesn't feel like a minor event!" The fact is that most of us do not often undergo what might be termed "major events," i.e., 1) major life changes such as marriage, birth, divorce, retirement, job change, 2) serious transgression of religious or secular law, 3) danger to our physical or mental well-being. Most of the events we encounter belong in the category of relatively mundane, uncomfortable, frustrating, boring, or irritating trivialities.

To identify a triviality, it is helpful to ask yourself:

1. On a scale of 0 — 10, with "10" being a true catastrophe, where is this event?
2. How will I feel about this event twenty years from now? Will I be able to look back and laugh? Then it's a triviality. If it will still be painful, then it probably is not.

Our reactions to trivialities may feel like a "10" on the scale at the moment they happen.

"My daughter asked me to babysit while she went to a class. She assured me the baby would sleep the whole time, but he woke up soon after she left and cried for two hours. I had no way of reaching her. I thought I would go out of my mind!"

"When I realized I left the keys in the car and had locked the doors..."

"When the clerk told me he had to close up after I'd waited for two hours..."

"When I saw the dentist's bill ..."

Thus, you cannot always rely on your initial response to events to get a true picture of the seriousness of the situation. Rather, use objective means to evaluate the problem so that you do not waste valuable time and energy working yourself up over a situation which calls for detachment or calm problem-solving techniques. For example, dishes are meant to be washed, not dramatized. Children's mistakes are to be corrected, not made into major issues. Save your emotions and your time for many worthwhile causes and desperate needs of your fellow man, not superficial concerns or minor discomforts.

> Turn away my eyes from things of no value, that I may live in Your ways.
>
> (*Tehillim* 119:37)

The opposite of a triviality is a priority. Every event involves trivialities and priorities. Our task is to focus on the latter. Our priorities are doing *ratzon Hashem,* particularly acts of *chesed,* and protecting our own and others' physical and mental well-being. Get in the habit of saying, "This situation is a triviality in comparison to my priorities in life." Or, "This is a triviality in comparison to my mental health."

> *Example*: When I got engaged, I told my mother the kind of wedding I wanted. When she told me that they couldn't afford it, I felt disappointed at first. Then I realized that everything about the wedding was a triviality in comparison to my goal of getting married and maintaining good relations with my family.

> *Example*: When my father had to be hospitalized, I found it necessary to give up a number of activities and to bear certain physical discomforts in order to be with him. But all that was trivial in comparison to the mitzvah of *kibbud av* and the strengthening of a relationship which had been weakened over years of being away from home.

> *Example*: In honor of my husband bringing home a very important Rav for dinner, I baked a special casserole. Just as my husband was walking in the door, my two-year old pulled down the tablecloth and sent the casserole dish crashing to the floor. At the same time, my three-month-old baby started screaming. Thankfully, I had been to three EMETT

meetings by that time and was able to recognize that the loss of food, the broken dish, and the commotion were trivialities in comparison to the mitzvoth of *hachnasath orchim* and *shalom bayith* and I was able to handle the situation calmly.

Temper tricks us into investing ourselves in meaningless conflicts and insignificant discomforts. Maturity, however, demands that "a man should separate himself from anything which is not essential... " (*The Path of the Just*, p. 191). Even if you experience a strong emotional reaction, with possible jittery sensations or heart palpitations, you can tell yourself to focus on your priorities and divert your attention from those aspects of the event over which you have no control.

On the other hand, since everything in your life has significance, it is important to monitor your reaction to trivialities. The fact that you might get upset when you see dust on the shelves or don't get the *kavod* you wanted from someone in shul, is an important indicator of the need to examine your irrational demands, condemnations, and insecure thoughts. Thus, looking at your response to a triviality is like looking at a drop of blood to get an indication of the condition of the entire body. Furthermore, your seemingly excessive reaction to a minor event may be evidence of a profound pain:

> "My pain over my boss' criticism is really related to my deep pain over being in a very unstimulating and unfulfilling job."
>
> "That small act of forgetfulness on a certain person's part was merely a symptom of what I feel is an unfulfilling relationship. I overreact sometimes to these little things because I lack trust in this person and feel uncared for."

Such "tip of the iceberg" trivialities should not be shrugged off as minor any more than one would ignore even the smallest lump that might be the sign of a serious illness, God forbid.

### FOCUS ON ANNOYING TRIVIALITIES IN EMETT GROUPS

It is difficult and often discouraging to try and solve your most troublesome problem areas during the first few months of EMETT. Bringing up a major life problem can be overwhelming for you as well as for the other members. Since we work on an example for only fifteen minutes per person, it is important to choose an event which can be dealt with in that amount of time. Otherwise, you might feel that EMETT is ineffective and other members might feel that they are not getting the opportunity to work on their own problems. For this reason, we ask members to discuss events which would not be overwhelming to themselves or the group, yet which caused enough emotional charge to make it worthwhile to discover the insecure thoughts behind their negative response. Also, the best way to build confidence and develop the expertise necessary to deal with more painful events is to start with smaller situations where you had some success.

### PREPARE YOURSELF MENTALLY TO EXPECT TRIVIALITIES IN CERTAIN AREAS

It is helpful to "predispose" yourself to the fact that certain situations almost always involve discomforts and trivialities: food, money, material possessions, bodily aches and pains, social snubs, traveling, other people's poor manners, etc. Tell yourself, for example, "Money is a triviality in comparison to my ultimate goals in life — no matter what the amount." Unless the loss or discomfort involves a major transgression or damage to health and welfare, most of the frustrations, startles, and losses in life are trivialities.

A great tzaddik, Rav Mendel Futterfass of Kfar Chabad, spoke once of an incident which occurred when he was exiled to Siberia. He was incarcerated with a tightrope walker and wondered to himself, "Everything Hashem does has significance. What could be the purpose of my being with this circus performer?" So he asked the man how he kept from falling off the wire. The performer told him, "I never look down. I always keep my eye on my goal." Rav Futterfass realized that the same philosophy applies to life in general. We can assume that our possessions will eventually get lost, be stolen, wear out, get stained, shrink, become obsolete or break down. People will not always be courteous, efficient, thoughtful, or cooperative. Life will not always go smoothly. The more of these events we can put in the category of "triviality," the calmer we will be. The very word has a calming effect. In this way, we are more likely to retain our sense of harmony and not fall off that "tightrope," even when faced with pain and loss.

> *Example*: My kids were being a bit wild and one of them broke something. I immediately took him aside and told him, "What you broke was a triviality in comparison to you. You are my priority. You are more precious than anything. However, you did break something and we'll have to figure out how you can pay for the item by doing extra chores."

### NEEDS ARE PRIORITIES; WANTS ARE TRIVIALITIES

> The right way [is that a man] will desire only that which the body absolutely needs and cannot do without.
>
> (*Shemonah Perakim*, 1:4, p. 47a)

> Who is rich? He who is joyful with his portion.
>
> (*Avoth* 4:2)

One way to distinguish between a priority and a triviality is to ask yourself,

"Is this present desire a want or a need?" The word "need" implies that if you do not get it, some major disaster might result. Be careful about how you use the word "need." Don't say, "I need a vacation" or "I've got to have a new suit for that *simchah,*" when you really mean, "It would be nice to have some peace and quiet for a couple of hours," or "It would give me a lot of pleasure to put on something new."

We all have certain needs for food, shelter, and the basic physical comforts that allow us to lead a healthy and dignified existence. Beyond these are what can be called "meta needs," such as creativity, communication, intellectual fulfillment, order, and usefulness, etc. Individuals vary in their meta needs. You know you have come across a meta need if you feel that your life is extremely unfulfilling with that quality missing. One person might crave the security and stability of a very well-ordered, highly predictable life, while another craves a great deal of stimulation and variety. One person may long for deep emotional communion with others, while another person loathes anything more than polite, superficial contact. If your meta need is unmet, you can go on living, but you feel a deep, underlying frustration which no amount of rationalizing can eliminate. Yet if that need is met, you can go on living with a minimum of other satisfactions, which others might consider necessities. Do not let people with different meta needs tell you what yours should be, or that you should be satisfied without fulfilling them.

The path to tranquility is to reduce our needs to a minimum. We say each morning, "Blessed art Thou, King of the universe, who satisfies my every need." Note that the prayer says, "need," not desire.

| TEMPERAMENTAL NEED STATEMENTS | REALISTIC WANTS |
|---|---|
| "I must never fail." | "I want ever-increasing self-mastery." |
| "I need the people around me to always be loving, polite, communicative, competent, and undemanding or I feel disrespected and get angry." | "I want to help others be the best they can possibly be, not for my own selfish ego gratification, but for their happiness." |
| "I need life to go smoothly in order to feel good and be in control." | "I want the opportunity to give and learn." |

## WHEN THE TRIVIALITIES PILE UP ONE ON TOP OF THE OTHER

At times you may feel as if you are in the center of a veritable storm of trivialities. The very fact that you think of them as annoying but not very significant helps you cope more effectively, because it implies that although the situation is stressful, it is bearable. When you feel that your fuses are about to be blown by too many demands at the same time, focus only on your priorities.

### TRIVIALITIES VS. MAJOR EVENTS

It is not always easy to distinguish between a triviality and a major event. There is often a thin line between the two. One way to distigush between them is to ask yourself if the event is really going to cause a major life change or permanent damage. If not, then classify it as a triviality, no matter how upset you feel.

If you are going through a major life change or crisis, you may have more difficulty applying EMETT tools. You may think, "She was upset because her husband came home late, but I don't have a husband." "He's upset because he couldn't get away for a vacation, but I don't have enough money to make it through the month." Read the EMETT book or go to a class, even if you have a major problem. You are bound to find some words of comfort which will help you go away feeling strengthened and better able to face your pain.

### FOCUS ON A TRIVIALITY WITHIN THE MAJOR EVENT IN CLASS

If you are in the midst of a major event, it is helpful to bring up some triviality around the event in order to break it down into pieces which can be seen as opportunities for growth. In this way, you do not overwhelm the group and can focus on the four steps.

> *Example*: My doctor told me that I have a heart problem and have to go on a salt free diet. The first few days I lost my appetite. Life didn't seem worthwhile without salt. I recognized finally that not having salt was distressing but not dangerous, and that I could bear that discomfort for the sake of my health. Each time I worked myself up, I had to admit that not having salt was a triviality in comparison to my health.

> *Example*: We're moving to Israel. I had to sell one item which I really loved a lot. It seemed that all my pain was displaced onto that transaction. However, the item itself was a triviality.

### DON'T THINK EMETT IS SUPERFICIAL BECAUSE WE FOCUS ON TRIVIALITIES

EMETT is a complex system for encouraging improvement in awareness and *middoth*. However, if you work on major problems or events too soon, you will feel too overwhelmed to experience success. When you analyze your response to a triviality, it is much easier to accept that it is not the event itself which makes you unhappy, but rather some weakness in you which is being highlighted by this particular situation. It is far easier to break your negative habit patterns which are the real source of your pain.

> *Example*: I admit that I've been a *kvetch* for most of my life. By talking only about my major disappointments and losses, it seemed that my *kvetching* was justified. But I was only hiding from myself the fact that I become negative even over minor upsets. By catching my tendency to explode or sink into self-pity over trivialities, I am building my ability to deal positively with larger problems.

## DEVELOP MENTAL MODESTY BY THINKING: "NORMAL RANGE"

> Hillel said, "Do not separate yourself from the community."
>
> *(Avoth* 2:15)

Hillel's statement is meaningful not only in a physical sense. It is also psychologically important to feel interrelated with others, despite all our differences. If you think that no one else understands you or shares your concerns, fears, or attitudes, that you are outside what we might term the "normal range" of human behavior, you will feel lonely, resentful, or ashamed. This is why we stress the importance of seeing your own and others' behavior as falling within a broad continuum of what society considers normal. "Normal range" behavior or problems implies that you are dealing with a situation which is tolerable and acceptable, even though you may not like it at the moment. It implies mutuality and communality. It is behavior which falls within what we call the "bell-shaped curve." Any personality trait will fall somewhere on that continuum, with only a small percentage of the population at either end.

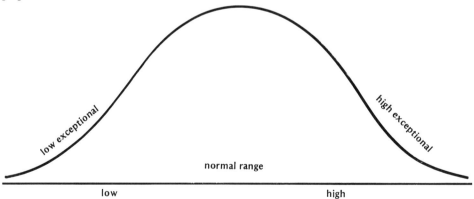

The more you see yourself as falling within this broad range of normal, the less anxious you will feel. The opposite of "normal range" is "exceptional."

Ironically, it is very normal to want to be exceptional. Children often assume that they are exceptionally bad or good, that their home life is totally different from that of anyone else, that they get more chores or less affection than anyone else, that their bodies, fears, feelings, impulses, and thoughts are different from those of others. They are terrified of being rejected or ridiculed. They crave acceptance and approval, and at the same time want to be exceptional, to have a cast on the leg or the best marks in the class or do something truly outstanding, either good or bad. Teenagers are especially prone to feelings of exceptionality because of all the changes they are experiencing. The more exceptional they feel, the more afraid they are to reveal themselves to others which, in turn, exacerbates their feelings of shame and abnormality.

One of the most important aspects of an EMETT group is the experiential value of finding out that one is normal, that others have similar problems and behave in a similar manner. If there is any doubt, the leader can say, "Is this an average problem?" "Was this handled in an average or normal manner?" "Do others ever feel this way?" The look of relief which comes over a person's face when he or she realizes that this is true is vital in order to grasp the power of this simple concept. Even when there are problems or reactions which do not fall within this category — and which are truly exceptional, (i.e., life-changing, highly unusual, or dangerous), the member can still look for parts of the event which fall within the normal range.

### STRIVE FOR THE GOLDEN MEAN

The Rambam says that we should avoid extremes or anything which would attract undue attention to ourselves, since this increases the sense of self-importance and arrogance. All extremes, except for the extreme of humility, are evidence of inner disturbance (*Hilchoth Dei'oth*, 1:7, p. 48a).

> Every human being is characterized by numerous moral dispositions which differ from each other and are exceedingly divergent. One man is choleric, always upset; another sedate, never angry.... One man is haughty to excess; another humble in the extreme. One is a sensualist whose desires are never sufficiently gratified; another is so pure in soul that he does not even long for the few things that our physical nature needs. One is greedy...another curbs his desires.... There are...the hilarious and the melancholy, the stingy and the generous, the cruel and the merciful, the timid and the stout-hearted and so forth. The right way is the mean in each group of dispositions common to humanity.... Thus a man should not be choleric, easily moved to anger, nor be like the dead without feeling, but should aim at the happy medium...not miserly nor a spendthrift...neither frivolous...nor mournful....If one only departs from haughtiness as far as the mean, and is humble, he is called wise.
>
> (ibid., p. 47a & b)

When you accept the fact that you are part of the normal range, you are able to avoid the self-preoccupation which arises from thinking that you are exceptional — either exceptionally good (a saint) or exceptionally bad (wicked or crazy). Thus, instead of spending time thinking about your image and your reputation, you are freed to devote your energies to the study of Torah and acts of *chesed.*

The essence of averageness or normal range is to strive for humility — to do the best you can without losing your sense of oneness with others. Humility connects us to each other with bonds of tolerance, love, and respect. Arrogance, the feeling of superiority or inferiority which often accompanies a belief in one's exceptionality, leads to intolerance and loneliness.

### HOW TO DETERMINE NORMAL RANGE VS. EXCEPTIONALITY

Our problems and the people we encounter may be exceptional; that is, they may involve a major life change, crisis, or the presence of acute mental or physical illness. However, we should view ourselves and our responses to these situations as within the normal range. The difference between normal range and exceptional is largely a matter of intensity and duration.

| NORMAL RANGE | EXCEPTIONAL |
|---|---|
| At times you feel despondent, lonely, tired, overwhelmed, crazy, withdrawn, resentful, angry, self-pitying, hostile, etc. | You feel that way a good deal of the time. |
| At times your mate is critical, uncommunicative, insensitive, talkative, selfish, lazy, etc. | He or she is that way most of the time. |
| Your children are uncooperative, *chutzpadik,* mean, unloving, unlovable, etc. | They are rarely happy or loving, are either hostile and aggressive or withdrawn and passive most of the time. |

If you live with an exceptional person or exceptional problem, you face unusual stress which most likely calls for the help of a Rav, doctor, or counselor. Normal range behavior, on the other hand, may call for indifference or attention-diverting tactics. Don't hide behind an attitude of "Well, it's normal," when you could improve the situation and help yourself or others grow healthier in mind or spirit.

Anything which happens occasionally and does not cause permanent harm or damage can be considered within the normal range: mild criticism, disorganization, thoughtlessness, or temporary "downs" are average for most people. Other normal behaviors are:

- husbands thinking their wives are too demanding, critical, or talkative
- wives thinking their husbands don't help enough or are uncommunicative or critical
- children being disobedient, wild, forgetful, bossy, dreamy, sloppy
- worrying about money matters, old age, what others think

Any behavior that is taken to an extreme becomes exceptional. The thought of exceptionality produces anxiety, especially if it is true. Any unusual situation places extreme demands on our physical, emotional, or mental resources. Thinking "It's average; it's within the nomal range," gives one flexibility, hope, patience, courage, love, and even humor about the situation.

The most destructive form of exceptionality is perfectionism. While we have an obligation to strive for the greatest *shleimuth* (moral perfection) that we can possibly achieve at any moment, the belief that perfection is possible guarantees our eventual feeling of failure. There will always be something more to learn, some improvement possible, something which is left incomplete. A perfectionist feels discouraged and ashamed of his incompleteness. Perfectionism is rooted in the feeling of inferiority and fear of failure. People strive for perfection because they mistakenly believe that this is the only way to win love and approval. The desire for attention and honor make it difficult at times to accept the humbling concept of "normal range."

> Since it is a person's nature to swell with self-importance, it is difficult to root out this inclination at its source.
>
> (*The Path of the Just*, p. 300)

It takes practice to define more and more of your experiences and reactions as in this category of normal. If in doubt, consult a Torah authority, counselor, doctor, or take a poll among your peers or at an EMETT class. Also, remember that what you consider average or exceptional might be different from someone else's opinion. A child might think he is giving you so much help around the house that it falls within the "high normal range" area while you think of it as "low normal range." By plotting such differences on the graph, you can talk more objectively about how to resolve problems, such as household chores, amount of communication, and other average areas of conflict.

It is important not to justify laziness, thoughtlessness, or bad manners by saying that "It's normal." This is a complete misuse of the concept. On the other hand, there are days when you don't feel well and you may have to lower your usual standards to a more realistic level in order to save your health. At such a time, just getting through the day may be considered "high normal range" while someone who sees the disorder in your home and does not know you are ill, may judge you as exceptionally disorganized.

*Example*: What a relief it was to find others with similar problems. I used to think my life, my marriage, and my children were so special. Knowing how average my problems are makes them far less upsetting and easier to handle.

*Example*: I was so anxious to have an exceptional *bar mitzvah* for my son that I was making life miserable for myself and everyone else. The smallest decision was agony. Finally, I decided to have a normal range affair, with the average mistakes and forgotten items which usually go along with *simchah*s. Only then did I calm down and find that I was able to treat others with sensitivity and respect.

*Example*: I used to want exceptional children, so I pushed them without respecting their individual capabilities or needs. It was only after I learned to give up my perfectionistic demands that I understood the source of so much tension and hostility around the house. Now, I strive for my children to have good *middoth* and to do the best they are capable of doing at any given time, not for my personal honor or public glory, but in order for them to serve God and man to the best of their ability. I thought I was being loving before, but I was so angry and intolerant that that love just couldn't come across. Now I am much more flexible and caring and the children are responding with equal warmth.

### WHEN THERE IS EXCEPTIONALITY, LOOK FOR THE NORMAL RANGE AS WELL

Even in the midst of an exceptional, once-in-a-lifetime event, or unusual situation, it is still helpful to look for the "averageness" or normal range.

*Example*: I've been undergoing chemotherapy for a serious illness. Even in the midst of my pain, it is comforting to know that others undergoing the same treatment have very similar responses, thoughts, and fears. The event is exceptional, but my responses are normal.

*Example*: When our baby was born with a serious heart defect and was not expected to live, the hospital got us in touch with another couple who had undergone the same experience just three months earlier. It was a tremendous help to us all to be able to share our similar fears and our pain. The sense of the normality of our responses helped us to be honest and confront our deepest feelings. When you go through something like this, you can feel so lonely. Being with others who understood made us feel a bond with them.

*Example*: I have an exceptional sensitivity to noise. It is a definite handicap and I used to feel ashamed about it. People were always telling me that I shouldn't pay attention to noise or that I was making a mountain out of a molehill. What a relief it was to find others with the same problem who validated how tormenting it can be to be subjected to loud noises. Among them, I'm average. To my husband and others, I'm exceptional.

Just as you should be aware of the normal range of acceptable behavior, so too should you be honest about true exceptionality. Do not apply the term "normal range" or "average" to events involving danger, abuse, mental illness, major life changes, or transgressions. Although they are frequent, they are not considered average. What is normal is our response to the event: joy, sadness, grief, pain, frustration, etc. It is very helpful to form support groups of others undergoing the same experience: cancer patients and their relatives, widows and widowers, divorced parents, single people, and the childless, etc.

# 4.

## *Learn to Recognize Temper and Combat It with Secure Thoughts*

The aim of EMETT is to help you to think and act in a constructive manner. However, at times you will find yourself feeling various emotions which hinder your ability to do this. For example, when you feel out of control, inadequate, or under attack, you may find yourself reacting irresponsibly and impulsively.

In particular, there are two negative emotional states which must be recognized and challenged before you can gain clarity about your situation. These are referred to as the anxious temper and the hostile temper. Once you recognize that you are in the grip of irrationality, you can begin to bring light into the darkness by thinking secure, self-strengthening thoughts and using other temper-reducing tools.

### THE ANXIOUS-RETREATING TEMPER

> Behold, God is my salvation; I will trust and not be afraid.
>
> (*Yesha'yahu* 12:2)

> I [God] am He that comforts you. Who are you that you should be afraid of mortal man...and have forgotten Hashem?
>
> (ibid. 54:12)

A certain degree of temporary anxiety is inevitable. After all, we do not know from one moment to the next what will happen to us. There are many mysteries to which we have no answers. We are constantly faced with disappointments, frustrations, and losses. We cannot help but be profoundly aware of our nothingness, of the ephemeral quality of our lives, "which passes like a shadow" (*Tehillim* 144:4). This existential awe (*yirah*) is a humbling reminder that the only true source of strength and protection is God.

On the other hand, there is a harmful habit pattern called the anxious-retreating temper which stifles the will to live and to love. It is rooted in a sense of shame, causing one to withdraw from responsibilities with the excuse that, "I can't cope." "I'm inadequate." "I can't control myself." "I won't do that task because it might bring rejection or require too much effort." Feelings of shame, inferiority, hopelessness, discouragement, and guilt characterize this destructive state. It can manifest itself in many ways, such as:

- constant self-deprecation
- excessive secrecy, shame, and fear of self-disclosure
- gloomy prognostications of possible future catastrophies, or breakdowns of body or mind
- exaggeration of discomfort with excessive emotionalism
- excessive guilt over transgressions and guilt over common human errors
- workaholism or its opposite — lack of drive, ambition, and goals
- intolerance for anything other than one's own narrow point of view
- constantly feeling trapped, victimized, powerless
- inability to relax, play, and engage in non-goal oriented pursuits at times
- constant fear of punishment over real or imagined sin
- hypersensitivity to disapproval, criticism
- lack of trust; inability to maintain close ties of emotional intimacy
- excessive dependency
- overindulgence and overprotectiveness
- obsessive thoughts and compulsive behaviors

In the hostile temper, the individual thinks, "The people around me are excessively inadequate and harmful. Therefore, I have to be on guard and attack back to protect myself." In the anxious temper, the person thinks, "I am excessively inadequate. Therefore, I have to withdraw because I can't really cope or stand up for myself." Like the hostile temper, the anxious temper is rooted in lack of trust in oneself which causes one to exaggerate the dangers or loss involved in everyday discomforts and demands. In hostile temper, a person thinks, "I'm hurt. Therefore, I must hurt back." In anxious temper, the person thinks, "I don't feel good. Therefore I don't have to function." Children may do this often: "I can't go to school because I'm tired." "I can't do the dishes because I have no strength." This can become a habit. The way to overcome anxious temper is to focus on solutions and learn to function despite discomfort. The same event can provoke a temperamental or non-temperamental response:

| TEMPERAMENTAL RESPONSE | NON-TEMPERAMENTAL RESPONSE |
|---|---|
| "Oy, all these demands from my family! I can't take it. Look how inadequate I am." | "These are normal demands. I'll do the best I can and not expect perfection."<br>"I'm not inadequate, I'm just inexperienced." |
| "She hasn't called for quite a while. No one really cares about me. I won't reach out to others until they start reaching out more to me." | "Most people are preoccupied with their own lives. That's okay. I can make an independent life for myself with my own projects. People care. They just don't always show it. I enjoy giving even without getting." |
| "Look at these filthy children! How can I stand all this extra work!? I'm just an unappreciated *shmattah*." | "A dirty child is a child who's probably been having a good time. I'm happy for him. Thank God I have kids to clean up after. Dirt is meant to be cleaned, not dramatized." |
| "I'm so depressed over the fact that people don't give me the attention, time, respect, and understanding I crave." | "Other people don't determine my worth or control my state of mind. I do. I'm going to make myself happy with worthwhile goals. |
| "I get depressed and lethargic just before a holiday or project and then do everything in a panic at the last minute." | "I make a lot of lists and trust my healthy inner core to pull me through. Sure, it's extra work! So what? I can do it." |
| "I made a mistake. I feel like *I* am a mistake!" | "So, I'm human. I see myself as being perpetually 'under construction.' " |
| "This illness will cause permanent damage." | "I will recover." |

The same thoughts which produce the hostile temper can produce anxious temper depending on your habit pattern, the circumstances, and the people involved. For example, if a person feels insulted by someone inferior or weaker than himself (such as a child) he might attack back. If the insult comes from someone with more power or prestige, he might cringe in discouragement and self-degradation. The important thing to remember is that when you are in temper, you attack or withdraw when you should be doing the opposite.

A person in anxious temper justifies his withdrawal from normal responsibilities or acts compulsively to win approval and avoid being attacked. He does this because he truly believes at that moment that he is victimized, helpless, unlovable, and inadequate. This thought can last a few seconds or a lifetime. Obviously, if it is true that the individual *is* under actual threat to his physical or mental well-being because of abusive people in the environment, serious illness, or some other real danger, then it is realistic to have a sense of helplessness and to be anxious about the possible harm or loss involved. However, when you are in an anxious temper, the threats are in your imagination and not in reality. Temper implies that your response is inappropriate or excessive:

> "When I didn't understand a difficult passage in Talmud, I felt like a complete failure. I couldn't bear the thought of the disapproval of anyone who might find out that I didn't understand."
>
> "A friend has failed to return an item which she borrowed months ago. Instead of asking her for it and risking her disapproval of me, I suffer in silent resentment. I feel cowardly, but I'm afraid she'll think I'm petty or will feel embarrassed that she hasn't returned it yet. I wish I could be more honest with people. But I'm too scared."
>
> "I'm ashamed that I just can't make it through the month on my salary no matter how hard I try. I feel like such a failure that it's hard for me to confront the problem."

### MANAGING ANXIETY

The best way to overcome anxiety is to find out if it is based on a real possibility of danger. Ask yourself:

1. "If I take my fears about this event or this relationship to their logical extreme, what is the worst possible consequence that I imagine will result? Are these fears realistic?"

2. "Am I capable of bearing that discomfort?" (e.g., of disapproval, criticism, rejection, temporary loss of control or prestige, loss of physical comfort or material loss, loss of fulfillment in some area)

3. "Am I having unrealistic demands for perfection from myself or from those around me?"

4. "What thoughts can I choose to think and what behaviors can I choose to do which will make me feel more in control and more self-respecting?"

When you feel anxious, try the following:

> Let the feeling be. Don't fight it.
>
> Label your discomfort level at this very moment on a scale of one to ten. Is it really awful this second, or are you making it worse by fearful previewing into the future?
>
> Focus on something manageable you can do in the present.
>
> Be proud of yourself for functioning with the discomfort and appreciate anything positive that you are able to accomplish.
>
> Recognize that most stressful events cause discomfort, but are not dangerous.
>
> Don't add frightening thoughts about possible future catastrophes.
>
> Don't worry about what others may think. Just do your best. Learn to give yourself a feeling of worth and not be dependent on outsiders for it.
>
> Notice that the fear rises and falls. Wait for it to pass while you take positive actions and avoid condemnations and gloomy predictions.
>
> Notice when the fear starts to fade.
>
> Expect it to reappear and do not be shocked when it does.
>
> Think of all that you have achieved.
>
> Plan what you are going to do next and focus on that goal instead of focusing on your feelings.

If you suffer from chronic anxiety and depression, you can also add the following:

> Don't blame yourself for your handicap. It is probably the result of inborn temperament or early childhood conditioning. You can function very well in life even with this handicap. The disciplines in this book will help you greatly.
>
> Don't blame others for your handicap. It's your particular obstacle which can drag you down or push you on to greater awareness and strength.
>
> Do not dignify your fears by paying undue attention to them. Divert your mind to worthwhile goals and positive activities.
>
> Keep a "happiness notebook" in which you write down all the good things that you have, that have happened to you, and that you have accomplished.
>
> Don't look for escapes. The biggest cause of depression is lack of meaningful goals. You can feel worthwhile whether you are scrubbing floors or tutoring a child. The important thing is that you are active, giving, doing. Stay functional. It's a well-known thought that givers tend to be happy people.
>
> Pray. Ask Hashem to help you overcome this problem.

Avoid excessive guilt over sadness. Many people struggle with bouts of depression or "blues" at times, even on a daily basis. It is certainly uncomfortable to function with this discomfort, but you can do it. The busier you are, the less you will focus on your feelings. Keep diverting your attention and endorsing yourself for whatever you do manage to accomplish.

Don't forget to nurture and nourish yourself or you won't be able to do so for others.

## THE HOSTILE-AGGRESSIVE TEMPER

> Whoever is in a rage is as if he worships idols.
>
> *(Shabbath* 105b)

> One who blames others for making him angry will fail to work on himself not to become angry. Rather, a person should take the responsibility on himself whenever he loses his temper.
>
> *(Hegyoney Mussar,* vol. 3, p. 12)

The Torah wants us to avoid anger, yet even a pious person is defined as "...slow to anger and abounding in loving-kindness" *(Avoth* 2:18). This seeming contradiction can be resolved by understanding the difference between healthy protective anger which rouses us to take action when action is necessary, as opposed to anger which results from an excessive desire to dominate others, from a desire for self-aggrandizement at the expense of others, and essentially is an expression of one's resistance to the reality of Hashem's will at that moment.

> Be angry only for a grave cause that rightly calls for indignation so that the like shall not be done again.
>
> *(Hilchoth Dei'oth,* 47b)

Anger is a power which must be used wisely. It is like a fire alarm alerting us to keep ourselves or others from being harmed. Once the alarm is sounded, it is no longer necessary to keep the anger alive. At that point, what you need is a clear mind so that your actions will be constructive. Sustained anger hurts the one who is angry and the one against whom the anger is directed.

> When a person gets angry and loses control, he loses his wisdom.
>
> *(Pesachim* 66b)

Thus we are told,

> Make no friendship with an angry man, and with a furious man stay far away lest you learn his ways and your soul be ensnared.
>
> *(Mishley* 22:24-25)

Anything more than momentary anger is termed temperamental anger, or the hostile-aggressive temper. This kind of temper is most likely to arise when you wrongly believe that someone is intentionally out to hurt you. Perhaps someone failed to cook the food the way you like it, forgot to mail a letter, kept you waiting, roughly pushed ahead of you in line, or in any other way acted thoughtlessly, carelessly, or impolitely. At such times you may experience a strong desire to use force to "teach that person a lesson," to forcefully get that person to improve his *middoth*, or to punish him into submission. Few people realize that such excessive attempts to manipulate and dominate are an expression of false pride and a resistance to the will of Hashem:

> "The desire to control everything" is a major manifestation of arrogance.
>
> (*Duties of the Heart,* vol. 2, p. 69)

The hostile temper is an overreaction to your not getting your way in relatively minor matters. Someone is impolite, uncooperative, inefficient, noisy, or slow. You take offense at what seems like an affront to your honor, a threat to your sense of power, or an obstacle in the way of your achieving a desired degree of comfort and pleasure. The result is that you become heedless of other people's feelings as you pursue the goal of having your wishes satisfied through force. You may shout, hit, criticize, give mean looks or condemn others mentally. You may use other cruel tactics such as the "silent treatment" in order to get your way. When you are in hostile temper, you do not care about others. You care only about making them give you what you want.

It's easy to justify temperamental outbursts because there seem to be so many provocations for them, especially around children or people lacking in sensitivity and understanding. That's when you most need to maintain your dignity under pressure.

### HOSTILE TEMPER HIDES THE PAIN OF POWERLESSNESS

Hostility is often an attempt to cover up feelings of inadequacy and helplessness. It makes a person feel powerful. Because you feel ashamed, you want to shame others. You want to satisfy your demands easily and quickly, without having to take the time for problem solving or patient conversations. Many people do not want to accept the fact that they are often powerless over others or incapable of getting what they want. They often think that they just haven't used enough force. While force is sometimes the best way to get something done, it should not be one's major view of relating to others. Force is addictive. Once a person starts using it, particularly on children, it is difficult to stop because the pleasure of feeling superior, of getting one's selfish desires quickly satisfied, is difficult to give up.

> *Example*: A very aggressive woman was barreling her way down the isle in the supermarket and bumped my cart as she headed for the tomatoes. I felt like bumping her cart right back and giving her a mean look. Thankfully, I was able to ask myself what that would give me. The answer was "an empty ego victory, nothing more."

> *Example*: My son was so slow in getting dressed in the morning. It was driving me nuts. The more I shouted and hit, the more he would go into a fog and resist. Finally, I realized that this particular child has difficulty getting organized. In the afternoon, we had fun practicing putting clothes on and off quickly. I made a game out of it with him and his brother. And I accepted the fact that he needs more guidance, especially in the morning. I stopped resisting the reality, calmed down, and just helped him get dressed without anger.

### TWO ERRORS IN THINKING PROVOKE HOSTILE OUTBURSTS

One of the false beliefs that encourages people to hurt others is the "provocationist theory" i.e., "He made me angry, therefore, I have the right to hurt him back." "He deserved it. Look at the mess he made! Did you hear how he talked to me?" People often forget that the Torah does not give us permission to sin just because others sin, make errors in judgment, or misbehave. Don't think, "I'm hurt. Therefore, I can hurt."

Another false belief is called the "ventilationist theory," i.e., "It's good to get this off my chest. It clears the air. I'll get an ulcer if I don't explode once in a while." Unfortunately, while you may gain temporary relief, the problems that result from the explosion are considerable. While it is often true that you must forcefully get your point across with serious intensity, exploding at others, especially family members, only makes them think that they have the same right. Thus, a vicious cycle is established. Frequent explosions are a symptom of a lazy will. Instead of tackling conflicts calmly as they arise, explosive people ignore problems until they think they can't bear it any longer and then explode as if they have the right to do so after such a long build-up of tension.

Be honest. If you have an outburst, recognize that you "angered yourself" over people's behavior or failed to take preventive action to solve the problem sooner. Certainly, there is a time to be aggressive in order to protect lives. But such instances are relatively rare. When they do occur, you are far more likely to react constructively if you have practiced staying out of temper on the minor upsets. If you get in the habit of catching yourself before you get into intense temper over someone putting his feet on the furniture or making noise while you are trying to rest, you will find yourself treating people in a much more loving manner. After all, there is *always* something to anger yourself about if you're looking for an excuse to put others down. Don't look for excuses to feel superior at anothers' expense. If you get in the habit of treating others with contempt or using excessive force to get your way, you will actually get more angry as time goes on, not less so. An expression of temper does not bring relief. The violent expression of hostile temper actually intensifies the anger. You get used to the pleasure of letting your emotions have free reign. You find that others give in out of fear and you enjoy the pleasure of an easy victory. Also, when you devalue someone, you think that the other person deserves abuse. Then you must maintain your negative attitude in order to avoid feeling shame for having hurt someone.

Interestingly, the word "mad" in English is synonymous with "insane." "There is really no difference between a person who lacks sanity and a person who behaves improperly" (Chazon Ish, *Shabbath* 56:4). When you feel anger, it is most effective to find some means of communicating your pain in a respectful, yet intense and serious, manner. And if the other person is unable or unwilling to listen, then you may be left feeling frustrated and helpless. However, you have not sinned by treating that person disrespectfully.

Temper provides the illusion of power and importance. But it is the mark of inner weakness. It is an attempt to bully or shame others into cooperation. The temperamental response is like a false fire alarm: The fire trucks go rolling out only to discover that there is no fire, or a fire so small that it could have been extinguished without all the drama and excessive emotionalism of temper. Imagine what it does to the body for you to be overreacting to illusions of great loss or danger! Before you react with anger, ask yourself:

"Am I overstepping the boundary between rightful concern as opposed to manipulation and domination?" "Do I have the right to interfere?" "Will my anger be helpful?"

"Is there another way of solving this problem more peacefully?"

"Do I want to teach the people around me that anger is justified as long as I am tired, tense, or upset? Do I want to teach them that it's okay to hurt others whenever I don't get my way?"

With hostility and punitive actions, you might get what you want momentarily. But in doing so, you lose the "whole of Torah," which, as Hillel stated, is based on the principle, "What you do not like to have done to you, do not do to your fellow man " (*Shabbath* 31a).

### THE HOSTILE TEMPER CAUSES YOU TO SIN

When you get into the hostile temper, you almost automatically transgress a number of Torah prohibitions, such as:

"You shall not hate your brother in your heart " (*Vayikra* 19:17).

"You shall not take vengeance or bear a grudge " (ibid. 19:18).

"...you shall not wrong another but shall fear your God " (*Vayikra* 25:17). (This is interpreted as not hurting others' feelings. See *Love Your Neighbor*, pp. 325-31 for details of the laws of this commandment.)

Some people think that they do not have to be strict about observing these commandments in the home — that the home is a place where good manners and sensitivity to others' feelings don't matter. Yet it is in the home where they matter most. The psychological health of children is determined to a large degree by the parents' ability to create an atmosphere of loving concern for each other. It is within the family that the true level of your spirituality is most apparent. Your home is your *beith hamikdash hakatan,* a holy temple in miniature. Angry outbursts and silent hatred should be considered as attacks on the very foundation of what is most precious to the Jewish people.

### THE DESIRE FOR HONOR PRODUCES HOSTILITY

Some people are quick to take offense at every grimace, shrug, or act of non-cooperation from others. Their excessive desire for respect (*kavod*) and approval keeps them in a constant state of angry temper. They assume that others are being deliberately lazy, selfish, and thoughtless out of lack of respect, instead of realizing that all human beings are sometimes lazy, selfish, and thoughtless and that it is not usually out of a deliberate desire to hurt you but rather because that is the way people act at times. If you want to reach and teach others, avoid making anger-producing negative conclusions such as:

"She didn't clean up because she doesn't respect me. I'll make her feel really bad."

"He didn't call because he doesn't care. I'm going to be mean and cold when he comes."

"My child was insolent in order to hurt me. A good slap on the face will teach him."

Your hostile temper can often get people to move quickly or stop what they're doing. But it does not awaken respect for you or greater self-awareness in them. On the contrary, it teaches people that force is the best way to get what you want and that other people's feelings don't count. We should strive for the level of Hillel the Elder, who "took offense at nothing and [therefore] felt not even a stirring of anger" (*The Path of the Just*, p. 163). Work at overcoming your desire to be honored at all times by everyone. This desire will make you so angry that you will not achieve respect for yourself or others.

> The desire for honor tugs at a person's heart more than any of the other longings in the world. If not for concern over his honor, a person would be content with whatever was at hand....
>
> (ibid., p. 171)

### RECOGNIZE THAT YOU ANGER YOURSELF

You do not have to take offense at other people's actions or shortcomings. If you do, say, "I angered myself," rather than "He made me angry." The former is a mark of maturity and responsibility. You will then be able to respond far more realistically when you are not upset: "Only that man whose character is pure, calm, and steadfast can reach correct conceptions" (*Guide to the Perplexed*, 1:34).

### MANAGING THE HOSTILE-AGGRESSIVE TEMPER

You may not always be able to control the spontaneous response of anger when you are upset, but it is vital to control its expression. The following suggestions may help:

- The Rambam recommends that if someone hurts you, you should 1) remain silent if you cannot talk calmly and respectfully, 2) remain silent if you feel that talking would not improve the situation or would be inappropriate, 3) share the pain you feel with "words spoken gently," with no sense of superiority or vindictiveness, and only with the goal of keeping the other person from sinning *(Hilchoth Dei'oth 6:8)*.
- "Just as it is a mitzvah to say what will be listened to, so it is a mitzvah not to say what will not be listened to" (*Yevamoth* 65b). Don't try to change personalities with anger. Don't think that the best time to educate the family members is in the heat of an argument or a crisis. Wait until others are receptive.
- Recognize that you may have unrealistic demands for maturity, competency, and honor that others are incapable of fulfilling. Keep your standards realistic.
- Recognize that you may not have to get angry or use force in order to change things.
- There are a host of other tactics to solve problems in a civilized manner. For example, try "role reversal," in which you ask the other person to act out your point of view while you take his in order to promote understanding.

Remember the *kedushah* you bring into the world by not getting angry: "The whole world exists only in the merit of one who bridles his mouth in a moment of strife" (*Chulin* 89a).

Avoid thinking that people are deliberately (*davka*) out to hurt you with their irritating or thoughtless behavior unless they have specifically told you so. And if that is the case, do something to heal the relationship instead of making things even worse by expressing hostility.

Recognize that you may be angry over the fact that people are imperfect.

Just as there are physical ailments, so too are there spiritual diseases which need to be healed with proper guidance, not hostility. Also, there are certain mental sicknesses which may not respond to any treatment. Don't assume that it's the task of other people to make you happy or comfortable. That's your own work.

Acknowledge that your being upset does not change other people's *middoth* unless they want to change. You maximize the possibility of their wanting to improve if you create a tolerant, loving atmosphere.

Use irritating situations for the improvement of your own *middoth*. Unpleasant people give you the opportunity to practice patience, respect, silence, peace of mind, etc.

Read and reread the many inspiring stories about our great Sages who responded to insult with humility, compassion, and even love. That will prove that it is not the words which upset you, but rather your own desire for greater control and *kavod* than other people are capable of giving you at that particular moment. Accept that reality. Resisting it does nothing but make you tense and unhappy.

Stay objective. Say, "This behavior is interesting," or "That's very challenging," if the behavior is merely irritating and does not involve an actual transgression.

### DO NOT SUPPRESS ANGER: EXPRESS THE UNDERLYING PAIN WITHOUT THE HOSTILITY

Even though you are working on the realization that you "anger yourself" unnecessarily over many events, do not try to deny your anger. Don't pretend to yourself that you are not angry when you are. If you do this, you will miss the opportunity to change your attitude or correct a problem in your environment. If you are angry, acknowledge that reality. However, do suppress the manifestations of anger, such as silent treatments, name-calling, grudge-bearing, yelling, or hitting. The fact that you are angry alerts you to the fact that something needs to be done. Do it! Don't confuse temper with action. If you take enough time, you can express the deepest feelings with great intensity and seriousness, yet without hostility. Keep your voice low to maximize communication and minimize defensiveness.

*Example*: My husband very innocently said something about his mother's cooking again after I had told him that it bothers me. Finally, I took the time to get my feelings across to him with greater intensity. We'd been doing EMETT examples at home and he asked me what my insecure thoughts were. I told him that the comparison made me feel like I was inferior to his mother. Then I understood that I often get angry to cover feelings of inadequacy and fears of rejection. That helped us both understand my touchiness.

*Example*: My wife said something in front of the kids which I didn't like. I asked her to go into another room where we could talk quietly, and explained that it really made me furious when she did that. I think it's vital for a child's emotional well-being for him to see that his parents love each other and support each other. I asked her to disagree with me in private. When she saw how seriously I felt about the subject, she agreed that I was right, and that we should support each other in front of the children.

*Example*: My mother is in a nursing home. I was angry at her for constantly accusing me of not visiting enough, when in truth, I was visiting her each day. And I was getting very impatient with her constant accusations against the staff, that they were taking things out of her room and treating her badly. I would argue with everything she said, trying to point out the truth. In desperation, I sought out the hospital therapist and he said that her situation was very typical of people with her illness. He gave me a technique to achieve emotional detachment similar to the "mental helicopter" trick I learned in EMETT. I would imagine myself watching her negativity from a position of safety and neutrality. He also told me not to argue, but to sympathize with her feelings and promise to do all I could to make things better. I stopped being angry when I became more accepting of the fact that she is really ill and that we can no longer have the relationship we once had.

*Example*: I had one child who seemed to constantly be provoking everyone. I was getting angrier and angrier by the day. I just wanted to throttle him half the time. I thought, "I just can't use EMETT on this kid. He's too difficult." I was ready to accept the fact that this would be my "failure child." That week, however, I went to EMETT class and people were talking about how important it was, especially with boys, to maintain emotionally close contact so that they would not become cold and uncaring later on. I saw other mothers with similar problems. I decided to use a technique my EMETT leader had mentioned as one of her PMAs. She wrote down every little positive act which her rebellious daughter did during the day in a little notebook: every time she helped, or did not criticize, or make a nasty face, the mother noted those times. At the end of each day, she read the list back to her daughter. She said that within a week, there were positive changes. I decided to try this with my son. My anger wasn't getting me anywhere — except more angry. It would have been easy to give up on him, yet I know he can teach me a lot about the improvement of my own *middoth* while I patiently heal our relationship.

## DEVELOP FAITH: LEARN TO THINK SECURELY

If one trusts in God, his heart is tranquil...but one who does not...is always troubled and in a continual state of anxiety....

(*Duties of the Heart,* vol. 1, p. 361)

Behold, God is my salvation. I will trust and not be afraid.

(*Yesha'yahu* 12:2)

Two students came to the Magid of Mezeritch and asked how it is possible to fulfill the Talmudic obligation of blessing God for misfortunes with the same joy as when one blesses Him for good fortune (*Berachoth* 54a). The Magid advised them to ask Rabbi Zushe who lived in extreme poverty, with only a dirt floor and barely the necessities of life as well as painful physical ailments. The students went and found Rabbi Zushe studying Torah. They put the question to him and received this reply: "I don't understand why the Magid sent you to me. I have never experienced anything bad in my life. Only good things have happened to me."

(*Midor Dor*, p. 216)

Many people do not realize that they have a choice as to how they can view events; that it is within their power to take a positive or negative view. You can turn any minor stress into major distress by adopting the attitude that an event is bad or damaging and that you are unable to cope with it adequately. One person hears children playing and thinks, "I enjoy hearing the sounds of children having fun." Another thinks, "All this noise! I can't stand it. I'll go crazy!" One person suffers a headache and thinks, "It's nothing. It will soon pass." Another suffers the same degree of pain and thinks, "It's mild now, but this is only the beginning. Soon the pain will be excruciating." You do a good deed for someone and the person fails to thank you. You can think, "What an ungrateful, selfish, terrible person. He has no respect for me." Or, you can think, "He just doesn't have the habit of showing gratefulness. Better for me to do things without thinking of reward, because that shows that my intention is only to do *chesed*." You see a family member doing something you dislike. You can think, "*Davka!* Just to hurt me!" Or, "He's just preoccupied with himself at this point. I'll find a tactful way of helping him become more aware."

In other words, it is not people and events which make us unhappy so much as our attitude toward them and our personal interpretation of the meaning of the event. If you look at situations with *secure thoughts*, you see them as opportunities for growth, and trust your ability to cope as adequately as possible given the circumstances. For example, even though evil exists, the fact that you are able to fulfill your purpose in life by opposing it is the positive aspect of the situation. Even though you may be in pain, the fact that you do not give in to depression or hostility is a tremendous inner victory. The more you choose to view events as offering the possibility of bringing good into your life, the greater will be your degree of love, trust, and inner tranquility. Secure thinking makes you feel loving, trusting, and enthusiastic. Insecure thinking makes you feel the opposite. The choice is yours: inner tranquility or inner turbulence. Both are products of the mind.

## YOU CAN CHANGE THE WAY YOU LOOK AT THE WORLD

A young boy ran excitedly into the house and informed his old grandfather, a recent immigrant from Europe, that "The Dodgers won, Zaidie! The Dodgers won!" The old man had never heard of the Dodgers, but he smiled at the boy and said, "If it's good for the Jews, then I'm happy with you."

(anecdote of unknown origin)

When you are completely convinced that something is for your good, you are happy, even though the situation may be painful. One aspect of our *avodah* (spiritual work) is to look for the good, to see each event as a learning experience from which we can grow. Some people do this more or less naturally. Others are highly insecure and tend to view even the most innocent remark or minor discomfort with negativity. Your upbringing has a lot to do with how you think. If you were the recipient of chronic criticism, harsh punishments, or parental neglect and indifference, you may tend to think that people don't like you and that you are unlovable and inadequate. You may feel secretly ashamed of your innermost self and may think, "I always mess things up" "I can't do anything right" "I can't cope." You may suspect that others are out to hurt you deliberately. Thus, you will be afraid to reach out or let others get close to you. You will view relationships negatively, awaiting the pain even in the midst of the good times. You may keep others distant with criticism and complaints or excessively submissive behavior which builds up silent resentment and sudden explosions.

Likewise, if you suffered from early childhood traumas such as severe illness, divorce, the death of a loved one, or severe parental disharmony, you may view the world negatively, thinking that disasters are about to happen and that life is not fair. You may think it's best to keep yourself in a state of unhappiness in order to ward off future catastrophes and to be prepared for the worst.

If you are an insecure thinker, do not despair. You can change this habit by recognizing that your mind has only two "stations": secure and insecure. It is your choice as to whether you choose thoughts which make you feel calm and secure or insecure and angry. Take time to integrate this concept. Think carefully about your ability to look at the same situation as either good or bad. Many people are shocked by the very idea, and even resist it for a while. This is because this fact gives you great power over your degree of serenity and joy at any given moment. And that is an awesome responsibility.

> *Example*: Every time my daughter was defiant, I used to think, "What a negative child she is. What a '*davka-nik*'." Then I changed my attitude to, "What a challenging child. What challenging behavior." My feelings about her changed completely, and her behavior also improved.

> *Example*: I was hanging out my wash one day and complaining to my neighbor, who was doing the same, about what a chore it was for me. She replied, "Dear, when I was in a concentration camp, I used to see the Polish women hanging out their wash. To me it was a sign of freedom. I never thought I would get out alive, but I did. Now it is one of my greatest thrills to have all this laundry to do for my family, a family I thought I would never have." When she told me that story, my muscles took on new life. I no longer felt burdened and fatigued. I too felt so grateful and happy that I could perform this task for my family, that we had money for clothing, and that I was healthy enough to be able to do all these things for them.

There are always two ways to look at any event:

| INSECURE (WEAKENING) JUDGMENTS, INTERPRETATIONS, CONCLUSIONS AND PREDICTIONS | OR | SECURE (STRENGTHENING) THOUGHTS |
|---|---|---|
| 1. *Others fail to live up to your standards:* | | |
| "My daughter is a spoiled brat." | | "She's expressing a normal desire for attention." |

| INSECURE (WEAKENING) JUDGMENTS, INTERPRETATIONS, CONCLUSIONS AND PREDICTIONS | OR | SECURE (STRENGTHENING) THOUGHTS |
|---|---|---|
| "I can't stand these terrible people." | | "We are all imperfect. I can still be loving." |
| "He's doing it *davka*." | | "He's preoccupied, tired, hungry, in need of excitement, variety, is curious." |
| "He's no good." | | "He's imperfect and inexperienced." |
| "She's out to hurt me." | | "She's not aware." |
| "This will last forever." | | "It's a temporary problem." "We'll work it out." "We'll get help." |
| "She's exceptional." | | "Her behavior is within normal range." |

2. *Insecure thoughts about oneself*:

| | | |
|---|---|---|
| "I'm a loser, a failure, unlucky, inadequate, unlovable." | | "My worth is not dependent on external successs. I'll put forth my best efforts. I'm not inferior, just inexperienced." |
| "People don't like me." | | "The more I give, the more I'll be liked." "No one is liked by everyone." "My worth isn't determined by others." |
| "I can't cope with this pain, these burdens, this family, etc. I'll collapse, get slightly crazy, etc." | | "It's distressing, but not dangerous. I'm doing an adequate job. I don't have to have things easy or perfect." "I can trust my inner strengths to pull me through." |
| "I'll never be successful." | | "What counts is effort, not success." |
| "If I need to ask for help, it means I'm inadequate." | | "It just means I need help." |

| INSECURE (WEAKENING) JUDGMENTS, INTERPRETATIONS, CONCLUSIONS AND PREDICTIONS | OR | SECURE (STRENGTHENING) THOUGHTS |
|---|---|---|

3. *The outcome is in suspense*:

"I'm sure the medical tests will reveal the thing I fear most."

"I hope for the best and refuse to think of the worst until I know for sure."

"I know what others are thinking of me behind my back."

"I'm not a mind reader. I'll assume that they're not all that concerned or that they like me, unless I know for sure otherwise."

"He's not on time. He's been in an accident."

"I will not contemplate those thoughts until I know for sure. In the meantime, I will pray."

"I'm not going to give because if I give an inch, she'll take a mile."

"I'll help and deal with the consequences later."

"I'll never get all I want in life."

"I don't need anything other than a life of mitzvoth."

"This child is showing negative character traits. I'll bet he'll be awful in twenty years."

"This is a stage. I won't strengthen it by giving it excessive attention. I'll give a lot of positive reinforcement and it will pass."

"It's going to be awful."

"Things work out most of the time. I can bear the discomfort."

4. *The outcome is known and it involves major loss, danger, or pain*:

"I don't deserve this."

"Hashem is running the show and He knows what is best."

"I can't go on."

"I will use this pain as a ladder to greater faith and refinement."

"This is bad."

"Whatever Hashem does is for our good."

↓

| helplessness, hopelessness, hostility | hope, love, constructive action |
|---|---|

If you are very anxious about an event, it is most helpful for someone else to ask you to express insecure thoughts. While it is possible to unravel them yourself, you will find it easier to be objective and to stay focused if another person is there with you:

> *Example*: "Oh no! The maid just called to say she's not coming! Oy, a disaster. Insecure thought? The place will be a mess. Then what? I'll feel ashamed if people see it like this. Then what? That will be distressing, that's all. I'll just have to work harder today and if it's not perfect, so what?"

> *Example*: "My wife's parents are coming to stay with us. Insecure thought? It'll be a lot of extra work for her. She'll have less time for me. I'll have less space and privacy. The extra expenses will be a big burden. Then what? I'll be tense and upset. Then what? I'll get mean and grouchy and won't want to be home. I might say something not respectful to them and be ashamed of it forever. I guess my biggest insecure thought is that I'll lose control, money, prestige in my own and their eyes, and have to give up my own selfish pleasures."

When you notice a trait in a close family member that bothers you, ask yourself if you think it will lead to a permanent handicap or great danger. If so, the trait will bother you much more than if you think it's temporary or harmless. When you get upset about a social snub, ask yourself if you think other people are rejecting you because of some terrible imperfection you have which can never be corrected. If you think you deserve to be insulted or that your worth is dependent on getting other people's approval, you will be far touchier to criticism. When you see an imperfection in another person, especially a close family member, ask yourself if you think that this is a reflection of your own failure as a human being/parent/friend. If so, you will be far more upset about their shortcomings.

Insecure thinking can keep you from taking action:

> *Example*: "I know I should seek counseling. I'm losing my stability, screaming a lot, and the children are being very hurt by the situation. But I can only imagine that it will be worse afterwards, and that my wife will respect me less if I go."

You can anger yourself endlessly with insecure thoughts:

> *Example*: "Whenever anyone does anything that I don't like, I assume that it is a deliberate attempt to hurt me."

Insecure thoughts can keep you from doing acts of *chesed*.

> *Example*: "I'd like to do more *chesed*, but I'm always afraid that I'll be rejected or that people will take advantage of me."

Insecure thinking can produce apathy:

> *Example*: "I know I should take him to the doctor, but I'm afraid that he'll find something really wrong so I keep putting it off."

Insecure thoughts can keep you in a continuous state of unhappiness:

> *Example*: "I'm always thinking about what I don't have and how I'll never be happy because I'll never have all I want."
> *Example*: "People have to prove they love me by doing and being everything I want."

Secure thoughts make you feel hopeful, calm, loving, and confident. Insecure thoughts have exactly the opposite effect. You can only have one or the other at a time. If you give in to a negative impulse, go back later and try to figure out what your insecure thought was the second before you gave in to it. It might have lasted only a fraction of a second, but it was enough to cause damage. This may feel like difficult mental work at times, but it is well worth the effort.

### DO NOT USE SECURE THINKING TO RUN AWAY FROM RESPONSIBILITIES OR FEELINGS

Do not use secure thinking as an excuse to be callous, lazy, or to deny your feelings, e.g.:

> "I'm going to stick it out in this abusive situation because it's a *kaparah*."
> "I won't go to the doctor. I'll just hope for the best."
> "My child is lying, stealing, and beating other children up. And I scream and hit a lot, but I'm sure he'll turn out just fine so I won't take action.
> "I don't have to take action. Whatever is, it's all for the best."
> "I don't feel that I have to help that person. If Hashem gave him the problem, I'm sure Hashem will give him the strength to cope with it."

### WHEN YOU OR OTHERS ARE ANXIOUS OR ANGRY, EXAMINE YOUR THOUGHTS

When you are upset, get in the habit of asking yourself, "What am I afraid of experiencing?" Or, "What is the worst that will happen?" Keep asking, "And then what?" until you get to your "final destination," that is, your final insecure thought. Then ask yourself if it is realistic or not. Help others to do this also.

*Example*: What will happen if I speak up and make a fool of myself? Others might laugh at me. Then what? I'll feel embarrassed. Then what? I'll worry that some people won't like me. And then what? Nothing. I'll just wonder for a few minutes what others are thinking and will have to take the secure thought that they probably don't really care all that much.

*Example*: I'm afraid to keep my son home from school even though he says he doesn't feel well. What's my insecure thought? That if I keep him home one day, he'll want to stay home every day and then I'll have a real fight on my hands. Then what? He might try to manipulate me into staying home because then he'll get attention. Then what? He'll go through life wanting to be sick in order to get attention and I'll be to blame. In the meantime, I'm taking the insecure thought that if I give an inch, he'll take a mile and that I won't have the strength to fight him. Is this realistic thinking? Not really. My secure thoughts are that he's rarely sick, that he's generally cooperative, and that I'm not going to let him stay home if I think he's well. I'm often afraid of asserting myself with my children because I take the insecure thought that then they won't like me. My secure thought is that they like me better when I set firm limits. Good. I'll let him stay home today!

*Husband*: "I'm really upset that you forgot to mail that check."
*Wife*: "What is your insecure thought?"
*Husband*: "That if you really loved me, you would have done it, that you did it deliberately to hurt me, that your forgetfulness might cause a disaster."
*Wife*: "Are you thinking realistically? Am I generally unreliable and unloving?"
*Husband*: "No. As a matter of fact, this is the first time you've forgotten in a long time. I guess I was having insecure thoughts based on old habits. I'll take the secure thought that you love me, and that you just forgot."

## AVOID THINKING OF PUNISHMENT IN A NEGATIVE WAY

One of the major insecure thoughts is, "I'm a failure. I'm a bad person. I'm inadequate and therefore deserve to be treated badly or to have bad things happen to me." These depressive thoughts prevent you from finding the positive in pain and loss. If you are full of self-deprecation, you cannot think of how you are meant to grow or what you are meant to do about the problem. Instead, you stew in self-pity, resentment, and anger against man and God. It is better to use the Torah approach and view suffering as a *kaparah*, an atonement and cleansing (*Mishnah Berurah, Orach Chayim,*

222:4). It is best to think of all suffering as an opportunity to see where our strengths and weaknesses lie.

> On one level my suffering bothers me because I am unable to study and pray properly. But I suspect the truth is my suffering bothers me because I lack a sufficient amount of acceptance.
>
> (*Chochmah U-mussar*, vol. 1, p. 347, cited in *Gateway to Happiness*)

Rabbi Moshe of Kobrin said that we are allowed to say that the situation is bitter, but not that it is bad. Nothing Hashem does is bad. However, like medicine, it is beneficial in the long run although bitter in the present (*Or Yesharim*, p. 57, ibid.). Maintain your sense of worth and dignity even when you are in pain.

> *Example*: I have a handicapped daughter. I used to think of her as a punishment, that it was a sign to the world that we were both bad people or else this would not have happened. Thankfully, I began to realize that her condition is an opportunity to strengthen certain *middoth*, such as patience and acceptance of Hashem's will, and to develop the strength not to be so needy of the approval and understanding of mankind. The more I focused on these positive aspects, the more able I was to treat her with love and appreciation for her presence. My previous coldness, resentment, and bitterness slowly faded as I worked on my attitude.

Remember that we often cannot understand our particular *goral* (fate).

> It is not for us to understand the suffering of the righteous or the good fortune of the wicked.
>
> (*Avoth* 4:15)

### RECOGNIZE THE CONNECTION BETWEEN ATTITUDES, IMPULSES, AND FEELINGS

Insecure thinking makes you anxious and angry. In that state, it is much harder to control your impulses:

> "When I think my children or spouse are doing something *davka*, I want to explode."
> "When I think that I'm inadequate, I fall into a state of lethargy and despair."
> "When I think that I have to have something and can't get it, I get frantic."
> "When I think I'm being used, I get hostile."

While some people are insecure thinkers about just about everything, others have a habit of thinking insecurely about particular topics such as cleanliness, food, travel, relationships, illness, money, old age, children, etc. Get in touch with your insecure thoughts. Ask yourself if you are needlessly upsetting yourself over events which are not in your control or which do not call for so much emotionalism. This is illustrated in a beautiful story:

> The great *tzaddik*, Rabbi Aryeh Levin (1885-1969) lived with his family in Jerusalem in abject poverty. One of the few items of any material value in their possession was a set of china dishes used on Shabbath. One *motzaey Shabbath* the rack on which they were drying came loose from the wall and the dishes smashed to the floor. The Rebbetzin ran with great joy to the synagogue where her husband was studying and told him, "Aryeh, Aryeh, a wonderful thing has happened. Thank God, we have been saved from a terrible misfortune. Hashem decided to take the dishes from us instead of inflicting pain on us or the children."
>
> (Telephone conversation with Harav Rafael Levin, in Jerusalem)

## PAIN AND EXHAUSTION MAKE YOU MORE PRONE TO INSECURE THINKING

When you are well-rested and feeling good, you have greater resistance to irritations. When you are not, your resistance is lowered. At such times it takes greater effort to organize and control the barrage of sensory stimuli impinging upon you at any given moment. You feel more vulnerable and edgy. Noise, commotion, disorder, demands, pain, become magnified. In an instinctive effort to protect itself, your brain, which is part of your nervous system, adopts a flight or fight response. That is, you either withdraw mentally and/or physically, or become hostile and aggressive in an effort to ward off further stress. By taking secure thoughts, you can calm down somewhat. You can tell yourself that the situation is temporary, that you can cope, and that there is no real danger to your mental or physical well-being. You can also make PMAs (Positive Muscular Acts), such as taking warm baths, listening to soothing music, or increasing your personal quiet time or your peer-group interaction.

It is important to recognize the symptoms of excessive sleep-deprivation so that you will know to put forth extra effort to think securely. You may suffer from slight body tremors, anxiety, mental confusion, loneliness, feelings of unreality, lack of vigilance, and weepiness. You may adopt a kind of "doom/gloom/disaster" attitude. Everything may look bleak — from your relations with others, to your own ability to cope adequately and the state of the world in general. While the brain often reacts to sleeplessness with a sense of danger, it is up to you to reassure yourself that people do not die from lack of sleep. Nor do they go crazy, though you may feel that that is happening. Sleeplessness alone does not produce mental illness. Keep your thoughts positive, even if those thoughts seem to be waging a losing battle. Do not condemn yourself or others at this time. You are worthwhile even if you cannot fulfill your usual high standards. Human beings have a core of inner strength which pulls them through the most difficult situations. Trust your inner strength. Remember, in Hebrew, "faith" comes from the word, *le-hithamein*, "to practice." And there is no more important time to practice increasing your degree of faith — in yourself and in God — than when you don't feel well.

Also, the body cannot relax if the mind is gripped with thoughts of danger and disaster. Any act of control will make you feel more secure. If you cannot control your outer environment, you can work on disciplining your mind by suppressing gloomy thoughts and disciplining your muscles by breathing slowly and avoiding the impulse to strike out at others. You may need extra help. Don't look at this need as a sign of inadequacy. Rather, endorse yourself for being self-protective and realistic.

Insomnia is a common side-effect of many drugs on the market today. See if there may be other ways of solving your problem, such as relaxation therapy or biofeedback. If you are able to sleep but can't because of a new baby or sick family member, find some way to grab "cat naps" now and then. Accept the fact that you may not feel like yourself when you suffer from sleep deprivation, that you may feel more frantic and "touchy," just like your children when they are overtired. Your compassion for yourself will awaken compassion for them. Every act of self-restraint can promote self-esteem, if motivated by love and not temper. At this time, you need self-esteem more than ever.

### ATTITUDINAL CHANGE IS OFTEN NOT ENOUGH

If you change your attitude toward a person or event and find that you feel calmer, more loving, compassionate, and confident — that's fine. You may not need to do anything more. But if you try to change your attitude and find yourself becoming more resentful, depressed, or anxious, then you may need to take action. Your feelings are your guide. Stay in touch with them. You may need outside help to give you insight and direction and to provide support as you make necessary changes.

### TAKE SECURE THOUGHTS EVEN IF YOU'RE IN DOUBT

Don't be surprised if you experience a fierce inner struggle at times. One part of you may be saying, "I can't do it. I'm not worthwhile. I can't cope." The other may be saying, "I am worthwhile. I can control my impulses. I can improve myself." Keep taking secure thoughts until they defeat the insecure ones.

## EXPRESS INSECURE THOUGHTS TO EACH OTHER

The following example shows the importance of expressing insecure thoughts.

> *Example*: When I came home, my wife was feeling kind of down. My immediate reaction was to walk away angrily. I thought, "Not again! Will she always be like this?" But I overcame my temper and said, "Tell me your insecure thoughts. We talked about what was worrying her. Her mood brightened. Then I expressed my insecure thoughts to her. She said, "Please, let's do this often for each other. It's so important and it brings us so much closer to each other."

## MAKE FAITH A LIFETIME AVODAH

Rabbi Bachya ben Joseph Ibn Paquda, an eleventh century scholar, provides guidelines for us to check the level of our trust in God. One who trusts:

1. Accepts God's judgments in everything, thanks Him for both good and evil, and does not get angry when things do not go his way.

2. Is tranquil because he knows that God decrees everything for his good in this world and the world hereafter. One who does not trust is always anxious, wanting always to increase his possessions and hoard what he has.

3. Knows that profit and loss are God's will.

4. Gives away anything beyond what he needs for his maintenance and does so with a spirit of generosity. One who does not trust never feels that he has enough and is, therefore, miserly.

5. Does nothing to compromise his religious principles, for that is his greatest priority. One who does not trust will do anything, good or bad, to get what he wants because his interest is only in the present, not in the hereafter.

6. Is beloved by all classes of people. Others trust him because they know he will not harm them. And he who trusts feels safe because he recognizes that "it is not in any creature's power or control to benefit him or cause him injury...." That is in Hashem's hands. One who does not trust blames others if he is frustrated and dissatisfied.

7. Does not feel sad when a request is not granted or if something loved is lost. He does not grieve or rejoice about his future. He is fully present in this moment, which is all he has.

8. Is anxious and mourns over his shortcomings in the fulfillment of his duties toward God and does as much as he can to do more. He tries to improve throughout his entire lifetime. But one who does not trust is in a constant state of mourning over "the continuance of mishaps that befall him in this world; that things he loves are taken away from him and his wishes remain unfulfilled " (*Duties of the Heart*, vol. 1, pp. 361-67).

# 5.

## Temper-Reducing Tools:
## Practical Aids for Secure
## Thinking and Constructive Behavior

### INTRODUCTION

In the following pages, you will find a summary of most of our major stress-reducing tools. These tools should be taken in a total Torah context. If you are in doubt as to how to use any tool, consult your local EMETT leader or write to the author. If you have a religious question, see a Torah authority. And if you are having serious mental or physical problems, seek outside help if necessary.

If you are in the midst of a major stressful event or have suffered a great loss, EMETT will not make your pain vanish magically. However, it will help you to cope with that pain more positively. Deeply imbedded habits, especially those involving your essential system of beliefs about yourself and the world, take time to change. Habits which have permitted you to justify laziness and selfishness are particularly difficult to break since you may not be sure whether or not you really want to let them go.

The term "force of habit" is a physiological reality. The synaptic patterns established in the neurons of the brain have an electromagnetic power to make us think as we have thought before, and thus behave as we used to. Therefore, if a particular EMETT tool doesn't work the first time you use it, you may have to repeat it thousands of times until the new habit becomes second nature, and the old one fades away. This diligence requires a lifetime of effort.

> All service to Hashem is dependent upon mending one's character traits, for they are like garments to the mitzvoth and embody general principles of the Torah; and all sins are rooted in faults of character.
>
> (*Even Shleimah*, p. 1)

Do not become discouraged by initial failure. Some traits may get worse simply because you are paying too much attention to them. You will not win all your skirmishes against your *yetzer hara*, especially if you have been excusing yourself for many years by thinking, "I can't change." Change begins with an act of will, and is maintained through continuous acts of will. Think of how you feel when you first awaken in the morning. Perhaps you have been telling yourself for a long time that you should engage in five or ten minutes of exercise to strengthen your back or some other part of your body. Part of you wants to exercise. The other part wants to lie there for a few more minutes. The part that gets you to move is your *will*. If you have a weak, lazy will, you will avoid those exercises. If you have a strong will, you will do what you know is best for your health. The will is like a muscle. It requires constant use to keep it strong. The purpose of the following pages is to provide the exercises necessary to strengthen your will and keep it strong. You will not always feel like using the tools. However, by forcing yourself, even when you are enraged or in pain, to repeat them over and over, you will find that they bring you some measure of relief. Even if you start saying them without sincerity, you will eventually experience their power to bring light into darkness. What is left when you rid yourself of temper? Very simply-service to Hashem and your fellow man.

## SEE YOUR OPTIONS MORE CLEARLY WHEN TEMPER IS REDUCED

Many situations can be approached in two different ways, depending on the circumstances.

1. *Helicopter tactics.* These help you rise above the situation, watching the events from a position of neutrality, detaching yourself emotionally and/or physically from the people involved.

   > *Example*: My son was in a bad mood. I knew it would pass quickly, so I didn't say anything.

   > *Example*: A certain family member is always late to everything, whether it's a wedding or a plane flight. After trying condemnations, nagging, complaining, and criticizing, I decided that I would go by myself if it was important enough, or sit and study while waiting in order to keep myself calm. I now focus on this person's positive qualities, which are many, and use this problem as a means to increase my patience and compassion.

2. *Confrontational tactics.* These tools help you to be assertive without hostility.

> *Example*: My son was in a bad mood. I was concerned, since he had been moody for a few days. Before engaging in conversation, I gave him the benefit of the doubt and decided he didn't want to intentionally hurt me. Despite his initial resistance, I took the secure thought that I could make a connection if I remained patient. When he said something sharp to me, I forced myself to sit there. I said, "I want you to think about what you just said. Let me know if you feel that those words are good or bad for our relationship." When he looked remorseful, I told him that I was proud that he had felt badly about what he had said. I gave him a few more endorsements, and little by little he opened up.

> *Example*: A family member's continual tardiness was driving me up the wall. I finally decided to confront the situation and express my deep pain about it. I also suggested that we talk about what it was doing to our relationship in front of a third party, if necessary.

Some situations combine both approaches:

> *Example*: My wife asked me if I would watch the children for an hour while she went shopping. I wanted to say "no." I didn't want to deal with all the noise and demands. However, it suddenly occurred to me how selfish I had become lately. I had full freedom to come and go whenever I wanted, and to sleep when I felt like it, while my wife was always on the go, always having to be available to others, always having to share of her time and energy. What about me? What about the development of my own *middah* of *chesed*? How much do I really give of myself to the family? I looked at myself from that detached position and saw that I had always justified my selfishness with a hundred excuses. I decided that I wanted to change, to give more of myself in accordance with Torah principles. I felt a struggle within myself until I said "yes" to her. Then I knew it was the right decision.

## TEMPER-REDUCING TOOLS

### 1. HASHGACHAH PRATITH: ACCEPTANCE OF ONE'S LOT IN LIFE

*Hashgachah pratith* means the "personal supervision of God." Torah teaches us that, "The righteous will always feel joy and never feel sad about what God has decreed upon them because they realize that whatever He does is for their ultimate best " (see Ibn Ezra on *Tehillim* 33:4).

Every painful event is like a wound, which takes time to heal. Sometimes you can get over something quickly. With more serious losses, however, you must work a long time at being *mashlim* (at one, at peace) with what happened, even though it left scars and pain.

> *Example*: When my newly married daughter and her husband left for Israel, I felt very alone. It took a long time for me to accept that she was not there to talk to on a daily basis. Visits and phone calls don't make up for the loss of her presence in the same city, but I have learned to direct my attention to other activities.

> *Example*: It took time for me to accept the fact that a certain family member had an emotional disturbance which prevented anything other than superficial communication. But once I accepted that this was the reality, I stopped making unrealistic demands. With the demands gone and the judgments dropped, I have been more able to accept the situation.

Don't feel guilty about your feelings of resentment or discouragement. It simply means that you still need to work on achieving *hashlamah* in that particular area of your life, or that you're not sure which things you need to accept and which you need to assertively change. If there is absolutely no possibility of changing a situation, practice willing it to be as it is, since that is the reality. In this way, you make Hashem's will your will.

If you remain in a state of shock or in great pain for what is clearly an excessive length of time, don't hide the hurt or try to convince yourself that you don't really feel a sense of tragedy or harm. Such mental trickery is not effective. Suppressed pain often finds unhealthy ways of expressing itself, through depression or psychosomatic illnesses. You may need help in working through your feelings about an event.

### 2. PRIORITIES

The desire for prestige, power, and pleasure can turn us away from our higher priorities — which are to serve Hashem with Torah study and observance of mitzvoth. When we view incidents in their right perspective, we can determine which aspects are trivial and which are significant. Our task is to distinguish betweeen the two and base our priorities on them.

> "I like privacy and space, but I put *hachnasath orchim* above my personal pleasure."

> "I want my mate to instantly give in to my demands, but I put *shalom bayith* above my personal desires."

"I would often like to use harsh words on family members when they don't cooperate, but I put their mental health above my desire for instant obedience and find other ways to teach them thoughtfulness and respect."

"I sometimes find myself feeling bitter over my fate. But then I realize that being angry at Hashem is a waste of time. I have more important things to do, such as studying Torah, doing acts of *chesed*, and strengthening my faith in God.

### 3. CHOICES

We often have no choice regarding what happens to us, but we always can choose our attitude toward it. We can work up the discomfort with exaggerations, emotionalization, and erroneous conclusions, etc., or work it down with secure thoughts and constructive action.

### 4. FIND THE GOOD

There is a hidden *brachah* in every event. If we focus on that, we will be less upset.

> When you find yourself in a difficult situation, the first thought you should focus on is that the situation is a test and a challenge.
> (*Chochmah U-Mussar*, vol. 2, p. 158, see *Gateway to Happiness,* p. 244)

*Example*: My daughter was in a bad mood at the Shabbath table. I thought, "Where's the good in this one?" Then I realized that it was an opportunity to demonstrate many important *middoth*, such as patience and compassion for her. I didn't want a big power struggle with her, which is what she was used to. Instead, I began to tell stories from the lives of our *tzaddikim*. In between that, we all sang. In a short while, she came out of her mood and we rejoiced that we had weathered that storm without a big scene.

There is always some mitzvah to perform in every situation, even if it's only to give the benefit of the doubt. If you focus on getting joy from whatever mitzvoth you are doing, you will be less wounded by the event itself.

> The Divine Presence comes to rest upon one only through his rejoicing in a mitzvah.
> (*Shabbath* 30b)

While many religious observances demand strict self-discipline, a religious life does not require a dour and grim countenance. On the contrary, everything becomes more difficult when a person lacks joy, including Torah study and acts of loving-kindness. Even if you are in emotional or physical pain, a part of you can be happy for your ability to still perform mitzvoth.

It is no great challenge to be full of faith when things are going well. But the highest *madreigah* (spiritual level) is to "accept pain with love." That is the hardest task.

> Great suffering involves the danger that one might come, God forbid, to harbor resentment against the judgments of God. It may be hard for such a person to realize that "all God's judgments are true," (*Tehillim* 19:10) and that truth means that there can be not the slightest deviation, for better or for worse, from the standards of absolute fairness.
>
> (*Strive for Truth!*, vol. 1, p. 81)

### 5. NORMAL RANGE

Strive to view your thoughts and actions as being within the "normal range" for the people in your community, and to see others as being in that "normal range" as well. This discipline keeps you tolerant and makes events seem more manageable than if you see them as exceptional. If you think of yourself or the people around you as exceptional, you will tend to feel overwhelmed and angry. However, if events or people really do fall into the category of "exceptional," take appropriate action. [See chapter 3 for further explanation.]

### 6. COMPASSION

To have compassion for others, especially after they have hurt you in some way, may be difficult. You can achieve it by practicing the next three tools in particular:

a. *Benefit of the doubt*. When you feel hurt by another's actions, assume that the person forgot, failed to exercise self-control, lacked insight, maturity, skills, or intelligence. Realize that many times you do not know all the background information.

b. *Avoid condemnations*. Avoid judging others, but retain your right to evaluate their behavior as acceptable or not. Condemnations don't help people to change. They only provide a momentary feeling of prestige, power, and superiority. You never know what pressures another person is under, or what is their true potential or level of sensitivity at any given moment. People shouldn't be condemned for where they are at. Instead, they should be helped to improve whenever possible. But openness to change can only come in an atmosphere of respect. Tell yourself, "He's doing the best he can with the tools he has at this moment." Believe it. Why should you condemn someone for his ignorance any more than you should condemn him for being near-sighted or having diabetes?

c. *Depersonalize*. Take away the *davka*. Assume that people are doing what they are doing, not out of spite, but because of some inner weakness or outer disturbance. Avoid thinking of yourself as the target. Even if the person says he's doing something *davka*, assume that such a childish attitude is due to that person's lack of awareness, inner pain or inability to communicate with you in a more mature manner.

If you remember that everybody has something to teach you, then you look at all people as *shlichim* (messengers) from God, who came to test you and show you your strengths and weaknesses. You might not like what they're doing, but that's not *their* fault. Like it or not, some person or event is bound to highlight your defects. Bless those who show you where you need inner repair work. By fixing it now, you may prevent greater damage. (See p. 24).

d. *Forgiveness*. To forgive does not mean to condone other people's actions. It simply means that you put yourself in a state of objectivity and compassion so that you are not tempted to take excessively harsh measures if you must be assertive, or stew in resentful silence if there is nothing you can do about the situation.

> When we forgive others, we are helping ourselves as much as we are helping those whom we forgive. We are elevating ourselves and will feel much better when we forgive than if we would keep on adding more and more resentment. With the majority of people, if you ignore their insults and behave in a kindly manner toward them, they will feel embarrassed to continue insulting you and their insults will stop. If they do continue to insult you, you can feel the pleasure of overcoming your natural tendency of revenge and feel more elevated for your kindness.
>
> (*Gateway to Happiness*, p. 307-8 )

Even when someone does something deliberate to hurt another, he should be forgiven because at that moment he must have lacked intelligence or awareness, or he would not have behaved that way.

> With the measure a man metes, it shall be measured to him.
>
> (*Mishnah, Sotah* 1:7)

Don't let forgiveness lull you into passivity. Rather, use it to prevent yourself from carrying around a destructive burden of resentment which does no one any good.

> *Example*: When I first started using EMETT tools, I became so forgiving that I felt people were taking advantage of me. Then I realized that while I needed to drop my condemnations, I didn't have to drop my desire for respect, justice, peace and quiet, and thoughtfulness. Now, when I have to stand up for myself or reprimand a child, I do it firmly and assertively, but without the hostile condemnations which I had before EMETT. It took me a while to figure out the right balance.

*Example*: I went to the doctor with a terrible pain in my back. He said it was nothing. I got really angry. He did all these tests and took all these x-rays and couldn't find anything! I started to think he was incompetent. Then I realized that my condemnations were only keeping me from asking him the proper questions and taking more assertive action to find out what was causing the pain. It wasn't the doctor's fault that he didn't know what was wrong. I kept telling myself that he had tried his best, in order to keep myself calm.

*Example*: An hour after I had given a repair man a large sum of money to fix the refrigerator, it broke down again. When I called, he said he couldn't come out again unless I paid another $60 initial fee to look at it. I was about to explode. Then I thought, if this man is trying to cheat me, then I can go to the Better Business Bureau or Small Claims Court. There are other courses of action. Eating myself up with resentment would not change him, and would only harm me. I had to act. And that meant forgiving him for having that kind of money-hungry personality. I figure that I was given a brain so that I could study Torah, not to go around condemning people.

### 7. SEEK PEACE, NOT POWER: AVOID SYMBOLIC EGO VICTORIES

The desire to maintain a position of superiority by making others feel stupid, wrong, clumsy, or inadequate is a popular bad habit. These little "victories" which one wins at the expense of another's self-esteem are called empty, or symbolic victories because they lack substance. No one profits from statements such as:

"I told you that you shouldn't have tried to fix it yourself, you idiot!"
"How can you go out looking like that, you slob!"
"How could you have been so stupid as to leave the tickets at home!"
"Dummy, I told you to do your homework and not wait till the last minute."

Seemingly innocent, or teasing, sarcastic remarks also fall in this category. No one ever matured by being told, "Grow up!" It is not necessary to tell someone who has just broken something, "Don't be so careless." He already feels badly as it is. It is not necessary to point out when others make mistakes, unless you could really improve their behavior by doing so. If not, then it's best to be quiet. Don't give your personal ego a victory at another's expense. Rather,

> Be of the disciples of Aaron, loving peace and pursuing peace, loving thy fellow creatures and drawing them near to Torah.

> (*Avoth* I:12)

### 8. PRACTICE DETACHMENT FROM ALL THAT IS BEYOND YOUR CONTROL

> By learning to divert the attention, a person can have control over being afraid or not.
>
> *(Berachoth* 60a)

This is a powerful statement. It implies that you have a great deal of control over your inner environment (thoughts, impulses, sensations, and feelings) by learning to divert your attention and focus on your goals, rather than the minor disturbances or temporary aches and pains which may be affecting you. Divert your attention toward positive thoughts and your muscles toward positive activities when you have:

- obsessive thoughts of past pains, present problems, or future discomforts
- harmful impulses to hurt yourself or someone else
- physical sensations which you know are temporary and are not indicators of any serious ailment
- negative emotional states

For example:

"In order to go to that interview, I ignored the heart palpitations and butterflies in my stomach."

"In order to lift my spirits, I detached myself from the hostile silent treatment which a family member was giving me at the moment because I knew that if I got really upset about it, it would only last longer. I left the house and turned away all thoughts except the pleasure of listening to the *shiur* I attended."

"In order to serve the customers in our store in a patient and pleasant manner, I practice detachment toward their poor manners and nasty looks and focus on my goal of demonstrating Torah ethics as well as making a living."

There are times when this discipline is very difficult. You feel as though you have to bolt the door and triple lock it against allowing entry to destructive thoughts. Get used to saying, "Oh, this is interesting." "Hm ... an interesting challenge," instead of jumping to condemnations or fearful predictions.

Thoughts can be like stray cats. Once you feed them, they keep coming back. When you stop entertaining those thoughts, they may seem to be even more insistent. However, if you make a firm decision to ignore them and to turn your attention to other matters, they will eventually go away. If you cannot divert your attention, try the "mental helicopter" technique. You can imagine that although your body is in the midst of a stressful situation, your mind is observing the scene from a position of calm safety, patiently waiting until the commotion or pain subsides. A part of you may feel frantic and nervous. There is not much you can do about that. But another part of you can be protected and protective, untouched by the chaos and pain, and trusting of your ability to cope. And it is that part which gives you a center of calm reassurance in the midst of the storm.

> *Example*: I used to spend the entire school year in temper at one teacher or another for this fault or that. Now, I offer my help if the teacher is open to suggestions. I organize the other parents to oust teachers who are downright abusive and use violence against the children or humiliate them constantly. And if the teacher is the kind that simply must be borne in silence, then I force myself to "turn chilly" toward him or her and help my children practice detachment when they meet one of these types. It's certainly better than stewing in resentment.

> *Example*: My example is about getting older and how much time I've spent in temper, as if that's going to stop the process. I have to always remind myself that my looks are not a reflection of my worth, nor is my mental agility going to determine my value in this world. I have to practice detachment and be philosophical about aging, and keep my mind focused on Torah and mitzvoth. Ultimately that is all that really counts.

### 9. IS THERE AN ISSUE OF RIGHT AND WRONG IN THE EVENT?

This tool helps you to avoid condemnation when you notice someone acting in a way which you dislike, because you realize that his behavior does not fall in the realm of *halachah* (Jewish law). Rather, you take the secure thought that the behavior can be tolerated because there is no wrong-doing.

> "My husband thought I was wrong for wanting to go to work, but when he saw how much happier I was, he realized that he should alter his belief system and avoid trying to squeeze me into his rigid image of motherhood."

> "I'm not wrong for not wanting to spend the entire Pesach with my wife's relatives. I don't mind one day. But eight is too much for me."

You save yourself a lot of heartache by letting people be who they are and accepting your own unalterable personality traits. Just be careful not to deliberately hurt others, or become complacent or despairing in the process.

### 10. LEARN TO FUNCTION WITH DISCOMFORT

Most of life's aches and pains are not permanent. About these, we can say, "It is distressing, not dangerous." It is necessary to remind ourselves about the lack of danger, because the physical reaction to a sudden loss or disappointment may be all out of proportion to the ultimate meaning of the event. Even when the discomfort is great, there are moments of less or no pain. We can often say, "Bear the discomfort and comfort will come."

> "While sitting next to a very loud and talkative person on the plane, I told myself to bear the discomfort and comfort would come — when I got off."

> "I had to sleep on the hospital floor next to my son's bed because there were no extra mattresses. I just kept being thankful that he was out of danger and kept endorsing myself for bearing all the discomfort that his illness had brought."

A great and wise woman, Rebbetzin Avtzon of Detroit, Michigan, a mother of fifteen children, used to tell those who came to her for advice, "Do not pray for comfort. Pray for the strength to bear discomfort." That philosophy enabled her to bear many difficulties with a degree of faith that inspires all who know her. Comfort should never be a supreme value. If it is your object in life, then you will constantly be upset by food which isn't prepared to your specifications, people who don't meet your standards, and material possessions which break down or wear out. Endorse yourself for the fact that you remain functional even though you don't feel well. Endorse yourself for carrying on with determination and confidence when life does not go smoothly.

### 11. TAKE THE TOTAL VIEW

Use this tool when faced with a temporary, yet distressing situation. If your general health is good; if the children are usually cooperative; if your spouse is usually communicative and caring, then the temporary upsets can be dismissed or faced in a calm, objective manner with the realization that this is temporary, not permanent. It often helps to use the word, "now."

> "Now I feel overwhelmed. But soon I will light the Shabbath candles and everything will be calm."
> "He was so stubborn and uncooperative this morning. But usually he's a good kid."
> "This person does not approve of me. But most people like me."
> "Now I feel upset. But as soon as I get moving, my attention will be diverted and I'll feel better."
> "At this moment, I feel insecure about our relationship. But in general, things are O.K. between us."

Obviously, if the total view is negative, take assertive action.

## 12. PART ACTS

This is what you do when you feel overwhelmed by some task, or pain. You take things minute by minute, hour by hour, day by day, endorsing for every small effort to bear discomfort without bitterness, or to act with diligence, patience, or compassion:

> "I'd been up for three nights and was feeling awful. I took the following day minute by minute, endorsing myself for putting one foot in front of the other."
> "I don't think of Pesach cleaning as a whole. Rather, I endorse drawer by drawer as I go along."
> "When I thought of the wedding as a whole, I panicked. Then, I made lists and endorsed myself day by day for whatever I managed to do."

## 13. AVOID COMPARISONS

> ...the last commandment is against coveting, for this principle incorporates all the other nine....
>
> (*Zohar* 3:77)

We cannot help but notice the differences between us. But we can avoid plunging into temperamental self-pity, anger, or discouragement by restraining the impulse to evaluate ourselves or others as inferior or superior on the basis of what we do or do not have. How will the following make you feel?

> "Look at how well her child is doing in school and mine isn't doing that well."
> "Her husband helps so much more than mine."
> "Her parents are so much more generous in supporting them than mine are."
> "Look how lively and pretty she is. And me — I am so dull and plain."

To minimize the negative feelings which can result from comparisons, avoid rating your worth on the basis of others' accomplishments or talents. Recognize that we all have differences in aptitude, skills, and temperament. The major thought to avoid when noting these differences is,

> "Because I have more, I am more worthwhile, i.e., superior."
> "If I have less than others, it means that I am less worthwhile, i.e., inferior."

Such erroneous conclusions can cause you to work yourself into temper throughout the day. All you have to do is see someone with a fancier lamp or a cleaner sink and you feel inadequate and depressed. There will always be someone who has more or does more than you. Don't let this be fuel for temper. Focus on your own particular struggle in life, with the particular skills and abilities which Hashem has given you.

> The humble man rejoices in the portion allotted to him. For, if pride and self-aggrandizement enter a man's heart, the whole world and all that is therein will be insufficient for his support, because of his high opinion of himself and because he looks down with contempt upon the portion allotted to him. But if he is humble, he does not think of himself as having any special merit and so, whatever he receives of the world's goods suffices .... This induces tranquility of spirit and diminishes anxiety.
>
> (*Duties of the Heart,* vol. 2, p. 117)

There are two positive forms of comparison. One is to compare how we are now with how we were in the past, in order to recognize improvement and encourage further growth. The second is to compare ourselves with those whose *middoth* we want to emulate. Comparison is constructive if it inspires you to change, not if it leads to envy and anger.

### 14. CULTIVATE A SPIRIT OF GRATEFULNESS

> The true service of God is built on a foundation of gratitude .... It is our duty to be thankful to Hashem for all the good He bestows on us, and ... this is to be the motivation of our observance of all the mitzvoth .... Thanksgiving and gratitude are the bases of ecstatic devotion to Hashem.
>
> (*Strive for Truth!,* vol. 1, p. 153)

If you want to feel bitter, sad, or angry, you won't have to look hard to find excuses, since there is no such thing as total fulfillment of all physical, material, emotional, mental, and spiritual desires in this world. Pain results from unfulfilled desires. Lessen the amount of desires, and you lessen your pain. Instead, cultivate the habit of focusing on the small pleasures — being grateful for simply being alive and for each and every breath (*Midrash, Bereishith Rabbah* 14: 9 ).

> A righteous person eats [the minimum needed] to satisfy himself while the wicked are always hungry.
>
> (*Mishley* 13:25)

*Example*: I was in the hospital for eye surgery. I thought I would go out of my mind with boredom because I had to have both eyes bandaged. To keep myself from getting depressed, I would move each part of my body from the toes to the head and be grateful for each and every movement. I would be grateful for being able to hear the sounds in the corridor and the brief visits of friends. I was grateful for each precious moment with my wife. When I was through being grateful for all that, I would review the events of my life, being grateful for everything that had ever happened to me — both the good and the bad. It was easy to be happy about the good things. And the so-called "bad" things, well, I figured out how those events helped me to be a more understanding, compassionate person. So even the bad things turned out to be good. This discipline really helped keep my spirits up.

### 15. KNOW THAT YOU DON'T KNOW

The ultimate of knowledge is to know that you do not know.

(*Shaloh* 91b)

It is difficult to accept that our hunches, intuitions, predictions, or diagnoses are just that — guesses which may or may not reflect truth. We are not mind readers or fortune-tellers. Our "feelings" about what people may be thinking or what may be wrong with our bodies may not reflect objective reality. It is important to admit, "I know that I don't know," and/or "My feelings may not reflect facts."

"I feel she doesn't like me. That's an assumption, a hunch, not a fact."

"I'm afraid that my headaches may be a symptom of a brain tumor. That's a feeling but not a confirmed fact. I will tell myself to 'know that I don't know' until I get the results from the doctor."

"My husband spends a lot of time with his computer. I used to think that it meant he didn't love me. Now I tell myself that it's a feeling, not a fact, since the truth is that he does care. The feeling comes and goes depending on my mood at the time. I can eliminate it with objectivity."

"I was quick to condemn a relative who didn't return the money I had loaned him. But then I told myself, 'Know that you don't know' until I had confirmed the facts of the situation."

There are many times we must say, "I need to have the humility to admit that I don't know why this happened. I cannot understand the ways of Hashem." The result of this discipline is a decrease in hostility and anxiety. This discipline can also prevent you from accusing others of intentional misbehavior.

Humility implies the recognition that we often do not know the purpose or cause of many events. Nor do we know for sure what others are thinking or feeling unless they tell us. The more you practice "knowing that you don't know," the more you lessen your desire for excessive control over man or God.

The external marks of humility are "gentle speech, a low voice, meekness when exasperated and sparing in taking vengeance when one has the power to execute it," and the lack of all haughtiness when rebuking others.

(*Duties of the Heart,* vol. 2, pp. 117–23)

When he is passionately angry against one who reviled him in word or deed, and exercises self-control and forgives....

After he has sustained a severe monetary loss or is affected by a mishap to his relatives ... his patience overcomes the shock and he accepts the Creator's decree submissively and declares that his fate was just....

When he is praised for the good he has accomplished and pays no attention to it....

He "is patient when troubles befall him" unlike the proud man whose "fear is great and his patience small when troubles beset him — because his soul is proud and he is dissatisfied with the state of affairs."

He "does good to others, speaks well of them, judges them favorably, does not speak disparagingly of them, forgives them when they speak ill of him even if they do not deserve such forbearance....

(ibid., vol. 2, p. 73)

### 16. IT'S TEMPORARY

Unless you know for certain that an unpleasant situation is likely to be permanent, and that it will, God forbid, cause great damage and pain, assume that it is temporary. For example, unpleasant feelings cannot remain at the same level of intensity for very long unless fed by the continuous input from insecure thoughts and condemnations. If you've suffered an embarrassment, allow the pain to rise and fall, while taking the secure thought that the event will soon be an uncomfortable memory. Assume the same with illnesses, children's misbehavior, the discomforts of traveling, and the various mini-crises and conflicts which we all encounter.

Another tool to help you bear discomfort is to "predispose mentally," i.e., to prepare yourself for the fact that certain people and events are likely to be unpleasant:

> "I predisposed that I would have to stand in line, so I took a book along."
> "I predisposed that the encounter with that person would be unpleasant, so I fortified myself by reading *Pirkey Avoth*."

You can "predispose" for various events by getting extra sleep, taking a friend along for moral support, taking an aspirin if you know you will be in pain, and so on. Predispose to disappointments and discomforts throughout the day in order to help you take them in stride. No one's life runs smoothly for long.

### 17. CALMNESS GENERATES CALMNESS, WEAR THE MASK IF IT ISN'T COMPLETELY REAL

Forcing yourself to act in the way you want to become will often produce that behavior. For example, when you are in the midst of an inner emotional storm, tell yourself, "Calmness will generate calmness." Your mask of calmness will eventually calm you down and it will often do the same for others. It doesn't have to be real or sincere at first.

*Example*: I had a car accident last Friday. Thankfully, nothing happened to me, but the car was damaged, which meant a big financial loss for us as well as a great deal of inconvenience. I was very jittery and suffering from mental confusion and disorientation. But I told myself, "Calmness will generate calmness," as I went about taking down the details from the other driver and calling the police. When I got home, I forced myself to report what had happened to my husband and avoided dramatizing my feelings. Surprisingly, he took it far better than I had expected, which I attributed to the fact that I had become calmer and more philosophical about the whole thing by the time I got home.

You can also wear the mask of love to awaken that feeling in reality.

*Example*: My oldest daughter and I were locked in a kind of cold war for the last month. Finally, last week, I decided to break through by making a forced gesture of love. I bought her a small gift and left it on her bed. When she came into the kitchen, I made another gesture by giving her a slight hug to which she responded with warmth. Then we sat down and were able to talk about what was going on.

You can wear the mask of indifference to prevent a confrontation with a person in a bad mood, or you can pretend to be cheerful if you yourself are in one.

*Example*: I tend to be moody and *kvetchy*. I could easily burden my family members with a running recital of my pains and disappointments. To overcome this habit, I try to wear the mask of cheerfulness when I'm going through one of my "downs."

This discipline can bring great rewards in terms of personal refinement and *chesed*.

The sons of Rabbi Avraham Grodzinski wrote that their father worked for two years on acquiring a pleasant facial expression. This became so ingrained in his character that even during the darkest and gloomiest days of the Second World War, when he and his family were incarcerated in the ghetto of Slobodka, and their lives were in constant danger, his outward expression was always cheerful, thereby strengthening others.

(*Torath Avraham*, p. 11)

Obviously, we would not want to wear the mask of cheerfulness if, by so doing, we would be hurting ourselves or others.

*Example*: After my operation, I didn't know if I was suffering from temperamental fatigue or was truly physically exhausted. I pushed myself to keep going, but ended up getting sick again. I tried to be a hero and not share my feelings, but my family members finally told me that I had become distant and cold by keeping everything to myself. I was wearing too many masks, and it was preventing me from being honest.

Don't "wear the mask" if it promotes phoniness, cowardliness, or callousness toward others. Use it as a way of encouraging yourself to reach a higher *madreigah* (spiritual level) than you are feeling át the moment. It keeps you from infecting yourself and others with temper.

> *Example*: When the bank manager told us he couldn't give us a loan because our credit wasn't good enough, I felt like crying. Instead, I wore the mask of confidence, while my insides were in turmoil, and asked him for alternatives. In the end, he was able to come up with a solution.

> *Example*: We were having a lot of financial problems. It seemed there was no choice except for me to get a job. I hadn't worked since before I was married and felt very insecure and unconfident. But by wearing the mask of confidence, I was able to keep my anxiety at a bearable level and give a confident appearance during the job interviews.

We are told,

> Greet every man with a pleasant expression on your face.
>
> (Avoth 1:15)

This act may feel forced or insincere, but it often generates positive results.

### 18. LOOK FOR HUMOR WHENEVER POSSIBLE

> [Man has the ability to achieve] expanded consciousness or restricted consciousness. Through joy and humor man can make the transition from smallness to greatness. One can then study and attach himself to God.... This was the task of the two comedians mentioned in the Talmud. Through their humor, they were able to remove man's anguish. They could draw him close to God and elevate him.
>
> (Ben Porath Yosef, 49b)

Nothing cuts through temper like humor. It is our greatest ally and a sign of good mental health. The ability to laugh at ourselves and to take ourselves (but not others!) lightly, is a sign of humility. Humor reduces tensions and gives us a more objective perspective toward our aches and pains. Whenever we think we have nothing to smile about, we can always laugh at our "romantic" demands on life and people:

> "I want to be skinny — tomorrow!"
> "I want everyone to respect and approve of me — all the time."
> "Life should go smoothly! I don't want any 'downs' in life."

"I want my mate and children to always be understanding and in tune with my needs."

We can always endorse for finding humor in uncomfortable situations:

*Example*: My wife and I were having an argument over something. Just then, someone called to ask if I would be the cantor at the Yom Kippur services. I have no voice whatsoever! When I told my wife about the call, we both started laughing. "That would certainly be one service the congregation wouldn't forget," she said lightly. After that, we couldn't be so angry with each other.

*Example*: My roommate did something which would normally have caused me to explode. When she asked why I wasn't talking, I said, "I'm thinking of *olam habah* and that's keeping me from saying anything to you." It turned into a joke between us. Now, whenever someone is upset, he uses that phrase. It's really true: when you think of your ultimate goals in life, you take these minor disturbances more lightly.

*Example*: I turned my back for one second and that was when my one year old turned a cup of cottage cheese over her head and my two year old poured a bowl of rice on the floor. I wanted to throttle both of them or just run away. It seemed that everywhere I looked were signs of my inadequacy. I felt like I was on a merry-go-round from which there was no exit. I struggled desperately to control myself — both my thoughts and my impulses. Then I noticed a sign on the refrigerator which said, "Messes are meant to be cleaned, not dramatized." That reminded me of EMETT and all the other mothers who were experiencing the same kind of difficulties. I remember one mother who said, "Better this *agmath nefesh* (pain) than another." I could see myself giving this situation as an example in group and everyone, including myself, laughing about it. I thought, "Anything I can laugh about in a week can't be all that bad."

There is no question that humor is your best friend and temper your worst enemy in dealing with everyday discomforts. However, appropriate sadness should be expressed without feeling guilty for it. And, of course, you should not use humor to make others feel inferior with a callous, "Cheer up," or "Don't take things so seriously." Sympathize with those who are having serious difficulties or are in real distress.

## 19. HAVE THE COURAGE TO TAKE A RISK

Growth cannot take place without risk. You risk possible rejection or failure whenever you try something new. That is why you often feel insecure and anxious at the outset.

> The success of a person is dependent on those good deeds that are difficult for him to do. A minor good deed that is performed by overcoming a natural tendency is much greater than many good deeds that a person finds easy to perform due to their being consistent with his nature.
>
> *(Da'ath Chochmah U-mussar*, vol. 3, p. 118)

> The right of choice and freedom is extended to every person to check the drive of his heart's desire and to conquer his nature....
>
> *(Likutey Amarim — Tanya*, p. 62)

If your nature is to be overly submissive, it is important to learn to be assertive. If your nature is frigid and aloof, you should try to feel warmth and compassion. If you are overprotective or domineering, restrain your impulse to control others in order to allow them to grow and gain self-confidence. Do the thing you fear to do.

> *Example*: My daughter wanted to study for a year in Israel. It has been her heart's desire for many years. I had to overcome my tendency to be too protective in order to allow her to go.

> *Example*: I had an argument with a neighbor. The last thing I wanted to do was ask her for *mechilah* before Yom Kippur. I felt I had to conquer my nature in order to do it. Shaking inside, I told myself to have the courage to do what was most difficult, and I did it.

You never know at the outset whether your efforts will succeed. Endorse for effort, not success.

> *Example*: I had the courage to make a mistake. I tried to fix the plumbing myself and failed.

> *Example*: I had the courage to take a risk and tell my wife that I wanted to quit my present job and start a small business. Surprisingly, she liked the idea.

One of the reasons for EMETT's success is that no one in the group, including the leader, is perfect or has all the answers. We all make mistakes. We are all working on ourselves, taking risks, struggling to develop the *middoth* which Torah requires of us. This demands great honesty and awareness. Our ability to talk about our internal struggle is essential.

> *Example*: I sometimes have violent impulses toward people who act improperly. I felt so ashamed and hopeless until I came to EMETT and found that many people, including the leader, felt the same way. They

were all working to overcome their negative tendencies. I'm glad I had the courage to join a group and to risk talking about myself.

## 20. REALISM VS. ROMANTICISM AND INTELLECTUALISM

A lot of pain over events comes from your resistance to the realities of the situation. One way of manifesting such resistance is with "romanticism." The romantic thinks, "I don't want it; I don't like it; therefore, it shouldn't be." The romantic is surprised that life does not go smoothly and easily, that people are not at his level of refinement, efficiency, and politeness — i.e., that people act like people. The gap between his ideal and the reality brings him constant heartbreak.

While the romantic is busy trying to make his impossible dreams come true, the intellectual is trying to figure out why things are the way they are. Such types get so carried away analyzing the situation, that they forget to do anything about it. They often have a mistaken notion that with enough insights and just the right diagnosis, life will cease to be stressful. They may seek the "right" book or method to make their problems vanish.

The third type is the realist. While the romantic says, "If only I had greater wisdom/intelligence/wealth, etc., then life would be perfect," the realist says, "Even if I had everything my heart desires, I would still have the humbling task of working on my *middoth*."

> Do not rely on the excuses "If" and "Perhaps." Do not say "If I had attained such a degree of wealth or wisdom, I would have discharged what I owe in service to the Exalted Creator ...." They are nothing but lies ....
>
> (*Duties of the Heart*, vol. 2, p. 227)

To be a realist, set realistic standards for yourself, and raise and lower them according to the realities of the situation. Recognize that you might have a habit of complaining no matter what the circumstances. Remember that it's not people, places, and things which upset you so much as your attitude toward those events.

## ACT CONSTRUCTIVELY: SOLUTIONIZE

Often it is not enough to change your attitude. You may also find it necessary to *do* something to demonstrate that change. For instance, doing some positive muscular act may accomplish what thinking cannot. When you are upset, look for the "M and M's" — some mitzvah and some manifestation of a positive *middah* on which to focus:

> "I was so resentful because my husband never got around to fixing that item, that I took it out on him in subtle ways. Finally, I fixed it myself." Or, "Finally, I called a repair man."

"I was terribly anxious about my husband's refusal to make out a will. Finally, I called a friend who is a lawyer and invited him over on the pretext of a social visit. I explained the problem and told him to tactfully find a way to get my husband to do this unpleasant task. It worked." Or, "I got the necessary papers, did all the preliminary work, and presented it to my husband in an orderly way which made him feel less threatened."

Stewing in bitter hostility or despair can be deceiving because you feel as though you are doing something active about the problem. But these emotions do not magically bring solutions. Take the initiative to improve your life wherever possible. Form groups of people with similar problems, if you have an exceptional situation. Gather information on special difficulties. Seek the guidance of experts. Don't assume that a situation, being the will of God, must remain that way, unless, of course, you have exhausted all avenues to improvement. Many people justify passivity by calling it "faith," when, in reality, they are too fearful or too lazy to make the effort to change. Maturity requires taking responsibility for thought, speech, and action.

When dealing with stressful events, there are only a few basic Torah principles which you need to keep in mind, such as giving the benefit of the doubt, accepting pain with love, and remembering that everything Hashem does is for our ultimate refinement. But when it comes to action, the possible solutions are as infinite as the variety of problems. The purpose of the temper-reducers is to keep you functional and objective. No one can give you solutions to all your particular difficulties. That is something you must figure out for yourself, given your nature, level of awareness, and capabilities.

There are two extremes when it comes to responding to problems: aggressive use of force and stoic resignation. Both have their place, and both can be misused. In his commentary to *Vayikra* 1:3, Rabbi Samson Raphael Hirsch noted that the two most important sacrifices in the Holy Temple were the lamb and the bull (*bakar*). The bull represented resolute devotion to actively carrying out our obligations with "... every drop of our blood and ... every ounce of strength which He has given us... in accordance with His will." The lamb represented that part of us which is "shepherded," which submits passively to His will. It is important not to confuse the lamb, who has surrendered to God's will in total love and trust, even in martyrdom, with the pseudo-martyr. The latter responds out of fear and mistrust, is passive, dependent, and often masochistic, causing himself unnecessary pain and avoiding permissible pleasures and comforts out of self-hatred and the compulsion to have others' approval. Likewise, the true *bakar* should not be confused with the "bully." The former is motivated by a spirit of selfless devotion to the good of mankind. The bully, on the other hand, is motivated only by the desire to have his own selfish demands satisfied. Whichever side we choose on any given issue, the important thing is to act from purity of motivation.

Almost every situation requires balancing acceptance with action.

*Example*: I can't change the fact that my husband had a heart attack. I have to accept that he has a heart problem. But I now make sure that we exercise and eat properly.

*Example*: I can't change the fact that we have a small apartment and no money to move to a larger one. But I avoid self-pity over this fact, and I am compassionate with my children when they are upset about not being able to buy the things they would like.

Obviously, we often have no solutions to many disturbing situations. EMETT does not make our lives pain-free. However, it does help us experience the pain which is appropriate to the situation while avoiding the unnecessary torment produced by temper.

## ENCOURAGE GROWTH: USE ENDORSEMENTS

Once you have taken secure thoughts or acted positively, you can reinforce your behavior with endorsements.

> There was a small town with only a few inhabitants and a mighty king came upon it and surrounded it and built great siege works over it. Present in the city was a poor wise man who by his wisdom saved the town. Yet no one remembered that poor man.
>
> (*Koheleth* 9: 14-15)

> According to the Talmud (*Nedarim* 32b) the small town is the body; the few inhabitants, the limbs, the mighty king is the evil inclination; the great siege works is the preparation the latter makes to tempt one to do evil; the poor wise man is the good inclination. Why is it called "poor"? Because most people ignore it. "No one remembers that poor man" means that no one holds the good inclination in any kind of esteem.
>
> (ibid., *ArtScroll* commentary)

It is a sad fact that our small acts of kindness, self-discipline, and courage are often unnoticed or shrugged off with indifference unless they are truly outstanding. On the other hand, minor acts of impoliteness or misbehavior may arouse a strong emotional reaction. Behavior which gets noticed gets reinforced. Thus, paying too much attention to the negative in oneself or others actually strengthens that behavior. According to various studies, the average family member makes approximately twenty-five negative comments or commanding statements for every one word of praise, appreciation, or polite request.

One way to correct this imbalance is through a discipline called "endorsing." This is a mental or verbal pat on the back for any positive thought, word, or deed. In order to override the pleasure of bad habits, endorsements substitute a pleasure of a higher level — the joy of increased self-awareness and self-respect which comes from restraining harmful impulses.

> *Example*: I overcame the temptation to say *lashon hara* (and the pleasure of feeling superior) by experiencing the pleasure of self-control.

> *Example*: When my daughter forgot to give me an important message, I calmed myself down before speaking to her by endorsing myself for not yelling at her. Only then did I speak to her about the seriousness of writing messages down and putting them in a place where they can be seen. I really got pleasure out of being firm but calm instead of expressing my usual hostility.

> *Example*: I wanted to overeat when I came home from that unsuccessful *shidduch*, but I decided that my self-esteem needed raising, and that required self-restraint, not self-indulgence. After the initial effort, I really felt that the pleasure of self-worth was better than any meal.

No one will endorse you for these unseen victories except yourself. Few people will celebrate or even notice the endless acts of self-sacrifice and self-discipline required to overcome temper, laziness, and selfishness. These events often pass on, forgotten forever, even by yourself, unless you stop for a moment and give thanks for this divine power of self-restraint.

> The smallest victory that you win [over the *yetzer hara*], the least increase in your power over him, regard as important so that it may be to you a step to greater victory.
>
> *(Duties of the Heart*, vol. 2, p. 23)

Recognize the positive so that it will be reinforced. Remember that adults are not that different from children in wanting a word of encouragement and appreciation for positive acts.

To avoid flattery or pride, endorse behavior and *middoth*, not people as a whole. Such limited endorsements do not lead to arrogance. On the contrary, by focusing on *middoth*, you are reminded that the process of character improvement is endless and involves constant vigilance, not smug self-satisfaction. Avoid "global" praise such as "perfect child" or "best in the world" because the label is not true. Such phrases may have a counter-productive effect, since one cannot live up to the image. It is less threatening and more effective to describe the specific *middah* which is being displayed such as: *chesed*, patience, thoughtfulness, tolerance, self-discipline, silence, and persistence, etc.

> *Example*: I made a little "endorsement notebook" for myself when I was going through a very difficult period and was fighting feelings of low esteem. It lifted my spirits to write down the positive things I did each day. I realized that I did have inner strengths which I had been ignoring before.

> *Example*: I made a little endorsement notebook for one of my children who was being particularly difficult. I wrote down all the things he did during the day which pleased me and ignored those that didn't. Each night, I would mention his positive behavior and the *middah* which it displayed. In a matter of weeks, our relationship improved. He not only saw himself in a new light, but I also stopped feeling so negative about him. After a month, I was able to ask him, "What *middoth* do you think you need to work on tomorrow?" He was able to give his own answers and became more aware of his need for growth without me having to say one word of criticism.

Endorse for effort, not success. The former is up to us; the latter up to a Power beyond our control.

> *Example*: I put together what I thought was a very special evening for the parents of the children in my class. But only a small number of mothers came. I kept myself from getting into temper by endorsing myself for effort, not success.

Endorse for "part acts" whenever a situation seems overwhelming.

> *Example*: The idea of moving to a new city seemed overwhelming until I endorsed for "part acts," one box at a time.

> *Example*: The staff had left for the day and I was going over the computer printouts to check if everything was okay for a big project which was due the next day. I found a serious mistake which required that I stay at the office the entire night redoing all the printouts. When I first looked at that huge pile of papers, I suddenly felt very tired and helpless. I told myself to take it in "part acts" — one page at a time. That's how I got through a very long night, endorsing all along.

Endorse for the "small gains."

> *Example*: I have a handicapped child. We don't know what the prognosis is at present. All I can say is that I focus on the "small gains" in her improvement and hope for the best.

Appropriate endorsements, done with tact and sensitivity, are usually received with quiet pleasure by others, even if they don't show it at the time.

> *Example*: One word of endorsement or encouragement from my spouse gives me the strength to go on when things are difficult. It's amazing how my spirits are lifted by the smallest sign of appreciation and caring.

Endorse immediately when you are so overwhelmed by temper that you can't think in terms of Step 2 or 3. This will give you something positive on which to focus.

> *Example*: I had an unpleasant encounter with a close family member. I got so upset that I had a strong impulse to retaliate. For a few seconds, I just stood there speechless, telling myself to endorse for breathing, endorse for not lashing out at the person, endorse for endorsing.... After a few minutes, I began to get in touch with thoughts which would help me take proper action.

Endorse yourself for going against old habit patterns.

> *Example*: My daughter was late for school and asked me if I would make her a sandwich. I wanted to tell her that it was her own fault that she was late and that she should accept the logical consequences by going hungry. I have a firm principle of not doing anything for my children that they can do for themselves. But it suddenly occurred to me that this was an opportunity to stop being such an *akshan* (stubborn one). I felt that I could endorse for flexibility if I made it for her instead of sticking so compulsively to my rules all the time.

A rigid kind of mother can endorse for flexibility and acts of kindness, whereas the type that martyrs herself for her children can endorse for teaching them independence and self-reliance.

Use written endorsements for yourself and others. They have special power.

> *Example*: I was furious about something and went in the bedroom, slamming the door and locking it behind me. I was sitting on the bed fuming when suddenly a little slip of paper came sliding under the door. On it, my seven year old had written, "Endorse yourself, Mommy." Well, the balloon of temper burst instantly. I smiled to myself and began to use my other temper-reducing tools.

Giving notes in lunch boxes or taping them to mirrors where others will see brings great rewards. Endorse yourself out loud every once in a while to bring lightness and humor into situations and let others know if they are being excessively critical.

"I know the project didn't turn out right, but endorse for effort, if not success."

"You might not think I'm doing a great job, but considering the pressures I'm under right now, I'm actually doing very well."

Keep a "mental photo album" of endorsable acts you or others have done to give you hope at a time when temper is making things look far worse than they actually are. When you are feeling resentful, tell the other person about some act that you remember him doing which pleased you last week or twenty years ago in order to awaken positive feelings in you both. If you feel you "never do anything right" or "never have self-control," counter those false beliefs with memories of endorsable acts from the past.

Teach others the power of endorsement by your own example.

"Kids, I'm not feeing very well right now, but I'm endorsing myself for functioning with discomfort."

"I'm endorsing myself for giving you the benefit of the doubt instead of assuming that you did what you did on purpose."

If someone complains that an endorsement is flattery, tell that person that flattery is a way of manipulating others for your own good. An endorsement simply encourages others to be all they are capable of becoming. It does not matter who or what you are endorsing. The important thing is that you are habituating yourself to look for the positive. Seek the beauty in life and in people.

| CONDEMNATORY ATTITUDE | NON-CONDEMNATORY ATTITUDE |
|---|---|
| My spouse is late. How selfish! | Something unexpected must have come up. |
| My child is being uncooperative. What a brat! | Something must be bothering him. |
| The house is a mess. What a bunch of slobs! | We need more organization, more charts, more discipline and more positive reinforcement around here. |
| My spouse is uncommunicative. He's mean. | He doesn't have good communication skills. |
| This clerk is an idiot! | She must be new or is having a hard day. She must not have the skills. |

## DROP THE "RIGHT" AND "WRONG" IN MATTERS OF PERSONAL TASTE

Every act, no matter how seemingly trivial or mundane, can have an aspect of right or wrong when seen in terms of our highest priorities in life.

> ... all human actions fall into the categories of good and bad, of commanded, forbidden or permitted ....
>
> (*Duties of the Heart*, vol. 2, p. 217)

Before acting, we should think, "Is this behavior in keeping with the will of Hashem? Will it enhance my own and others' mental and physical well-being?" However, we should be careful not to impose our own sense of right and wrong on others in matters of taste. A great deal of interpersonal strife, particularly in families, arises from judging right and wrong in areas which have to do with custom and personal taste.

We have an enormous body of religious laws (*halachah*) which tells us what is right and wrong. Anything outside that category should be kept separate from that judgment. The term "right" implies an inflexible obligation to behave in a certain way. It adds a certain necessary stress in our lives because it forces us to accomplish various tasks in a certain way and by a certain time, such as Pesach cleaning and candle lighting. We should not add to this pressure by imposing a judgment of right and wrong on others where it does not belong. When in doubt, ask yourself if the event you are judging has to do with actual law or is merely a personal preference. For example, there is really no right or wrong in the following areas unless you are deliberately trying to hurt someone by acting this way:

- matters of food, travel, household chores, and clothing, as long as it does not violate *halachah*,

- giving babies pacifiers,
- serving fancy or simple meals,
- giving children an allowance,
- holding your fork with your right hand or your left,
- laundering certain items every week or every month,
- giving fancy gifts, simple ones, or none at all, etc.

Unfortunately, there are many people who decide that whatever they think is right is actually right, as if to say, "If it feels good to me, it must be good." Or, "If I like it, it must be right." People often try to define their own personal desires as the only right way to live, eat, and dress. They then justify the imposition of their will on others by claiming that this is the way it *must* be and that they will feel terribly hurt or insulted if it isn't that way. They may even give their own interpretation of Torah laws in order to satisfy their own selfish desires. Needless to say, this is a gross misuse of *halachah*. Such intolerance and excessive desire to dominate others wreak havoc in family life by denying the important and healthy right to hold one's own opinions and have those opinions respected.

Be as flexible as necessary about man-made rules and customs, but as firm as possible about ultimate priorities and values.

> A man should be soft as a reed, and not hard like a cedar.
>
> *(Ta'anith 20b)*

*Example:* I told my husband that it was silly to take the baby to the doctor, since he only had a slight fever. But my husband said he wanted the reassurance of an authority and that there was no right or wrong. When he said that, I relaxed and actually urged him to go.

*Example:* I used to have a lot of negative judgments about the way my wife did things, which were different from how my mother did them. Only when I realized that these were matters of taste, style, and habit, was I able to control my criticizing.

*Example*: When my four year old was going through a difficult period and having many nightmares, I allowed him to come into my bed for a short time, and then, I put him back in his own bed when he calmed down. The stage lasted only a short time, and he hasn't come into my bed since. Previously, I would have been inflexible about such things, and would have thought it was wrong to ever let a child into my bed.

To understand the importance of this discipline, you can go back to the story of Adam and Chava. God told Adam that he could eat of all the trees in the Garden of Eden except the Tree of the Knowledge of Good and Evil.

However, when Chava told the snake about this commandment (some say it was Adam who had misinformed her in order to make sure that she would keep the prohibition), she said that they were not allowed to eat *or* touch it (*Bereishith* 2). It is said that this small addition created the opening which led to their sin. Therefore, we are told,

> He who adds to the Torah, subtracts from it.
>
> (*Sanhedrin* 29a)

Before you take the law into your own hands, check with a Torah authority. And if you receive an opinion different from that of a friend who follows another Torah authority, be tolerant. Accept that there are often many ways of looking at the same issue, and that one need not feel superior or self-righteous becuase his way differs from that of another.

## AWAKEN COMPASSION BY SAYING:
## "HE'S DOING THE BEST HE CAN WITH THE TOOLS HE HAS "

The Baal Shem Tov said that when we see people doing something which displeases us, we should think to ourselves that, given the same personality and situation, we would probably do the same. Another way of looking at such behavior is to say, "He's doing the best he can with the tools he has at this moment, with his present level of awareness, with his past conditioning, and the passions and pressures impinging on him at this time." Giving the benefit of the doubt means believing that this attitude is true. This statement reminds us that we never have all the facts about what is going on in the inner world of another person.

You may have to repeat the phrase hundreds of times. Keep saying it even if you do not believe it at first. As a result, you will become more objective and forgiving, and eventually be able to give the benefit of the doubt with true compassion, even if the person's behavior is not to be condoned.

> *Example*: My two year old was being very defiant about getting dressed and I was feeling more and more inadequate and angry. Finally, I said to myself, "He's doing the best he can with the tools he has." As a matter of fact, he is supposed to be defiant at this age! He doesn't know any better and he's not out to get me. I stopped feeling inadequate and dealt more calmly and assertively with the problem.

> *Example*: I had a very difficult childhood and harbored a lot of resentment toward my parents. Finally, I started repeating over and over to myself that given their personalities and their own backgrounds, they really did the best they could with the tools they had. They simply did not have many tools to know how to get along together or how to treat

children any differently. They really did the best they could. After months of repeating these words to myself, I could feel the hostility fade away and in its place was a real acceptance and love.

The Chazon Ish stressed the importance of being sensitive to one's own minor faults while overlooking even the most obvious faults of others. This, he said, was the mark of a refined nature (*Emunah U-bitachon*, 1:11). While we can often tell ourselves that we could be doing better, when it comes to others, we should excuse rather than accuse whenever possible.

> Do not judge another until you have come unto his place.
>
> *(Avoth 2:4)*

The truth is that you can never really be in another person's shoes completely. You will foster compassion and forgiveness if you humbly assume that others are doing the best they can with whatever resources they have at the moment. If they could be more loving, sensitive, efficient, or mature, they would no doubt be acting differently. If there is any hope for change, it will be promoted by an atmosphere of compassion, not condemnation.

> *Examples*: "Hm ... that is interesting behavior from a three year old. I've never seen that before. Now I have to think of what to do."
> "Hm ... what a challenging situation to have an adult act in this way. Let me think if it's best to respond or to just walk away."

## DEVELOP IMMUNITY TO INSULT

It is most difficult to avoid grudge-bearing and vengeful behavior when you are insulted. While no one would recommend tolerating abuse if it is possible to help the other person correct his behavior, there are many times in life when you will be dealing with people who are temporarily or permanently in a state of irrationality and are taking out their pain on those around by insulting them. Some people are more sensitive to insults than others. They feel as if they have received a kind of emotional beating. And certainly, if you are constantly insulted in your own home by a close family member, this is precisely what is happening. However, on an infrequent basis, insults can be useful opportunities to practice mitzvoth and to use EMETT tools.

> Rabbi Chanina ben Dosa was bitten by a poisonous lizard while praying, but did not interrupt his prayers. His disciples asked in amazement how he managed to do this. He answered, "I take an oath. Because my heart was intent on my prayers, I felt nothing!"
>
> *(Talmud Yerushalmi, Berachoth 5:1)*

If your mind is focused on compassion for the insulter or on other mitzvoth, you too may not feel the pain.

Rabbi Zalman of Volozhin was traveling with his brother, Rabbi Chaim, when they stopped at an inn. The ill-tempered innkeeper shouted insults at the brothers and refused to allow them to stay. As they were leaving, Rabbi Chaim noticed that his brother was crying and said, "Why are you crying? I didn't take what he said to heart and neither should you." Rabbi Zalman replied, "I'm not crying because of his insults, but because when he shouted, I felt a bit of pain. I am crying because I didn't reach the level of being oblivious to insults."

(Rabbi Yechezkel Feivel, *Toldoth Adam*, cited in *Love Your Neighbor*, p. 297)

A disciple of Rabbi Yechezkel Levenstein said that he once saw his teacher in a great state of cheerfulness. When he asked the reason, Rabbi Levenstein said, "Someone greatly insulted me and I didn't say anything in return. For this I am joyful."

(*Marbitzey Torah U-mussar*, vol. 4, p. 212)

One EMETT member found the following to be helpful.

*Example*: When I am insulted, I think to myself that by not answering back, perhaps I am bringing Mashiach one step closer. I'm so happy thinking about the effect that my self-control is having on insuring inner tranquility, and perhaps world peace, that I have no chance to dwell on hurt feelings.

## DO NOT PLAY MIND READER:
## TAKE AWAY THE DAVKA OR INTENTION TO HURT

One of the most anger-producing thoughts of all is that others are *davka* (intentionally) out to hurt us when they misbehave, fail to cooperate, or disappoint us in some way. When you assume *davka*, you are adopting an arrogant position, for you cannot really know what is in the heart or mind of another unless that person has specifically told you how he feels and thinks. Your insecure interpretation of another's behavior can upset you:

"I know why he didn't show up on time. It's because he has no respect for me."

"I know why he's being so uncooperative. It's because he wants to drive me crazy!"

"I know why he's being so uncommunicative. It's because he does not love me."

Some people have severe paranoia: they think that others are out to hurt them no matter what they are doing, even if they are being nice! While few people go to that extreme, most of us indulge in this habit at times. However, once you recognize it, you can discipline yourself to avoid condemning the individual and focus simply on whether you approve or disapprove of the act.

Or, you may simply notice, "That's just what's happening" without making an evaluation of inferiority or superiority.

| BEHAVIOR | INSECURE INTERPRETATION | SECURE INTERPRETATION |
|---|---|---|
| neighbor scowls at you as you walk past | "This person is *davka* trying to hurt my feelings." | "He's having a hard day. Maybe I did something to annoy him. I'll go talk to him about it." |
| child doesn't come when called | "He has no respect for me! He's deliberately trying to get me upset." | "He must be preoccupied, maybe dreaming or having fun doing something else. I need to work with him on the discipline of respecting my orders." |
| friend cancels her visit | "She doesn't like me anymore." | "Oh, she cancelled. We'll have to set another date." |
| child is in a bad mood | "*Davka*, now, right before candle lighting! He wants to destroy my sanity." | "She's in a bad mood. Everybody has the right to be moody sometimes." |
| mate leaves items lying around | "*Davka* he's doing this to be inconsiderate and thoughtless. He's trying to show me that he does not really love me." | "He forgot. He doesn't know how important it is to me." "He knows how important it is to me but doesn't have the self-discipline at times or sometimes forgets. I know he loves me even if he doesn't always do what I want." |

We are obligated to search for mitigating circumstances whenever anyone does something wrong (*Makkoth* 7a). Thus, when others cause you pain, inconvenience, disappointment, or unnecessary expense, assume that it is because they:

1. forgot,
2. failed to exercise self-control,
3. were preoccupied with themselves because of fatigue, pain, hunger, some kind of internal or external problem, or simply daydreaming,
4. are lacking in awareness, skills, intelligence, information, or maturity,
5. are mentally ill and are therefore incapable of acting in any other way at this moment.

Domestic life in particular requires the continued use of this discipline. Otherwise, every misplaced item, forgotten message, or display of poor manners becomes a source of conflict and resentment. Before making a judgment, get the facts directly from the person involved. When that is not possible, observe the behavior without making a negative evaluation about the motivation behind it.

> *Example*: I had a hard day and came home wanting only to have peace and quiet. But the kids were noisy and my wife wanted to talk. I started to think, "*Davka*, they are doing this to make me explode." Then I realized that it was my assumption of deliberate intention to hurt which was making me so upset. When I realized that they simply wanted some attention, I calmed down and delayed my desire for rest for an hour until I had time to be with each one.

> *Example*: I used to get so upset at a cetain relative who was always giving me advice. I used to think, "She must think I'm a total idiot! *Davka*, she's trying to make me feel inferior and inadequate with all these endless suggestions." Then I realized that she had no intention to hurt. She has a lot of opinions on how to do things and she is sure that she will make my life better if I do everything her way. Once I took away the intention to hurt, I was able to tell her in a humorous way that we should establish a "comment quota" so that I could develop my own skills as a homemaker and establish a sense of trust in my own ability to work things out. She was very accepting of my response because I said it without any hostility. Then I mentioned that advice can sometimes make people feel inadequate. She was very surprised, but I could see that she gained a new awareness about people.

> *Example*: It was just before Shabbath and I was running around frantically. A child was reading the newspaper calmly. I could never stand to be busy while others are relaxing because I always thought it was a sure sign of lack of respect or caring. But this time, I thought to myself that he probably thinks I have it all under control. I don't have a

neon light on my forehead saying, "Please get dressed," or "Please vacuum the rug." I have to tell him. When I dropped my insecure interpretation of his newspaper-reading, I was able to ask for help without my former hostility. And he was responsive — more so than he has ever been before.

*Example*: One of my children started displaying very disturbing behavior around the age of two. He was super-sensitive, moody, often aggressive toward others and sometimes even cruel. He seemed to lack the awareness of other people's feelings that my other children had. I used to think he was doing this *davka* to be hurtful. Then I started to give him the benefit of the doubt. I realized that he simply lacked awareness, skills, and maturity. It wasn't his fault. He needed extra time to become part of our world, so to speak. There were times when he was so obnoxious that I wanted to really beat him hard. But I thankfully thought of the importance of not seeing children as doing things intentionally, because that thought only made me angry. I was able to discipline him firmly, strictly, but without the angry hysteria which had sometimes gripped me previously. Little by little, with a great deal of physical warmth and extra attention, he began to improve. After five years, he is almost completely normal — i.e., loving and helpful most of the time. The discipline of "dropping the *davka*" was the most important tool to me during that time.

The following story illustrates how we should use our imagination positively and creatively to give others the benefit of the doubt.

A man from the Galilee hired himself out to someone in the south of Eretz Yisrael for three years. Before Yom Kippur, he said to his employer, "Give me my wages so that I can go home and feed my wife and children."
"I have no money," was the employer's reply.
"Then give me fruit," suggested the man.
"I have none," answered the employer.
"Give me property."
"I don't have any."
"Give me pillows and blankets."
"I haven't any."
   The man slung his belongings over his shoulder and went home with nothing. After Sukkoth, the employer brought the wages plus three donkeys loaded with food, drink, and delicacies to the home of his employee. After they had eaten and the salary was paid, the employer asked, "When you asked me for money and I said that I didn't have any, what did you suspect?"
"I thought that you might have spent your money on a bargain that had just arisen."
"And when I told you that I had no livestock, what were your thoughts?"

"I thought that you might have lent them to others."

"And when I said I didn't have any property?"

"I assumed that maybe it was leased to others."

"And when I said that I didn't have any fruit?"

"Perhaps you hadn't separated *maaser* (tithes) yet."

"What did you think when I said I hadn't any pillows and blankets?"

"I thought that you might have dedicated all your possessions to the Beith Hamikdash."

"I make an oath, that that is exactly what happened! Just as you have judged me favorably, so too should God judge you favorably."

(Shabbath, 127b)

We are taught that the Second Temple was destroyed because of unfounded hatred (*sinath chinam*) between people (*Yoma* 9b). The *tikun* (spiritual correction) for this tragedy is for us to do the opposite, to practice *ahavath chinam*; i.e., to show love and respect for others even when it seems that they are not deserving of it. This mitzvah not only benefits others but ourselves as well, for,

"He who does *chesed* receives *chesed*. And the more *chesed* he does, the more he receives."

(The Path of the Just, p. 229)

## AVOID THE CONDEMNATIONS IMPLIED IN NAME CALLING

There is a well-known saying that, "Labeling is disabling." The names we call ourselves and others can leave emotional scars that may last a lifetime. Labels tend to be self-fulfilling prophecies. You drop something and say, "Oy, what a klutz I am." And before you know it, you are actually behaving more and more often that way. When you use words like, "crazy," "pushy," "cold," "slob," "brat," "pest," or "monster" on yourselves or others, you often condemn yourself and others to continue acting that way. It is as if by hearing the words often enough, you come to think, "I *am* my label." Then, because human beings have a natural tendency to select those behaviors or phenomena which fit into their preconceived belief about how things are or should be, they discount anything which does not fit into that label. This kind of "selective blindness" is referred to as "cognitive dissonance." It is a phenomenon whereby people see what they want to see. Thus a person can claim he doesn't have the capacity to be any different than he is. For example, an overweight person may say, "I have no will power." Yet such a person displays countless moments of self-restraint without realizing or giving importance to those times. Or, a person will say, "I'm so untogether," completely forgetting that there are many areas of competency and times when he does manage to behave in a very normal, adequate manner.

Labels are a license — often seen as an actual obligation — to act negatively. For example, the following questions are not really questions. They are statements of fact to which there is no positive response. One is left with a feeling of hopelessness from the implied condemnations:

"Why don't you ever understand your studies?"
"Why must you always walk away every time I try to talk to you?"
"Why do you have to argue about everything I tell you to do?"
"Why do I always have to be so late to everything and so disorganized?"
"Why must you always create tension at the Shabbath table each week?"

Such statements are often internalized as unalterable facts. People usually do not realize that first they inflict these condemnations on themselves and others and *then* they get angry or depressed. They fail to realize that the source of their negative feelings is their own negative attitude.

1. I saw the mess.
2. I thought to myself, "What an irresponsible, lazy slob she is."
3. Boy, did I get furious!

1. I got lost on the way to the meeting.
2. I thought to myself, "I'm such a failure. I can't do anything right!"
3. I felt so inadequate and gloomy about myself that I got more mixed up than before.

Certainly we cannot help but notice that we and those around us sometimes fail to live up to certain standards of efficiency, maturity, intelligence, and thoughtfulness. But calling constant attention to this behavior is counter-productive. Constant criticism reinforces the very behavior we are trying to eliminate, instead of doing something positive about it. Watch for the "small gains" in people. Search for and highlight those times when others act as you wish. After all, no child is always uncooperative, sloppy, or obnoxious. No mate is totally uncommunicative. No one is a complete failure, although temper would have us believe otherwise! You are never totally incompetent. If we reinforce behavior with a nod, smile, word of appreciation, or written note, we will encourage improvement.

Furthermore, many negative character traits can be seen as positive traits which have been carried to the extreme: thrift became stinginess, assertiveness became aggression, acceptance became apathy, etc. We can often help ourselves and others see themselves in a more positive light by pointing out the positive source beneath the unhealthy extreme.

"You have good leadership qualities. However, sometimes you get very overbearing."

"It's great that you have such confidence that things will work out all right. But sometimes that trust leads you to be too passive."

But within every family, there is almost inevitably one child or another who, at one time or another, plays the role of dreamer, wild one, boss, *klutz*, fearful crybaby, clown, slob, or bully. Roles may switch depending on age and circumstances. It is very easy for these labels to become hardened realities if we fail to be realistic in our demands for improvement while avoiding the demand for perfection. Perfectionism often causes others to become anxious and resistant. Then they sink further into the negative habit pattern or adopt another which is equally aggravating.

When Yaakov rebuked Reuven for his rashness and Shimon and Levi for their excessive violence, (*Bereishith* 49:4-5), he did so not in order to condemn them to a life sentence from which they could never escape, but to make sure that they were aware of their need to exercise self-restraint. This is only one example of instances in which our forefathers waited until they were near death before rebuking their children. Rashi (*Devarim* 1:3) says that this was done to save the children excessive shame and despair. This teaches us to avoid the temptation to rebuke over and over again, thereby creating even more resistance, and to maintain loving relationships.

Obviously, we need to recognize where we and others need improvement. When we can admit our faults, then we can begin to change.

## AVOID SELF-CONDEMNATIONS:
## CULTIVATE SELF-ESTEEM, NOT SELF-IMPORTANCE

> Do not be wicked in your own estimation.
>
> > (*Avoth* 2:18)

> Do not be overly righteous or excessively wise. There is no man so wholly righteous that he always does good and never sins.
>
> > (*Koheleth* 7:16-20)

One of the most important disciplines necessary for maintaining inner peace is to avoid the judgment of inferiority or superiority. The former shows lack of respect for oneself and the other manifests lack of respect for others.

> The important thing is for a person to know his value, to recognize his positive character traits and those of his forefathers, the greatness and importance of these traits and how beloved he is by Hashem. He should strive always to be aware of these positive traits and strengthen them daily, to draw closer to Hashem through them. Then, if he begins with small steps, he will gradually improve himself. He should act in a manner that would not shame him before his forefathers, but should be in accordance with the best of his ability. The result of this will be that when he is tempted to act wrongly, he will be ashamed before his forefathers and

> will think, "An important person like me, who has so many good qualities, and is the son of great men, how could I possibly do such a terrible thing before my fathers." But if he does not recognize his inner greatness, it will be far more easy to sin.
>
> (*Sha'arey 'Avodah*, p. 1)

A sense of self-respect is the foundation for loving relationships. It is the source of self-confidence in the midst of stress. It is good to be self-critical, to be aware of where one needs to improve. But excessive self-criticism stifles growth. It is as much a manifestation of the *yetzer hara* as pride, and just as destructive. You do not have to be perfect to be deserving of love and respect. Character improvement is always possible, which implies that no one is perfect. Nor do you have to be productive every moment of your life in order to think of yourself as having value, for such an attitude prevents you from being able to relax and enjoy life. It can also cause depression if you become sick or incapacitated, God forbid.

We have worth because we were created *be-tzelem* Hashem, in the image of God (*Bereishith* 1:27). Even though we sometimes make errors in judgment and fail, our intrinsic worth remains the same. Although our *madreigah* (spiritual level) does change depending on our thoughts and actions, our intrinsic worth does not. We should not allow our self-esteem to fluctuate like the stock market, depending on how well we are coping at the moment.

> *Example*: When the house is organized, and my learning is going well, and I'm in total control, I have good self-esteem. When things are messy or my children don't get good marks or are misbehaving, or I haven't been able to solve some difficulty, I feel inferior. I'm a nervous wreck from worrying about what others are thinking of me, and whether or not I'm living up to my sometimes impossible standards.

It is useless to try to figure out whether or not you have worth. You do by virtue of having been created. As for comparisons, you can always find people who cope better, are more beautiful or smart. That does not make you less worthwhile. You do not know their level of intelligence or competency. You may be trying harder and achieving less because of greater handicaps. The important thing in life is to work at achieving your own personal level of excellence at any given moment, taking into account external pressures, internal awareness and health.

A psychologically revealing incident concerning the importance of self-respect is seen in *Bamidbar* 13:33-14:11. After Moshe sent twelve of the finest men of Israel to spy out the land of Canaan, ten came back with an "evil report." Although there are other interpretations of this event, Abarbanel says that the sin of the spies was that of self-deprecation — for the moment that they lost confidence in themselves, they automatically lost faith in their leaders and in God, "doubting the reality of His intervention in earthly matters" (Rabbi S.R. Hirsch, ibid., 14:23). Note the sequence well: self-devaluation leads to helplessness leads to hopelessness leads to hostility leads to loss of *emunah* and *bitachon*.

| BIBLICAL ACCOUNT | PSYCHOLOGICAL INTERPRETATION |
|---|---|
| 1. The ten said, "We were as grasshoppers in our eyes." | 1. You devalue yourself. |
| 2. "And we were as grasshoppers in their eyes." | 2. You think that others lack respect for you. |
| 3. "Then the whole congregation gave way to defeatism and despair." | 3. You, and often those around you, give way to defeatism and despair. |
| 4. "They turned on Moshe and Aharon saying ... it would have been better to have remained in Egypt or died in the wilderness." | 4. You look around to see who is to blame and begin to think irrationally, seeing evil as good and good as evil, lacking in gratefulness for what you have, despairing of improvement. |
| 5. They turned against God saying that, "God brought us into this land to fall by the sword." | 5. You become temporarily paranoid, thinking that your present difficulties are a cruel punishment which is undeserved and purposeless. |
| 6. They urged each other to stone Calev and Yehoshua. | 6. You want to "stone" those whom you think are responsible for your present sorrow. |
| 7. Finally, God became visible to Moshe and says, "How long shall they have no confidence in Me with all the signs I have shown in their midst?" | 7. You lose faith in God, in His wisdom and goodness. |

To avoid this negative habit pattern, practice respecting and valuing yourself and others, as you are at this very moment, even though you know that there could always be an improvement. Encourage yourself and others to think, say, and do only what will promote self-respect and dignity. If you fail, remember that,

> A righteous man falls seven times and rises up; the wicked stumble under adversity.
>
> *(Mishley* 24:16)

If you feel low, remember that any act of self-discipline or *chesed* enables you to experience your inner strength and worth, and, thereby, lifts your spirits.

## APPROVAL SEEKING: A RESULT OF LOW SELF-ESTEEM

> Woe to a person who is not aware of his faults, for he does not know what he has to correct. But double woe to a person who is not aware of his virtues, for he is lacking the tools for correcting himself.
>
> *(Aley Shur,* pp. 168-69)

> The Torah writes about the faults and transgressions of even the greatest of our forefathers. This is to console us and to teach us that while it is normal to have faults, we should continuously strive with all our might to elevate ourselves.
>
> *(Shi'urey Da'ath,* vol. 2, p. 158)

> Every man should have a pocket on either side of his coat. When he is feeling angry at not getting his way or superior to his fellowman, he should reach into one pocket and take out the note that says, "What is man? Dust. A zero. A nothing." But when he feels dejected and afraid, he should reach into the other pocket and read the note which says, "The whole world was created just for me."
>
> *(Sanhedrin* 37a; story from the Kotzker Rabbi)

> The goal to strive for is that it should be equal in your eyes if others praise or insult you.
>
> *(Duties of the Heart,* vol. 1, p. 45)

Many people try to cover feelings of low self-esteem by seeking others' approval. This is one desire which can never be satisfied. No amount of approval from others can make up for one's sense of unworthiness. When you constantly seek approval, you are forced to lie, even to the point of harming yourself:

> "I didn't ask the doctor for my x-rays because I was afraid he would disapprove of me if he knew that I wanted a second opinion."

You fail to be assertive with others:

> "A certain person is always putting me down. And I'm afraid to tell her, because she might ridicule me for being so touchy."
>
> "A certain person spoke *lashon hara* and I was afraid to stop him."

You cause yourself unnecessary discomfort:

> "When I visit my married children, I would prefer to stay in a quiet hotel, but I don't let them know, because I don't want them to feel insulted and be angry with me."

You fail to pursue the achievements which would give you joy and meaning:

> "I would like to take an exercise class but I'm afraid others will think I'm a *klutz*."
> "I would like to take some stimulating classes and work part-time but I'm afraid of the disapproval of certain relatives who believe I should be home full time."

You set yourself up for anger and resentment since no one can be totally approving one hundred percent of the time. Clerks, family members, and strangers will not give you all the respect, love, and honor you crave. Your response is likely to be a temperamental one if you are dependent on outside approval for your sense of worth.

People with low self-esteem tend to project their feelings of inferiority onto other sects, nations, or individuals. You can overcome this tendency with a simple exercise: practice looking at people without allowing yourself to feel inferior or superior. Simply notice them as a child might, paying attention to various details without evaluating their worth. Every person deserves to be treated with respect, yourself included. The most important principle to remember is to avoid judgments which lead to an attitude of personal inferiority or superiority because this stifles love of self, man, and God.

## RESPECT PEOPLE AS THEY ARE, NOT AS YOU WANT THEM TO BE

> When demands begin, love departs.
> (Strive for Truth!, vol. 1, p. 132)

You may think that it is a sign of love that you want to push a person to reach a certain level of excellence. This is true if the individual wants your help. But if he does not, you may stifle his independent motivation and actually reduce his ability to develop and perform. Acceptance precedes growth. It also promotes it. Acceptance implies respect for what the person is at the moment, without bitter resignation or indifference on your part.

Constructive criticism may be welcomed as long as the person with whom you are dealing is having success experiences and is self-motivated toward a particular goal. However, if inner motivation is lacking, your pressure is likely to produce a great deal of tension and resentment, and destroy your relationship in the process.

The awareness of very distinct personality types has fascinated great thinkers for centuries. It seems that each of us has certain sensitivities and talents which pull us in the direction in which we were meant to travel. Some things give us a deep sense of satisfaction and others don't. You can't force a person to change his interests any more than you can force him to like a food which he hates. You can try to motivate a person to take interest in being more communicative, assertive, or quiet, but don't become hostile if your efforts fail. .

> *Example*: I very much wanted my older daughter to go into teaching. She tried it and said that she couldn't stand the noise and commotion. She's not very people-oriented and prefers working with things. She found it far more satisfying to work in a laboratory. But my son, who was hyperactive as a child, loves his teaching job and disliked having to sit and learn all day, which is what I had wanted for him.

Just as we don't condemn people for their God-given physical qualities, so too we should avoid condemning them for their personality structures. Some people are innately slow-moving or fast-paced, warmly passionate or cool and aloof, impulsive or cautious, fastidious about order or more easygoing, domineering and aggressive or passive and unassertive, demonstrative or inhibited, desirous or intense, emotional interaction or prefer superficial relationships, etc.

Much hostility is generated by trying to get people — family members in particular — to be what we want them to be, without regard for their own needs and capabilities. The more we push, the more they pull away. Don't fight nature. You'll lose. People change only when they are deeply motivated from within.

## DEAL ASSERTIVELY WITH ABUSIVE PEOPLE

> Do not answer a fool according to his folly lest you become like him.
>
> (*Mishley*, 26:4)

> Do not reprove a scorner, lest he hate you; reprove a wise man and he will love you.
>
> (ibid., 9:8)

> There is an outstanding and elevated type of individual whose devotion to Hashem is so strong that it leads him to try and avoid the company of the wicked altogether.
>
> (*Strive for Truth!*, vol. 1, p. 238)

Of course, there are many intolerant, unrefined, and cruel people. However, it does not help you or them to be in temper over this fact. You should do everything in your power to bring them closer to Torah and mitzvoth. At the same time, recognize that you may be adversely affected by the frustration of talking to people who are resistant to all your efforts and who resent your interference. You can view such people as a supreme test of your *middoth*: not to return an insult with an insult, to have compassion, to be diligent in trying to help others, etc. At times you will need the courage to disengage from them, either emotionally or physically. At other times, you need the patience and determination to withstand their negativity in order to awaken a spark of goodness within them.

> It is irrationality and poverty of spirit [to] patiently endure injuries which might be averted. This sort of humility is found among foolish and ignorant people [and is not really humility], but rather spiritual poverty and blindness.
>
> (*Duties of the Heart,* vol. 2, p. 75)

When dealing with abusive people, remember that passivity and propitiation often make them more aggressive and contemptuous of you. These people respect power and you will have to use it to control them, while avoiding the sin of vengeance. EMETT in no way encourages people to unnecessarily tolerate or condone abuse.

### BE AGGRESSIVE WHEN DEALING WITH ABUSIVE TEACHERS

Teachers who are hostile, critical, and physically abusive to children with slapping, hitting, and pinching, are a threat to your child's mental and physical health. Take prompt, swift action. Such teachers can leave lifelong scars on the child's psyche. If your child balks at going to school, complains of frequent aches and pains, and has become more aggressive at home, find out if there is an abusive teacher at school. This is not the time to take the secure thought that "everything will be all right."

# 7.

## Foster Healthy Relationships with Communication Techniques

He who loves a fellow Jew loves God, for he contains within himself a part of God above. Love for him, for his inward self *is* love of God.

(*Kuntres Ahavath Yisrael,* p.5)

*Regesh* (feeling) is composed of the same letters as *gesher* (bridge). It is through our feelings that we truly connect to each other.

(said by Rabbi Meyer Goldberg at the *brith* of Moshe Bezalel Adahan, 5740)

We have an obligation to "Love thy neighbor as thyself " (*Vayikra* 19:18). It does not say to love only those who are intelligent, polite, and kind, but rather to love all those with whom we come in contact. And if we do not feel loving, then at least we must act in a loving manner. (Obviously, this does not refer to *resha'im* — evil doers). One way we create loving relationships is by sharing our likes and dislikes, our feelings and worries, our hopes and dreams with each other. Sharing builds trust. Mutual sharing implies that you care enough to try to understand the other person's personality and his way of looking at life.

Many people mistakenly think that when you love someone, you should avoid mentioning the things which bother you. In reality, the opposite is more often true. If you are hurt by an incident or repeatedly irritated by someone's behavior and you suffer in silence, it can build up a wall of coldness over the years. Or, you may suddenly mention the behavior tactlessly in the heat of anger, causing far greater damage than if you had spoken about it calmly and patiently sought solutions.

It is also essential to ask for validation of possible rejection if you have an insecure thought about someone's behavior. Your feelings are not always accurate reflections of reality. Before you jump to conclusions, ask:

"I have this insecure thought that you're not happy with me because of 'X'. Is that true?"

"When you told me you were busy, I had this suspicion that it wasn't true — that the real reason was that you didn't want to be around me. Was I right? Do you feel I've been making too many demands lately?"

People differ vastly in their desire for and ability to communicate on a deep level. One with a high need level may see someone with a low need level as aloof and uncaring, while the latter sees the other as demanding and dependent. Don't anger yourself over other people's communication style. Rather, be accepting of the reality and then figure out how you can resolve your differences in a mutually respectful manner. As with most habits, the more you push others to either share more or talk less, the more likely you are to reinforce the very behavior you would like to eliminate. When it comes to basic personality traits such as communication patterns, it is wise to be very patient and to approach change in a non-demanding way. Respect people's differences, especially those of your own family members. Remember, no two human beings can ever share the exact same reality. What is important to one may not be so to another. One person may want only very polite and superficial relations. Others are at the opposite extreme. Often, there is not a great deal that can be done to alter this trait. If change is possible, it will come only through patient effort.

## AVOID COMMUNICATION ROADBLOCKS

The ability to be open and honest about one's feelings is important. Most people feel vulnerable when they share their pain. If he feels invalidated, ridiculed, or rejected by you at that time, he may never open up to you again. Then you'll have lost the opportunity to make a deep connection with that person, and he won't gain the relief and objectivity which he needed. The following "communication roadblocks" shut people off. While some of them may be useful at times, they should not be used when the individual is expressing a deep feeling. EMETT class members should be familiar with this list and strictly avoid them at all times in class.

*Analyzing*: "I know why you didn't show up on time. You have a deep unconscious need to be rejected."

*Arguing*: "You don't really feel like that." "It's not the way you see it." "No wonder you're in such pain. Why didn't you take my advice?"

*Commanding*: "Leave that job!" "Go on a vacation!" "Cheer up!"

*Counseling*: "Now, I'll tell you just what to do. First thing, put an ad in the newspaper." "A divorce is best."

*Diagnosing*: "I know exactly what's wrong: it's your hormones/ the weather/ a vitamin deficiency/ lack of calcium...."

*Generalizing*: "All women make too many demands on their husbands." "All men do whatever they can to get out of being with the kids." "All children that age do that."

*Guilt-tripping*: "How can you be so unhappy when Hashem has given you so much?" "You're so selfish and ungrateful. That's your whole problem."

*Maximizing*: "How can you be so calm about this? How can you be so blind? It's far more serious than you think."

*Minimizing*: "I can't see why you're so upset. It's really nothing." "Be happy!" "Ten years from now it won't matter."

*One-upping*: "Humph! That wouldn't have bothered me one bit!" "Humph! I never have one second of doubt."

*Over-identifying*: "You don't have to go on. I know *exactly* how you feel!"

*Philosophizing*: "Well, life is no bowl of cherries."

*Probing*: "Now, give us the real, underlying reason why you felt like that."

*Reassuring*: "Don't be upset. Everything's going to be fine."

*Self-disclosing*: "You think you have it bad? Let me tell you what I'm going through."

*Shaming*: "How could you have been so stupid?" "You know what? You're just feeling sorry for yourself." "It's all your fault. You brought it all on yourself."

*Simplifying*: "With kids, it's all a power struggle. Just don't ever give in. That's all there is to it." "Just be happy and everything will be fine."

*Warning and threatening*: "If you don't act immediately, I can't begin to tell you what terrible consequences you will suffer."

Note that all of the above put the person in pain in a "one-down" position and the "receiver" in a "one-up" position. This inhibits the flow of communication, which is best achieved from a position of mutual respect and concern.

## RECONNECT DAILY

A famous rabbi recalled that when he was told as a child that he had to pray three times a day, he got out his *siddur* and said *Shemoneh Esreh* ninety times, one after the other. Afterwards he proclaimed, "Now I'm finished for the whole month!" Obviously, this is not the way prayer works. There is a reason why we pray three times a day. We need to remind ourselves continuously that we love God and that He loves us. The same is true of those around us. The mitzvah of love requires that we try to understand the unique world which each of us inhabits and that we take the time to let others know that we care. We often think,

"What does she want? I told her just last month that I love her!"

"He should know I love him! I make him a good meal every night."

"I'm afraid I'll turn my kids into dependent, spoiled brats if I tell them I care."

Many people feel alone and insecure at times. Reconnections are necessary and comforting.

Words of endearment and encouragement, a squeeze of the hand, or a few minutes of special time together bring calming reassurance. Modern medical research proves what our Sages knew well: that the immunological system is strengthened and the spirit uplifted in this way. A loving word is spiritual nourishment — as important as food is to our bodies.

Death and life are in the power of the tongue.

(*Mishley*, 18:21)

Pleasant words are...sweet to the soul and health to the bones.

(ibid., 16:24)

Anxiety bows the heart down, but a good word makes it cheerful.

(ibid., 12:25)

This is not always easy. People often need love most when they are least lovable. Children, in particular, often manifest their fear of rejection and need for reassurance with obnoxious behavior. One kind word, or five minutes of holding, or storytelling at that point can save us hours of tension and years of alienation.

## THE ART OF PROBLEM SOLVING: ATTACK PROBLEMS, NOT PEOPLE

Conflicts between people are inevitable. We have differences in temperament, talents, tempo, and cravings. We have differences in the amount of tension we experience concerning various emotionally charged issues such as child rearing, money, household chores, degree of religiosity, social events, and relations with relatives. Instead of stewing and grumbling about our conflicts, we can build self-esteem in ourselves and others (even children as young as two or three) by saying, "We have a problem. How can we solve it in a mutually respectful manner?"

Take other people's feelings and ideas into consideration. This is far more likely to gain their respect and cooperation. However, be prepared that this is not always going to work. If people think their behavior is correct and beneficial, they may not care about what you want. Therefore, you may have to first find out if they are comfortable with the present situation before instituting changes.

Conflicts can bring out the best or the worst in us. One way to bring out the best is to try the following six-step problem solving technique.

1. Define the problem in the simplest terms possible.
2. "Brainstorm" — i.e., think of all possible solutions without attaching any evaluative description such as "good" or "bad" to any of them. Allow time for the free flow of ideas no matter how silly or farfetched they may seem at the time. Sometimes a seemingly "wrong" idea will work or will spark one that will.
3. Evaluate which one or ones would be most effective. Then, weigh the advantages and disadvantages.
4. Make a firm decision to act on the solution. Set a date by which you hope to put it into practice.
5. *Optional*: Decide on a penalty if it is not carried out.
6. Set a date to meet again and see if the decision has been effective. Endorse everyone for their efforts, patience, ideas, and honesty!

People, especially children, are far more willing to cooperate if they have been part of the decision-making process and have been given a chance to give their input. Decisions concerning use of the phone or car, chore schedules, and special celebrations, etc. can be easily made and carried out in such an atmosphere. Discuss, don't dictate whenever possible. If you do have to dictate in times of conflict or crisis, your word is far more likely to be accepted because you have established a foundation of mutual trust and respect.

## MAKE CONTACT BEFORE YOU COMMUNICATE SOMETHING OF IMPORTANCE

Before speaking to Adam about his transgression, God said, "Where are you?" And with Cain, He first asked, "Where is Abel, thy brother?" (*Bereishith* 3:9 and 4:9). The Almighty obviously knew the answers to these questions. However, He demonstrated an important principle: before making a direct confrontation, find out where the person is mentally. He may be physically present, but a person is really where his thoughts are (*Chasidim Misaprim*, story 19). People are generally preoccupied with their own thoughts and feelings. If you have something important to say and you want someone to listen to you, you have to take a moment to find out if he is with you, and not thinking about the bank or some other place. By first mentioning some words of endearment or endorsement, others may respond more quickly.

> E.g., to wife: "That was a great meal. How was your day? Are you in the mood to talk about these bills? If not, when would be a good time?"
> E.g., to child: "Remember yesterday when you helped me out? I really appreciated that so much. I thought about it all day today. Now, I need your help again ...."

Do not be surprised if you meet people who seem unable to make anything but superficial contact. Unfortunately, it is a common experience usually stemming from severe childhood trauma (neglect, abuse, illness, or death in the family). Being in temper over their inability to relate will not help either of you. Be accepting. If there is hope for change, that is the only way to get it.

### QUICK ICE-BREAKER

If you are in a temperamental deadlock with someone, one quick way of getting into contact is to say: "Tell me two things you like about me and I'll tell you two things I like about you." [Note, you don't ask if there are two things. You make a statement which presupposes that there are!] Then, say, "Now that we're on a positive wavelength, let's talk about this conflict."

### GENERAL RULES FOR GOOD COMMUNICATION

1. To encourage self-disclosure, listen to the other person carefully. Avoid judgments and evaluations when a person is sharing pain. Avoid comments like: "It's not true that you're trapped or unappreciated." Accept people's feelings. Don't argue with them. Get on the person's side by saying something like, "I'd probably feel the same way if I were in your shoes," or "I can see that you're really having a rough time."

2. Avoid labeling or name calling. Don't throw out words like "crazy," "hysterical," "paranoid," "slob," "nagging witch," etc.

3. Try to understand the other person's point of view and get him to understand yours by *role reversal.* You take his side and he takes yours. Or, you take the side of the teacher/boss/store manager/clerk/relative, etc. and have him play himself.

4. Stay in the present. Don't be diverted from your goal of understanding and problem solving. If the other person tries to divert you with excuses, defenses, previewing of the future, or reviewing of the past, come back to the present problem.

5.  State precisely what you want without excessive drama.

> "I want five minutes of your time to share the day's events each night."
>
> "I would like you to endorse me twice a day for something — anything."
>
> "I want you to help me in the kitchen for ten minutes after dinner. I'll set the timer so you'll know I won't ask for more."
>
> "I want my money back."
>
> "Please keep the kids quiet when I'm studying unless you're feeling overwhelmed. Then tell me and I'll help."
>
> "I'd like you not to be on the telephone between these hours."

6.  Reassure others of your love and concern. Don't assume that people automatically know it or don't need words of endearment or endorsement. Every positive expression is like a candle that expels the darkness of temper.

> "I want to tell you three things you did today that pleased me. Then you can tell me three things too."
>
> "You know what I like about you? It's that you ..."

7.  Accept individual differences and don't see disagreement or failure to implement your desires as a sure sign of the other person's lack of love for you. Some people are by nature and/or conditioning more efficient, confident, communicative, expressive, and organized than others. If someone lacks awareness or skills, teach, don't preach. Discuss, don't dictate.

## THE SPECIAL PROBLEM OF
## COMMUNICATION AND EMOTIONALITY BETWEEN MEN AND WOMEN

In general, men are socialized not to express their emotions freely or to value emotional expression as much as women. Men tend to see the exchange of information as more important than "contact communication" — i.e., words of endearment, sympathy, and support. To help bridge this gap, it is important to let your spouse know what pleases or displeases you without temper. If the gap in communication styles is very great, it is wise to see a counselor. The lack of an emotionally fulfilling relationship is profoundly painful to a very feeling individual.

## AVOID MAXIMIZING: "IT'S AWFUL"

When we are in temper, we tend to maximize our own pain and minimize the pain of others. The tendency to complain and to exaggerate ("awfulize") mundane frustrations and discomforts has a number of negative side effects: it makes you think that you don't have the self-control or capacity to cope adequately with the task, which you really do have; it leads others to think that you do not have that ability; and it makes things look more complicated or uncomfortable than they are, so that they really do become more of a burden. The loss of trust in yourself and of others' trust in you, lowers your self-esteem and harms relationships. Others may not tell you what you need to know. Many children who have "awfulizing parents" withhold necessary information from them for fear that, "Daddy will have a heart attack, God forbid, and Mom will be hysterical." Thus, you distance yourself from others with such awfulizing. Furthermore, you may come to believe that things really are awful and thus overprotect and stifle others so that they do not develop self-trust and self-confidence. If you "awfulize" rejection, you may become excessively permissive, giving in to others' demands out of fear of how "awful" it would be if they rejected you. As a result, you often end up feeling that they took advantage of you.

> *Example*: I used to awfulize doing the dishes. I'd be tense and self-pitying about all the housework I had to do. Finally, I decided to change my attitude. I decided to be grateful for the fact that we have dishes and good food to eat. I put on music in the kitchen or would sing to myself. Without a word to my children, they began to help more on their own instead of always trying to find excuses to get out of it. And my husband even started coming in to chat or help me out. I was amazed at how my changed attitude affected the whole family without my saying a word.

> *Example*: A neighbor asked me to deliver Shabbath candles and cake to the Jewish patients in a hospital near our home. At first, I thought, "Oh no, I can't do that. What if someone gets angry at me? What if I see someone with a terrible illness? What if I say the wrong thing?" Then I realized that I was awfulizing. None of these events would be unbearable. I can handle my uncomfortable feelings in order to do this important mitzvah.

It is usually a mistake to tell others that they are "awfulizing." They might not have told you the whole truth and are really facing a serious problem. Or, they might feel put-down by your telling them that their perceptions are untrue. You don't know the depth of another's pain. If appropriate, you can ask them to measure the pain on a scale of one to ten. That often brings insight. If they say that the situation is a "ten," don't argue. Empathize.

Common areas for excessive emotionalism are: minor disappointments in relationships, food, money, cleanliness, dress, and social events. Get in touch with your own particular "sore spots":

> "I can't stand it when someone ..." (shows up late, criticizes me, leaves the lights on unnecessarily, uses too much hot water, etc.)
> "I hate the thought of ..." (going to the dentist, cleaning, asking for help, not getting enough sleep, etc.)

Don't say "I can't stand it ..." when you could substitute, "I don't want it or like it." Awfulizing is a subtle form of self-denigration.

## AVOID MINIMIZING: "IT'S NOTHING"

As frustrating, irrational, and sometimes dangerous as it is to awfulize, the opposite habit, called "minimizing," can be equally problematic. Chronic minimizers are apt to say, "It's nothing, don't worry, everything will be just fine, just calm down" even *before* they know what is going on. They may refuse to take the time to examine the realities of the situation. And even when they do know that real pain and hardship are involved, they minimize the difficulty and distress involved, perhaps saying, "They can handle it," "They deserve it," or "They're used to suffering." Minimizers are uncomfortable with feelings. They tend to see the display of emotions as a sign of weakness or impending collapse.

Minimizing is a positive strategy which is useful for those who over dramatize. But when this becomes a lifelong, compulsive character trait, it prevents the development of truly caring relationships. It may also cause one to avoid action when there is a situation that calls for prompt attention because he feels ashamed or inadequate. A parent may not want to face that his child has a real physical or emotional problem because he thinks it implies that he is a failure. Others may want to deny the reality of an incompetent teacher, the possibility of financial collapse, or the pain of physical and/or mental abuse. They may be afraid to face the unknown, afraid of the discomforts of change, or fearful of public censure or rejection if they try to change. So they say, "It's not all that bad," and lull themselves into passivity.

Temper can cause you to minimize or maximize. Either way, it keeps you from reacting appropriately to the situation.

## EMPATHY: TZEDDAKAH ON THE EMOTIONAL LEVEL

> Compassion is the feeling of sympathy which the pain of one being of itself awakens in another; and the higher and more human the beings are, the more keenly attuned are they to re-echo the note of suffering which ... penetrates the heart .... Do not suppress this compassion ... especially with the sufferings of your

fellowman. It is the warning voice of duty, which points out to you your brother in every sufferer ... and awakens the love which tells you that you belong to him. ... Do not suppress it! If you thrust it back too often, it will no more well up of itself and you will have cut yourself off from the company of your fellow creatures .... Your heart becomes a stone, and there no longer sounds in it the voice of God, reminding you of your mission. Yet be on your guard against letting sympathy degenerate into a hypersensitivity which identifies itself with the sufferer to such an extent that it retains no composure or power or strength to help.

(Horev, pp. 55-56)

One of the most loving forms of compassion is empathy. Empathy consists of:

a. *Acknowledgment*: To acknowledge the other person's pain.
b. *Duplication*: To awaken a similar feeling within your own heart.
c. *Reflection:* To reflect back that experience in your own facial expression or voice.

The key to empathy is the willingness to put aside your own thoughts, feelings, and evaluations of the situation for the moment in order to share the other person's experience. The less said the better.

"Oh, that must have been so embarrassing!"
"How painful that must be for you."

Empathy does not work if you say these words condescendingly or superficially, without real feeling. If you cannot spontaneously feel along with the other person because his experience is not common to your own, then awaken a memory of when you felt similarly about some other event. This is especially true of small children, whose losses and pains may seem insignificant. However, if you think of a time when you felt jealous, embarrassed, sad, frustrated, or rejected, it will help you empathize with him.

*Example*: My son lost some trivial item which had great value for him. I was about to reprimand him for making a mountain out of a molehill when I thought of how I might feel if something I valued had gotten lost. By thinking of this, I was able to awaken a sincere feeling of pain and sympathize with him. He calmed down almost immediately and began thinking of solutions.

Empathy can free others from the pain of loneliness.

*Example*: My wife was complaining about how tired she was. She got really upset when I said, "It's not my fault. Just stop complaining." Finally I realized how callous that sounded. I said, "Wow, it's really hard to function when you've been up all night with one sick kid after another. Is there anything I can do to help?" It was like magic. She brightened up and said that now, at least, she didn't feel so alone.

Empathy is the symbolic "touch" which can make an emotional bruise feel better. If the other person's pain is slight, you will usually find that a minute or two of empathy is enough to bring relief. If there is greater loss or real grief, it will take longer and you may have to go through this process over and over. Do not worry that the person will get "stuck" in this painful state. The opposite is true: people who can't talk about their pain are the ones who get stuck in negative emotional states. Empathy creates a bond which reassures others that they are not alone and brings people out of their isolation. A famous Chassidic tale illustrates this point:

> The wise man of a small village was told of a young man who had gone crazy. The latter had locked himself in a small room, undressed completely, and crowed like a rooster day and night. No one could reach him with logic or threats. Finally, the wise man climbed in the window and joined the man, undressing and crowing just like him. Little by little, the wise man established contact and the forlorn soul was thereby returned to health.

> (anecdote of unknown origin)

Empathy allows a person to release his pain, at least momentarily, like an electric current which has finally found a terminal. This is especially important if someone has a chronic problem (illness, childlessness, major life change, etc.), but also helps release the smaller fears and disappointments. To encourage a person's full expression, you should keep asking, "Is there anything else you want to share?"

Empathy can often win cooperation far more quickly than orders:

> "I know it's hard to stop what you're doing, but I really need your help right now."
> "I know you're disappointed about my decision. Tell me your feelings and let's focus on alternatives."

Empathy can keep a person from feeling exceptional, weird, or abnormal:

> "I also felt like throttling the guy who cheated us out of so much money."
> "I also feel like I'm going to break apart into little pieces when I have twenty different demands on me at the same moment."

Empathy can open up communication:

> "I see that you are hurt. I feel badly for you. Do you want to talk?"

There are some general rules to follow when being empathic:

- Be congruent: don't go above or below the pain level of the other person.
- Use precise words to reflect back your understanding of the other person's feelings: e.g., "I can understand how disappointed/jealous/rejected/humiliated/trapped/bored you feel."
- Never argue with what the other person is feeling. A person's feelings *are* his reality at that moment. Saying, "You don't really feel that way," creates distance and antagonism.
- Don't philosophize or reassure at the moment of another's pain. Just listen.

Do not pacify thy fellow in the hour of his anger, nor comfort him in the hour when his dead lies before him.

(*Avoth* 4:18)

- Let the other person express himself fully before you reflect back.
- Don't try to smooth things over with expressions like, "This too shall pass," "It doesn't really hurt all that much," "You think you have problems? You should hear about my poor neighbor."
- Don't scold. "You're such a *kvetch*. You should be counting your blessings instead of complaining."
- Don't pretend to empathize if you really don't care about the person or the problem.
- Keep your comments simple: "It's so difficult." "That's really painful."
- Compassion is a mitzvah. Endorse yourself for taking the time to show that you care. An essential aspect of loving others is to take the time to see things from other people's point of view even if you disagree.
- If someone resists your empathy, stop.
- Watch for visible changes in the other person's face and body. If he shows a release of tension, he may be ready to move on to Step 3 type thinking and take secure thoughts or think of some possible action. At this point you might help him see alternatives, gain insight, or find new direction by asking: "How are you managing to cope in the midst of all this?" "What tools are you using to keep going?" "Where do you go from here?"
- If you find that the person is getting even more upset, then he probably is having insecure thoughts. If appropriate, ask, "What are your insecure thoughts? What are your worst fears?"
- You can teach others to be more open with you by using everyday events to demonstrate empathy.

"You probably feel embarrassed about that mistake. I know how it feels."

(Not, "You idiot! I told you to be more careful!")

"That's a big disappointment. How do you feel about it?"

(Not, "Stop feeling sorry for yourself.")

"It's very frustrating to be in such a situation."

(Not, "Don't worry. Everything will be just fine.")

When you love someone deeply, compassion is a spontaneous response to the loved one's pain. By expressing empathy, you strengthen love, or awaken it when it may have been weak or absent.

### LIVING WITH AN UNCOMPASSIONATE PERSON

There are many unfortunate people who, in the words of Rabbi Hirsch, have hearts which have turned to stone. Recognize such people when you see them. Don't be angry about their defect. Childhood traumas have caused them to be as unresponsive to others as others were to them. They are often critical and easily angered. If the disability is not too great, it can sometimes be corrected with therapy. If the crippling is severe, you may have to learn to accept the sad reality of this all too common phenomenon.

Living with such a person is like being sentenced to an "emotional Siberia." If you feel deeply and have a desire to communicate, you will no doubt need help in learning how to cope with your lack of fulfillment in this area.

### HANDLING OTHER PEOPLE'S ANGER

It is a tremendous test of character not to retaliate when someone is angry with you. The following suggestions may help.

1.  Acknowledge their feelings even if you do not agree with their views.
    "You have a right to be upset." (They do have that right!)
    "You have a point."(Everybody does always have a point.)
    "I'd probably feel the same way if I were in your shoes."
    Empathize. Beneath anger you will often find fear, frustration, and feelings of inadequacy, helplessness, or despair. Say:
    "I'm sorry that you are in so much pain."
    "I hear you. I feel badly that you are upset."
2.  Agree:
    "You're right."
    "I was careless. I'll try harder."
3.  Apologize if you did something wrong.
    "I'm really sorry."

4. Delay and/or divert.

"Give me time to think about this."

"I'm taking this issue very seriously and will give you an answer this evening."

5. Walk away. "He who walks with fools suffers harm; he who walks with wise men will become wise" (*Mishley* 13:20). If the person is being irrational and it would be useless or possibly harmful for you to do or say anything, it might be best to leave.

6. Be assertive.

"I will only talk to you if you can speak to me respectfully."

"I will not respond to threats and intimidation."

"I cannot give you what you want."

7. Get the person to state his insecure thoughts.

"What are your worst fears of what will happen if this continues?" If the person has high level insecure thoughts, help him to recognize whether or not they are realistic. Then get the person in touch with reality:

"Do you think your requests are reasonable and average?"

"Do you think I am exceptional in any way?"

"Do you think your fears are realistic?"

8. Get the person to focus on solutions rather than feelings.

"I know you're upset. Now, let's think of what we can do about this problem."

"What exactly would you like me to do in order to help you?"

9. Keep him from bringing up his list of past hurts.

"Let's focus on the present. I want to talk about what's happening right now."

10. Reassure: An angry person is apt to think that you have done something deliberately to hurt him. Reassure him.

"I really love you. Do you believe that?"

"Do you think I don't care about you?"

"I am doing my best. I have absolutely no intention to hurt you. Do you believe me?"

11. Ask: "Do you want to hear my side of the story or do you want to believe your own version?" If the person says, "No, I don't want to hear your side," then you haven't wasted words or energy in talking. If he does want to hear, then his "Yes," has obligated him to listen. Ask that question first before you defend or excuse yourself in order to get the angry person's attention. Then you can say that you forgot/lost the message/were tired/lacked self-discipline/were lazy, etc.

12. Sign a contract. Put into writing your decisions about certain highly

charged matters, such as household chores, how much to spend on clothing or holidays, visits to relatives, how to divide the budget, etc.

13. Use compromise, arbitration, and rewards as alternatives.

"Let's have the phone off the hook for one hour each evening."

"Let's put a certain amount of money in a cup. We'll use it for a special treat. Each time someone gets angry, we'll take a certain amount out."

"You can go to classes three nights a week if I can go twice."

14. Get the person to focus on priorities.

"Is what you are doing now good or bad for our relationship?"

"Is this going to bring *shalom bayith*?"

15. Get outside help. Go to a third party if you cannot resolve your differences or talk about matters calmly. Go to a financial counselor for money problems.

16. Reverse roles to increase consciousness, awaken compassion, and get people out of their narrow point of view.

Also, think about preventive measures. During nonstressful times, hold family conferences to air out differences and make new rules and schedules. Once a week ask family members, "What have I done recently that might have irritated or offended you." Don't ask, "Have I done anything?" It's a pretty sure bet that if you're living in close quarters with another person, something probably caused them discomfort, even though minor, which should be talked about before it builds.

Remember, when a person is angry, it's not the time to be angry at him for his anger. It's not the time to moralize or philosophize. That makes the person feel misunderstood and invalidated. Stay objective. Avoid the impulse to hurt back and you are likely to find that even the most temperamental people soon lose the "joy" of their temper when they find that they can't pull you into their negativity.

## REBUKE: SANDWICH IT BETWEEN LOVE

While rebuke is a positive mitzvah (*Vayikra* 19:17), putting people down is not.

Who is lowly? He who tries to lower others.

(*Ahavath Meishorim*, p.216)

Shame is the greatest pain.

(*Tosafoth* to *Shabbath* 50b)

He who could have kept the members of his household, his fellow citizens, or the whole world back from sinning and refrained from doing so is held responsible for their guilt, and even if his own life is exemplary and blameless, he gets judged and punished first of all if he has kept himself to himself and not done everything to improve his fellow men.

(*Shabbath* 54b and 55a)

Shame is such a great pain that if you are not careful, your rebuke is likely to be taken wrong and will simply cause the other person hurt, not improvement.

"I should be surprised to find anybody living in our times who is ready to accept rebuke," said Rabbi Tarfun. And his colleague, Rabbi Azarya, said, "There could hardly be found anybody who could give it correctly."

(*Arachim* 16b)

It is important to become familiar with the laws of rebuke so that you know how, when, and whom to rebuke without causing more damage. If you are feeling vindictive, angry, or are bearing a grudge against the other person and want to get back at him, it is not the time to give rebuke. Better share your feelings first with "I messages" ("I feel hurt, misunderstood, and rejected," etc.) and avoid the "You messages" ("You are the source of my pain because you are so cold, thoughtless, and uncaring.") Only after you have established a relationship of respect or, at least, compassion for the other person can you rebuke without having the secret desire to hurt, and thereby feel superior. If you look carefully at the sequence in the Torah, you will see how essential it is to sandwich rebuke between love and even then, only after ridding your heart of any hatred.

1. "Thou shalt not hate thy brother in thine heart."
2. "Thou shalt rebuke...thy neighbor but not incur sin in so doing" (i.e., not hurt his feelings by making him feel ashamed, especially in public).
3. "Thou shalt not take vengeance nor bear a grudge."
4. "Thou shalt love thy neighbor as thyself."

(*Vayikra* 19:16-19. See *Love Your Neighbor*, pp. 278-92, for advice on how to rebuke lovingly.)

In other words, not hurting someone takes precedence over rebuke, because if you rebuke someone and hurt his feelings in so doing, you are likely to make the problem worse. On the other hand, if you approach the person correctly, with sincere love in your heart, like a doctor who has to perform a lifesaving operation or administer a painful drug, then the hurt will be minor in comparison to the appreciation he feels at the opportunity to improve himself. But be careful how and to whom you administer this powerful medicine. It is not something to be thrown at someone in a fit of anger or moment of weakness:

> Do not reprove a scorner, lest he hate you. Reprove a wise man and he will love you.
>
> (*Mishley* 9:8)

Do what you can to correct others. Use a pleasant, soft voice (*Hilchoth Dei'oth* 6:7). Train yourself to speak in a low tone to minimize the hurt you may cause with your words, whether intentional or unintentional (*Igereth Ha-Ramban*). And make sure to have both halves of the "sandwich": i.e., to start and finish with words of encouragement and love. It often takes courage to rebuke. Think of it as a manifestation of your love.

> Whomever Hashem loves He reproves, like a father the son in whom he delights.
>
> (*Mishley* 3:12)

Children are especially vulnerable to rejection. Make sure your voice conveys real concern. If you are harsh, children might try face-saving tactics, such as denial or counterattack.

Rebuke is a powerful weapon. Like fire, it can heal or destroy. Use it sparingly or you will cause others to lose trust in you and in themselves. Make sure you are accepting of the other person even though you disapprove of his behavior. Don't use it when some other tactic will be more effective, such as positive reinforcement.

### WHAT TO DO WHEN REBUKE ISN'T APPROPRIATE? TRY ACCEPTANCE

Many EMETT members have experienced a fascinating paradox. After giving an example of great frustration with a child or adult, they reach a certain degree of relief and accept the fact that that person may not change in the near future. Then they return home and find to their great surprise, that that individual is no longer so negative! It seems that when the member stops being so resistant and upset about the behavior, the other person often stops acting that way because he no longer feels the same power over the EMETT member. Most of this reaction is not at the conscious level. But it proves that people are sensitive to our emotional states, even though we may not say anything directly.

*Example*: I gave an example last week about my four year old and how exasperated I was with him. I just didn't like him anymore. I could hardly keep myself from doing something violent at times because he kept everybody in a constant uproar. I was amazed that so many other mothers said that this was average, especially in cases where there are a number of siblings spaced close together. I went home feeling more relaxed and accepting of him. Without my saying a word, he was calmer that day. I was able to think of creative ways to keep him occupied and gave him extra cuddling. He's still my difficult one, but I managed to stay more accepting until just before Shabbath, when it started up again. Then I had to go through an EMETT example with my husband in order to remember what had calmed me down.

*Example*: I have a difficult relative, a holocaust survivor, who disliked everything about me. Nothing I could do would win her respect or approval. Everything I did was wrong, from how I cooked to how I cleaned. I couldn't be in her presence without wanting to jump out of my skin. Then I realized that a lot of my pain came from resisting who she was. I tried to develop compassion by remembering what life in a ghetto must have been like and how that had crippled her. I used my imagination to see myself not being bothered by her, to see myself being accepting of her illness. As I did this, I was able to be more calm in her presence.

## AVOID DOMINATION MASQUERADING AS HELPFULNESS

> All Jews are responsible one for the other.
>
> (*Shavu'oth* 39a)

We should do our utmost to help each other improve. However, there is sometimes a thin line between healthy caring and excessive domination. The latter can be seen in the following:

"I'm going to drag my neighbor to the EMETT meeting."

"I told my daughter what I wanted her to do with her birthday money. I don't know why she got so angry. After all, teenagers don't know how to be practical."

"Every time I visited my neighbor, I told her that she should stop eating sugar and caffeine and then she wouldn't have such a nervous stomach. I don't understand why she doesn't invite me anymore. My advice is so sound."

"I kept telling my daughter-in-law that she's spoiling her kids by holding them so much, and that they'll be tyrannical little brats if she gives them so much attention. Now she's cold to me. I don't understand why. I was only trying to help. It's for her own good."

It is a sign of spiritual refinement to want to help others. However, domination is a sign of arrogance and insensitivity. Domination often masquerades as advice giving, nagging, criticism, and overprotectiveness. The difference between love and domination is that love urges others to fully develop and explore their potential according to their own temperament and talents, and it is rooted in trust and respect. On the other hand, domination conveys the message, "I have no faith in your ability to cope adequately. Therefore, I will have to take control." Domination and overprotectiveness are forms of rejection. They cause others to lose faith in their ability to cope, or to withdraw in angry self-defense.

Before you tell someone, "Let me do that for you," see if your help is really needed and wanted. Remember, the more control a person has over his life, the more confident and secure he feels. If you take control where it is not wanted, you increase the other person's sense of self-doubt. You might think you are doing someone a favor in telling him how to dress, eat, or make money. You may have excellent advice about how this one should quit his job or stay put and how that one should treat his children. But if you see that your well-meaning help is creating resistance, hold yourself back unless you want to risk losing the friendship. What you may think of as constructive criticism may be viewed by others as one-upmanship and may be causing resentment.

Even children, who must be respectful of our wishes, should not be overprotected, because it produces anxiety and stifles initiative. Many immature adults were psychologically crippled by parents who never taught them how to cope with frustration or function with discomfort. Teach your children to do what they can by themselves, so that they will not be afraid of independence. Teach them to master basic life skills, and do not catastrophize every mistake they make, so that they will develop self-trust and self-leadership.

## AVOID EXCESSIVE RESPONSIBILITY

A more subtle form of domination is called excessive responsibility. You know you have overstepped the boundary betweeen healthy involvement and excessive responsibility when you feel guilty for your inability to make people happy all the time or to solve their problems for them.

> *Example*: My parents are not observant. They always tell me what a heartache it is for them that I became a *baal teshuvah*, and they blame me for their illnesses. I do my utmost to be respectful towards them and to model Torah principles. But I stopped feeling excessively responsible for their feelings of rejection over the fact that I now wear a *kipah* and keep kosher.

> *Example*: The evening before a party, my daughter asked me to stay up half the night to finish a dress she was making. I debated whether or not to do it. Finally, I had the courage to say, "No." It would have been excessive responsibility to do so, since she never gave me any advance notice. In the past, I would have done anything to keep her from

experiencing failure or frustration. Perhaps this is why she has learned to procrastinate.

*Example*: My daughter has three small children and no outside help. I was afraid she might collapse under the burden of so much to do. I kept offering to pay for a maid, but she refused. I was eating myself up with worry until I decided that this was excessive responsibility and domination in the guise of helpfulness. I have to trust her, and let her build trust in herself.

One of the sources for domination and excessive responsibility is unrealistically high standards. When your standards are realistic, you instill enthusiasm and self-respect in others. But when they are too high, the opposite occurs: people lose their motivation to excel because they keep experiencing frustration and failure. When necessary, lower your standards for yourself and others if it will help your performance rise and lessen your anxiety.

*Example*: Before leaving to visit my children in Israel, I tried to get everything on the long shopping lists they sent to me. I was wearing myself out trying to accommodate everybody. Then I realized that for the sake of my inner peace, I had to lower my standards and drop my excessive responsibility. I would do my best in the time I had, and avoid panic if I couldn't buy everything.

*Example*: I have very high standards for how the house should look. However, each time my wife has a baby, I have to lower my standards for a while. She used to wear herself out taking excessive responsibility for everything, and then she would get sick and we'd all be miserable.

*Example*: Some relatives who are not observant wanted to send their problematic teenage daughter to live with me so that I could "straighten her out." I was in a panic wondering how I could reach her. Then I realized that I could not take excessive responsibility for her. I will try my utmost to demonstrate and teach Torah principles. That's all I can do. The rest is in the hands of a Power beyond my control.

# 8.

# Understanding Your Emotions

*Shir Ha-Shirim* shows how all earthly feelings that we experience are only to help us understand the only thing that really exists, that is, the love of God.

*(The Book of Our Heritage, vol. 2, p. 310)*

Our feelings are vital, internal indicators of the true state of our minds at any given moment. A good example of the importance of emotional honesty is seen in the encounter between our forefather, Yaakov, and his brother Esav. When Yaakov was informed that Esav was advancing toward him with an entire army, Yaakov "was greatly afraid and he was distressed" (*Bereishith* 32:8). There are many interpretations of this phrase. The Midrash says that he was distressed in part because he thought that he had reached the level of such perfect faith in Hashem that he would have no fear of mortal man. His feeling of fear also caused him to reflect on the possible transgressions which he might have committed toward his father and in his dealings with Lavan. In the midst of his distress, he accepted the fact that he was afraid. He then took realistic, positive actions: he divided his camp to protect his wives and children, he prayed, and he prepared gifts to appease Esav.

Any unpleasant, distressing, or so-called "negative" emotion is an opportunity for growth. These feelings point out areas of weakness. If you deny their existence or suppress the fact that you are feeling resentful, envious, inadequate, or hurt, you will miss the opportunity to learn more about yourself, to do *teshuvah* or to change something in your environment. Jealousy, for example, may be a sign that you need to work more on the *middah* of gratefulness. It might also mean that you need to be more ambitious and persistent about having your reasonable desires fulfilled. Resentment may be a sign that you are resisting a painful reality and need to work on accepting what cannot be changed. On the other hand, it may mean that you have failed to take action and communicate your feelings to another or seek help from a counselor or other outsider.

Above all, guard thy heart; for out of it come forth the issues of life.
(*Mishley* 4:23)

Maintain emotional honesty with yourself and, as far as appropriate, with those around you in order to keep you and your relationships healthy.

## SADNESS: APPROPRIATE AND TEMPERAMENTAL

There are various sources of sadness. There is the very real grief one feels when a loved one is in pain. There is the longing for those who are distant. There is the sadness we feel about the fate of our fellow Jews who live in spiritual darkness or the torment of imprisonment under totalitarian regimes. There is the sadness we may feel about not living a more meaningful life; the empty feeling which can bring one to *teshuvah* or to more active participation in community events. And there may be sadness and pain because of a physical, emotional, or mental disability in oneself or a close family member. We acknowledge real pain, yet retain our faith in God and our ability to go on living with meaning and purpose. We trust that "Hashem is righteous in all His ways and holy in all His works" (*Tehillim* 146:17).

> *Example*: The night before my son's wedding, I felt great sadness, almost grief. At first I told myself that this was silly, that I should only be feeling joy. But I couldn't shake the uneasy feeling. Finally, I just gave in to it, not knowing what was behind the pain. As the tears came forth, I realized that I needed time to mourn, to let go — let go of my little boy, let go of my youth and the dreams which could no longer be fulfilled because of my age and circumstances. So many lost opportunities. So much to say which must now remain unsaid. I needed to cry in order to let go. In the middle of it all, my husband walked in and I shared my feelings with him. He said that he, too, was feeling a jumble of emotions. It helped to talk. When we emerged from the room, we were both better able to face the company which had gathered, and we felt released from the pain so that we could be truly happy about this momentous event.

Then there is "temperamental sadness" which is largely the result of self-pity and inertia. In this state, a person thinks to himself, "I can't be happy because I don't have everything I want." Since, "No man dies with even half his heart's desires fulfilled" (*Koheleth Rabbah* 1:34), a person can be continuously unhappy because no one ever has all he wants.

As a child, such a person might have gotten others to give in to him by pouting, sulking, and being silent for a long time. Many hope that, as adults, the same techniques will work, i.e., that acting miserable will make them happy, but it doesn't. Such passivity induces lethargy. And when a person gives in to passivity, he loses faith in himself, becomes dependent on others, and ends up being more and more depressed. A mature person takes active responsibility for his happiness and does not wait for others to bring it to him.

There is nothing unusual about short periods of dysphoria (sadness, "blues") if it leads to greater insight or meaningful change. But when it makes a person feel unlovable and unloving, discouraged, and hostile, then this state can be self-defeating.

> Sadness itself might not be a transgression, but no transgression hardens the heart so much as sadness.
>
> (*Siach Sarfey Kodesh*, vol. 1, p. 115)

It might seem strange to think of this sadness as a hardening of the heart (*timtum ha-lev*) because it appears that the person is full of feeling. However, the individual might be quite out of touch with his real feelings. Rather, the head might be full of unrealistic expectations, harsh condemnations, and immature beliefs. For example:

> "I have nothing important to contribute to the world."
> "Things will never work out."
> "Nobody loves me."
> "I can't be happy unless I'm getting what I want from life and people."
> "If I stop being miserable, I won't be able to manipulate others into giving me what I want."
> "If I'm happy, people will think I'm superficial, callous, stupid, uncaring, or arrogant."
> "I'll lose my motivation to make important changes if I'm happy."
> "If I'm happy, something terrible is bound to happen to take my happiness away."
> "I don't deserve to be happy after all I've done."
> "If I stopped being miserable, I'd have to do something positive which I don't want to do."
> "Unhappiness is a way of warding off further suffering."

If you have long bouts of unhappiness, examine your beliefs. See if you are using sadness to get something which you could get by more constructive, direct means. Above all, remember that the true source of happiness is not in getting but giving:

> The person with a good heart has a continual feast.
>
> (*Mishley* 15:15)

Ironically, retaining your *emunah* in times of darkness brings greater understanding and faith, even though you may have started from a point of despair.

> We must have *emunah* in order to understand and know that there is *hester panim* in the world. And after we recognize and experience this *hester panim*, then suddenly there is no *hester panim*.
>
> (*Chasidim Misaprim,* vol. 1, p. 94)

There is a great deal about life which seems unfair or you may not understand. However, with practice, you will be able to see more good in everything. The fact that you search for that good is in itself a source of joy. Even if a part of you is in pain or doubt, keep another part focused on your ultimate goals, and on the challenge of facing loss with faith.

### SADNESS OVER MAJOR PAINFUL EVENTS

If you live with an emotionally disturbed person, particularly someone who is abusive or depressed, or if you or someone close is suffering from a chronic or serious physical ailment, it is more difficult to avoid a negative response. The words, "Don't be sad," are unlikely to be helpful. Rather, acknowledge the spontaneous and legitimate sadness which arises from time to time. However, avoid chronic self-pity, resentment, and depression which are signs of temper about the event. It is no use telling yourself that you are not upset about a situation unless that is true. Living with a serious mental or physical ailment means that you may not function as well as others. It's like trying to walk with a broken leg. You can do it, but there is a disability which you should not deny. Find someone with whom you can share your feelings. When you are upset, use the technique of allowing feelings to rise and fade. Then move on with your life to the best of your ability.

### DON'T SUPPRESS EMOTIONS

Only *tzaddikim* have complete control over their hearts (*Bereishith Rabbah* 34:11). What this means is that the rest of us have to struggle with envy, resentment, self-pity, and all the other unpleasant emotions which afflict us at times. Don't think you're bad because you feel bad. We all have moments of hostility and discouragement. The important thing is to figure out what you need to change in your attitude or behavior to overcome the negativity, and thereby lessen or eliminate the pain. It may be as simple as remembering to be grateful for what you have, instead of focusing on what you lack. On the other hand, you may need to act by getting to a doctor, moving to a new apartment, getting a maid, or making some major change in your life.

## GUILT: APPROPRIATE AND TEMPERAMENTAL

No one would question the fact that we should feel guilty if we have done something wrong. In that case, it is necessary to do *teshuvah* by recognizing the fact that a wrong has been committed; feeling deep, sincere remorse for having done it; taking steps to ask for forgiveness; and making sure that it does not happen again (*Duties of the Heart*, ch. 3). Once we have done sincere *teshuvah*, we are obligated to immediately forgive ourselves and to assume that Hashem has forgiven us as well. This means avoiding thoughts which would bring long-lasting depression and despair, for that would only lead to further sin.

Guilt is a powerful emotion. You need just enough to keep you from doing wrong and to get you to do *teshuvah*, but not so much that you are filled with self-loathing and thereby lose your ability to "rejoice with all the good that Hashem has given you" (*Devarim* 26:11). It is best to set aside certain times to feel genuine remorse for transgressions, and to avoid dwelling on depression-provoking thoughts outside of those times. Also, learn to recognize temperamental guilt:

> *Guilt over unavoidable mistakes and human imperfection*: "I should never make mistakes." "I should be able to always do and say the right thing."
>
> *Guilt over causing others pain unintentionally*: "I only wanted to help. I had no idea that I would only make matters worse. Now I feel guilty for offering my services."
>
> *Guilt over other people's imperfections*: "I should be able to get my friend to be less compulsive and critical. I feel like it's my fault that she hasn't improved."
>
> *Guilt over permissible pleasures*: "I feel guilty if I take time out from my usual goal-oriented activities to enjoy myself and relax for a while."
>
> *Guilt over feeling guilty or for having other normal feelings*: "I shouldn't be having these feelings of guilt, sadness, self-pity, resentment. I'm a bad person for not being able to rid myself of all unpleasant emotions."
>
> *Guilt over lack of omniscience*: "I should have known that this financial investment would turn out badly!" "I should have known it would rain."
>
> *Guilt over lack of omnipresence*: "I should have gone with them and prevented the accident, instead of going to work that day."
>
> *Guilt over lack of omnipotence*: "I should be able to make my friend lose weight." "I should always be in total control of everything."

*General guilt*: "I don't know what I did wrong. But I go around with this terrible feeling of guilt all the time."

If you have done something wrong, tell yourself, "O.K. I have this problem. I feel bad about my mistake, but I'm going to do my best to improve." Excessive guilt actually paralyzes positive action.

Avoid guilt manipulation. E.g., "I'll feel terrible if you don't have another piece of this delicious cake which I worked so hard to make." Or, "I'll have a heart attack if you don't do what I want." Use more honest, direct means of getting your message across to others. And avoid equating love with obedience. That's a sure way to make others (or yourself) end up with excessive, temperamental guilt.

## SHAME AND BLAME

Shame is the greatest pain.

(*Tosafoth* to *Shabbath* 50b)

God said [to Adam] "Where are you?"
[Adam replied] "I heard the sound of You in the garden and I was afraid because I am naked. So I hid."
And He said, "Who told you that you are naked? Have you eaten of the tree which I commanded you not to eat?"
The man said, "The woman whom You gave to be with me — she gave me of the tree and I ate."
And Hashem said to the woman, "What is this that you have done?"
And the woman said, "The serpent deceived me, and I ate."

(*Bereishith* 3:9-13)

When you feel guilty and ashamed because you have done something wrong, your initial response may be to ward off the shame by putting the responsibility on someone or something else. Blame is the outward manifestation of a guilty conscience and a refusal to take responsibility for one's actions. It is often based on the mistaken belief that, "If I do something bad, then I am bad. It's too painful to think of myself as bad, so I'll blame others. I'll make them the bad ones and then I'll feel better." The refusal to accept responsibility is a sign of low self-esteem and fear of rejection. Defending oneself unnecessarily against criticism is also a means of warding off shame.

Shame is appropriate if you have done something terribly wrong. But it is destructive to feel chronic shame over the fact that others have things that you lack, or that you are not as skilled or knowledgeable in some area as someone else.

Learn to endorse yourself for the good that you do. Avoid paying undue attention to your mistakes unless you can gain insight as to how to change.

You will not need to blame others for your mistakes and imperfections because you will take responsibility for your own self-improvement, seeing those mistakes and imperfections as challenges rather than obstacles to growth.

Obviously, you should also avoid shaming others. It could provoke retaliation, not awareness. Find face-saving methods to get others to improve.

### SHARE FEELINGS WITHOUT TEMPER: REPORT, DON'T DRAMATIZE

People have differing capacities for experiencing emotions and sharing them with others. Some people seem closed off to feelings, while others are overly aware or incapacitated by them. Some want to share their resentments and discomforts, like a running commentary, throughout the day. Others don't care to hear about what anyone else is going through. Before you share, note the other person's state of mind. If the person is unreceptive, you may have to make some preparatory comments to get his attention. If he still doesn't want to listen, don't force communication or you will only end up feeling frustrated or resentful.

Sharing feelings is a sign of trust and a way of building a relationship. But be sensitive to the other person's reactions. Try to report your feelings calmly if the other person is the type who does not value sharing or who is easily overwhelmed. Remember, most people tend to listen more attentively if you are not excessively dramatic.

| SHARING WITHOUT CONDEMNATIONS OR FOREGONE CONCLUSIONS | GIVING IN TO TEMPER |
|---|---|
| "I'm so disappointed that they cancelled at the last minute." | "They probably don't like us anyway. How inconsiderate!" |
| "I find it very irritating to see this place so messy!" | "I can't stand this mess! You don't care about anything but yourself! You're lazy and selfish." |
| "My back really hurts." | "I'm nothing but an old rag to you all! No one appreciates me!" "Soon I'll be a cripple." |
| "I'm upset that we're over our budget again. We need to sit down and talk about where we can cut back." | "You're so frivolous! I can't believe how wasteful you are. I have to go through the garbage to make sure you're not throwing anything valuable away. I just can't trust you." |

Obviously, there are situations where you must be dramatic in order to make a point or get action. Do so when necessary. Avoid it when not.

## RECOGNIZE THE FUGUE EFFECT

Like a piece of music which has many voices or parts going on simultaneously, you may often experience a "fugue effect" of emotions. You may simultaneously feel happy for another's good fortune, yet slightly jealous as well; resentful of children, yet happy for the *brachah* of parenthood; sad, lonely, and anxious over a major life change, yet excited about the new possibilities. Some people are more sensitive to a broader range of emotions than others. If you are in this category, accept this reality and do not compare or compete with those who seem to be calmer because of their more monotone emotional world. Also, do not be surprised if you do not understand their world or feel understood by them either.

## LET YOUR DEEPEST FEELINGS RISE AND FALL ACCORDING TO THEIR OWN NATURAL RHYTHM

Emotions are self-limiting. They come and go, crest and fade on their own, as long as you do not attach danger to the situation or condemn yourself for having those feelings. Temper can last for years. But the feelings beneath the temper will fade if you simply allow yourself to experience them fully, while avoiding condemnations or fearful predictions. The major nontemperamental emotions are loneliness, disappointment, frustration, fear, sadness, and embarrassment. Keep your mind quiet while you watch the feelings peak and fall. You may or may not want to take secure thoughts and engage in positive activities at the same time. Do not be worried about being overwhelmed by your feelings, as long as you stay out of temper.

> *Example*: After I made that stupid remark, I let the feeling of embarrassment rise and fall. I took the secure thought that I'm not a total failure socially and that people don't pay much attention to these things. I kept up the conversation as the feeling faded.

> *Example*: I walked for two miles on Shabbath to see a friend, only to find that she wasn't in. I let the feeling of disappointment rise and fall as I walked away.

> *Example*: When I saw what my son had done, I let the feeling of rage rise and fall before I opened my mouth, because I knew I would overreact.

> *Example*: I live with a chronic ailment. Sometimes the feeling of helplessness sweeps over me. I surrender to the pain and keep my

thoughts focused on serving Hashem as best as I can despite this problem. Since I've used this technique of letting the hurt rise and fall, I have pretty much been able to stay away from self-pity and despair.

If a one-year-old child falls down, he feels pain. But he doesn't add to the pain with self-recriminations like, "What a klutz I am," or fearful prognostications about the future, or diagnoses about the present such as, "Old age is overtaking me," or "There's something terribly wrong with my body." He experiences the pain as it is, and then moves on. This is what you should try to achieve with the "peak and fade technique."

If you lived in an emotionally suppressive environment as a child or saw close family members having long bouts of anger or depression, you might fear that this will happen to you. You might be suppressing your own emotions — either anger or anxiety — for fear of becoming overwhelmed by them. Such suppression may find an unhealthy outlet in criticalness, depression, hypochondria, overprotectiveness, obsessive-compulsive behavior, paranoia, hysteria, or withdrawal. When you suppress the feelings you think you should not be having, you also suppress your ability to experience joy, love, and enthusiasm to the same degree. However, as you learn to let your feelings rise and fall, you will be able to experience a wide range of emotions. You will be able to acknowledge them honestly, learn from them when necessary, and express them when appropriate.

Allowing your feelings to rise and fall does not mean that the pain of a tragic event will be gone. It only lessens the duration, so that you can go on with your life and pursue fulfilling goals without being tormented by the past. The following is a story of a woman who remained in prolonged grief because she could not fully express her pain after a tragedy.

> My only daughter was killed in an accident three years ago. Afterward, I found myself unable to express my real grief to anyone. I told myself, "It is God's will. Everything is for the best. It's a *kaparah*." But inside, I was bitter and angry at God. Little by little, I withdrew into myself. I felt that I couldn't express my feelings, so why venture out into the world. I stayed by myself more and more, getting more and more depressed. I couldn't listen to music or look at flowers. I stopped going out of the house. I stopped caring about anything or anyone.
>
> After two years of being housebound, my husband finally brought a special therapist to the house, a "grief therapist." For two hours each day, he let me talk about my pain, my doubts, my fears, and my anger. He was wonderful. He seemed to understand and accept everything I said. When I cried, I could tell he too was in pain over my loss. Sometimes tears would fill his eyes. Together we were finally able to

look at my daughter's picture and mourn the loss of this pretty little girl, who was so full of life and laughter and was now gone forever. He shared the profundity of my grief in a way which no one else had. He didn't tell me to keep a stiff upper lip or to deny my pain. He didn't tell me to suppress it. He allowed me to feel it fully, and his being there to share it with me helped me not to be afraid of it.

Within a month of these daily visits, I felt ready to face the world again. I was no longer angry at my husband, who had been able to go back to work. I realized that that was his own way of filling the void in his life. It didn't mean that he didn't care. But I also understood that he could not experience my grief back then, because he had a different way of expressing his pain. And it was all right for him to be like that. However, I needed this therapist to validate my reality — to feel what I was feeling. I no longer have to be stuck in a state of grief to show that I loved my daughter. I feel the hurt and then go on with my life. During our last session, I looked at her picture and felt the pain of the loss very deeply. It was strong at first, and then it receded. Then it was replaced by a feeling of happiness that she had been part of my life, even for a short time. I have learned how to go on living in the midst of pain.

There are many traumatic experiences which need to be expressed in a similar way. The loss of a close relationship, a divorce, the loss of a fulfilling job or of one's health, a move to a new city with all the losses that that entails — all these events can provoke profound emotional hurt which needs to be validated and, whenever possible, expressed. This helps facilitate the process of reaching *hashlamah* (acceptance). Even a small critical remark can be terribly wounding if it symbolizes the failure of a significant relationship. The "temper reducers" help you acknowledge your feelings. Then you are free to move on. If you find that, despite all your efforts to accept your situation and to be honest about your feelings, you are still depressed, anxiety ridden, or in a chronic state of resentment, take action. Any prolonged emotional state is a cry for help.

# 9.

## Avoid Temper with Children

We want to teach our children to be kindhearted and self-disciplined, both of which are based on a strong sense of self-worth. How can we accomplish this if we are cruel, indifferent, or overprotective? The following list describes the major negative habit patterns of parents. Beneath them are the messages which a child is likely to internalize, based on these behaviors. Remember, you might think that you are training the child to be quiet, respectful, and obedient. But he may be getting training of a different sort — training in temper.

> The chronically angry parent, or the one who uses yelling, beating, and other violent methods, trains a child to think that:
>> "Since my parents can't control themselves when they're upset, I can't either."
>> "It's okay to lose control as long as you're really upset about something — and as I see it, there's always something to be upset about."
>> "It's okay to hurt people who are weaker than yourself."
>> "Force is the way to solve problems."
>> "It's okay to hurt others to get what you want."
>> "Whenever I feel hurt, it's permissible to take my hurt out on others."
>> "I'm bad."
>
> The aloof, indifferent, cold parent, who does not respond to the child's need for guidance, reassurance, touching, holding, and attention, teaches the child that:
>> "To need help is a sign of inadequacy and weakness."
>> "You don't have to help people when they're in distress. Let them work it out for themselves."

"I'm a burden."

"It's not good to have feelings. There's no one to share them with. It's easier not to feel, not to reach out."

"No one really cares about anyone else. Don't put yourself out for anyone."

"No one will ever be there for me. I can't trust anyone."

The overprotective, overindulgent parent teaches the child that:

"I can't do anything for myself. I need the constant guidance and approval of others." "I'm weak and helpless."

"I hate to work hard! I shouldn't have to do it!"

"The world is a frightening place. I need protection."

All three types make the child feel unloved, inferior, and afraid. Children cope with these feelings differently, depending on their inborn temperament, birth order, and life circumstances. One child may become very cruel and aggressive. He may lie, steal, and constantly provoke fights. Another may become a passive, fearful, dependent type. He may withdraw into his own world where no one can reach him. He may not even be in touch with himself. Still another might become a compulsive "goody-goody," engaging in pleasing behavior, not from inner conviction, but to ward off punishment. Each of these children is trying to compensate for feelings of helplessness and inadequacy.

## CHARACTER TRAINING: OUR LONG-RANGE GOAL

A short tempered person cannot teach.

*(Avoth 2:5)*

The word "parent," *horeh* in Hebrew, comes from the word "to teach." Indeed, this is a parent's basic function. When you get angry at an adult, he closes up, gets defensive, and wants to hurt you back. How much more so a child, who is so vulnerable and easily overwhelmed by his own exaggerated fears of abandonment and bodily harm. Getting angry at a child often is bound to make the child indulge in harmful behavior: lying, vengeful acts in fantasy or reality, self-insulation against attack through daydreaming and emotional withdrawal, and displacement of his rage onto siblings, peers, animals, etc. In addition, because a child needs to think that his parents are good, for they are his only source of protection and security in the world, he becomes the "bad guy" in his own eyes, and thinks he deserves abuse and rejection. His shame is so great that he may develop all kinds of self-punishing behaviors.

When you are in angry temper at your children, they look far more powerful, destructive, and obnoxious than they really are, which makes you more violent or prone to feelings of helplessness or hopelessness. In order to justify your own anger, you have to think of the child as bad. This creates a vicious cycle — the child misbehaves, you think he is bad ánd get angry, he misbehaves more and you get even angrier, perhaps hitting and shouting at him, which frightens him into being more resistant.

If you label your children as "bad" or interpret their behavior as intentional attempts to drive you crazy, you will instantly anger yourself. There are so-called "child educators" who teach parents to think of their children as self-centered manipulators who are locked into a constant struggle for power and attention from the parents. Such thinking is bound to make the parents hostile. Assume that your children are doing the best they can with the tools they have at any given moment. If they knew of any other way to satisfy their very healthy need for love, attention, power, security, pleasure, variety, and stimulation, they would do it. But they do not have other resources until we teach them intelligent, creative ways to solve problems, keep order, and cope with disappointment. Take time to teach them the tools. They will learn more quickly if you are not hostile.

How you act around your children is the best indicator of the state of *your* mental health. Your children will play up all your weak spots. That's not their fault. They're just showing you where you need to grow. Don't be angry at them for pointing out your imperfections. They're doing you a favor!

A famous saying tells us, "He who spares his rod spoils his child" (*Mishley* 13:24). Unfortunately, some people misinterpret this as blanket permission to hit the child any time he misbehaves. They might not be aware of the many prohibitions against hurting another person's feelings or destroying a child's self-esteem.

Hit only with a light string.

(*Hilchoth Talmud Torah* 2:2)

Never hit an older child as you are apt to cause him to strike back.

(*Mo'ed Katan* 17a)

Hitting should be rarely used and only at times when the child is in danger or must be stopped immediately. Such action does not call for hostility. A parent who rarely uses violent methods will find that a quick slap on the hand to a two year old who is throwing food or getting near a hot stove is enough to teach the child not to do it again. On the other hand, a child who is used to being hit will not be as responsive, since the more the parent hits, the more immune and unreachable the child becomes. Hitting becomes addictive. There is no end to it. The child becomes more resilient and resistant while the parent uses more force to control the child until, God forbid, the parent loses all rapport with him altogether. It is especially important to avoid excessive harshness with male children, to keep them emotionally open.

The Rambam tells us that we may have to act stern and angry on the outside, but we should maintain a calm interior (*Hilchoth Dei'oth* 2:3). The emotional force of a parent's anger often obscures what he really wants to teach, such as keeping things neat and clean, not making noise when parents are sleeping, making sure homework is done, etc. Rather, the child learns cruelty. To help you respond constructively to misbehavior:

- Think, "Is it worth making an issue over this behavior? Will a little 'benign neglect' be better?"
- Try to understand the world of your child from his point of view. You want him to be orderly, compassionate, self-disciplined, and refined. Is he ready? Are you pushing too soon, too fast? Are your expectations realistic? Impatience denotes temper.
- Have a mental photo album in your mind. When he misbehaves, remember also the good things he has done. Remember how you treasured him when he was born, what a miracle you felt he was. Life may have been easier when he was totally helpless and you had all the power, but your task is to encourage independence and autonomy, not submissiveness.
- Welcome some degree of noncooperation. It's a healthy sign of a child who is struggling to establish his independence and sense of self-mastery.
- Say "yes" as much as possible so that your firm "no's" will be more readily accepted.
- Don't think of your children's mistakes and failures as your failures.
- You've probably done the best you could, given their personalities and temperaments. Look toward the future with greater hope and desire for improvement, not with condemnations and fearful predictions.
- Don't talk when you are angry. If you do talk, don't call names. Say the minimum, and in a low voice. They are more likely to listen if you don't scream. If you have habituated your children to be screamed at, take time to undo that conditioning.

## TO BUILD A CHILD'S SELF-ESTEEM

1. Whenever possible, avoid ordering your children to do things. Give explanations and credit for their responses. Then, when you do have to order them, they won't be so resentful.

2. Praise the child often for the smallest acts of self-discipline or kindness. You can start with a one year old (e.g.,"Thank you for letting me wipe

your nose." "Thank you for holding still while I change you."). He may not understand what you are saying, but he knows that you are expressing love.

3.  One of the most successful tactics according to veteran EMETT members is to keep an "endorsement notebook" for children who are over the age of four. Write down the endorsable acts they do each day, noting which *middah* was strengthened. Within a short time, they themselves will be aware of their *middoth*. In time, you can ask, "Now, which *middah* do you think you need to work on most tomorrow?" Four year olds can already do this. You can keep one notebook and put the initials of the child's name by the side as you jot down the things they do during the day. For example:

    D (David): Memorized three *mishnayoth* during his free time. (Torah study, self-discipline)

    M (Miriam): Wanted to hit, but didn't. (Self-discipline )

    Y (Yaakov): Gave in to his little brother. (Made peace )

    C (Chaim): Was happy for another's pleasure when sister got a gift and he didn't. He avoided making her feel badly by restraining his expression of jealousy. (Happiness for another's joy. Self-restraint )

    D: Helped with extra chores without being asked. (*Chesed*. Orderliness )

    M: Was honest when she admitted she did something wrong in taking away a toy from a friend. (Truthfulness )

    Y: Did his homework even though there were many distractions in the room. (Diligence. Perseverance )

    C: Thought of good solutions when mother forgot to turn out the light in the fridge for Shabbath. (Resourcefulness, accepting suffering with joy, flexibility, etc.)

    M: Gave the neighbor a gift from his own toys. (Kindness. *Chesed* )

    C: Didn't complain overly much when the trip was cancelled. (Acceptance )

    Y: Got a shot from the doctor. (Courage )

    D: Initiated a Shabbath study session for neighborhood children. (Spreading Torah study )

    M: Wanted to wake mother up, but didn't. (Love)

4.  Teach your child Torah thoughts and stories to share at the Shabbath table.

5.  Teach your child life skills: cleaning, cooking, repair work, etc. Endorse for his efforts rather than his successes.

6. Give plenty of opportunities for physical expression: pushing, pulling, climbing, running, jumping, swinging, etc. This helps establish a sense of self-mastery and self-confidence.

7. Create situations that will give him success in his weak points.
   a. Have a "slow learner" teach a younger child whatever he does know.
   b. Give a messy child one small area to clean, and praise him for orderliness.
   c. Let a bossy child "babysit" for ten minutes on the condition that there is no bossiness. Pay him a small amount for his time.
   d. Give the slow child the opportunity to practice various skills during non-crisis hours. For example, in the afternoon, set a timer and see how fast he can put his pajamas on and off and get into his clothes.
   e. Give the passive, fearful child small tasks to accomplish that require initiative.

8. Touch, hug, hold. Emotional maturity is established through touching and reassuring. Moral maturity is established through self-discipline. With reassurance and love, self-discipline and independence follow naturally. A child with low self-esteem needs extra doses of physical warmth. Hold him when you read to him. Hold his hand if you need to rebuke. Hug him when he does something good.

9. Give him success experiences. Have colorful charts to remind the child of his progress or to help him focus on a goal. For example, draw an ice cream cone at the top of a ladder with six or seven rungs. Each time the child does something in the particular area which you want him to improve, put a star on the next rung up. When he has done that thing the specified number of times, buy the ice cream or other small object which he desires.

## REWARD AND PUNISHMENT

Parents will sometimes say, "I have the kind of child who simply must be hit. He doesn't understand anything else." Or, "My little girls have personalities which make hitting absolutely necessary. One good whack, and I have peace and quiet for the next few days." If this is your attitude, it would be worthwhile to read the work of a famous educator, Rabbi Meir Munk, Rav in Torath Emeth, Bnai Brak. His book, *Schar Ve-hanashah Be-chinuch* has the *haskamah* of Rav Shmuel Vozner, *shlita*. Some of his major points are:

1. Before giving a punishment, you must be loved by the child. Also, it must be clear to the child that you love him. Otherwise the punishment will have a negative effect.

2. We are told, "Do not placate your fellow in the moment of his anger" (*Avoth* 4:18). This is because an angry person is not rational at that moment. You should also avoid giving *mussar*, which he cannot possibly listen to in that state of mind.

3. If a child loves you, then a nod of the head or a wink of your eye is enough to make him behave.

4. Punishment comes from weakness. It shows that the educator hasn't been able to influence the child with words. To correct this weakness, the educator should feel great pain that he had to use punishment (based on *Chazon Ish, Orach Chaim* 56:4).

5. Veteran teachers all know that positive statements have a much stronger effect in helping children grow than negative statements.

6. The teacher should smile at his students as much as possible. Then, the mere lack of a smile is enough of a punishment.

7. The teacher should work to see the positive and the beautiful in his students. Then he will be able to influence them because his students will want to do anything to please him.

8. The Chofetz Chaim's son said that his father never disciplined him through fear, only through love.

### DO NOT PUNISH IN ANGER

Rabbi Eliyahu Lopian wrote that he would not rebuke his children or students when he first heard about a wrongdoing, for fear that he might rebuke out of anger. He would always wait. Once, one of his children did something which so upset him that he waited a full two weeks before censuring him (*Lev Eliyahu*, vol. 2, pp. 26-27).

### DO NOT THINK YOUR CHILDREN DO THINGS DAVKA

Rabbi Shmuel Pliskin, *z.l.*, student of the Chofetz Chaim, always quoted the latter as saying that on Yom Kippur by night, we recite the verse that God should forgive all Bnai Yisrael because they transgressed unintentionally. How can this be? The answer is that if a person really understood that something was wrong, he wouldn't do it. Therefore, the person obviously lacks awareness and we should feel sorry for him. Have this attitude in mind before you rebuke your children.

## RECOGNIZE YOUR CHILD'S EMOTIONAL NEEDS AND HELP FULFILL THEM

> A parent needs to see his child as a precious diamond which needs to be polished
> in order to make him shine and glow.
>
> (Rabbi Zelig Pliskin)

It is fairly easy to satisfy a child's physical needs for food and shelter. It's the emotional needs which cause more problems, because they require that we give more deeply of ourselves. For example, all children have a healthy need to be held and cuddled by their mothers. In Biblical times, children were nursed for two years and slept in close proximity to their parents. The physical presence of the parents was a constant reassurance to the child. Now it is common for parents to view this need for reassurance as a manipulative attempt by the conniving child to trick them into giving him undeserved and unnecessary attention. Such parents often think they will "toughen the child up" by never touching him, except to feed and dress him. Many of these children grow up emotionally deadened and unable to form close, caring relationships with others. They become insensitive to their own and others' deepest needs.

Children need to be touched and stroked by a reassuring person, in order for them to internalize the *middah* of loving-kindness. Children who were responded to as babies, when they were in distress, need less reassurance in the long run. A well-loved, secure child is capable of treating himself and others in a loving manner quite early in life. Remember, a child's dependency needs must be satisfied if he is ever to become truly independent.

Children also need to learn self-mastery:

> Who is mighty? He who conquers his own passions.
>
> (*Avoth* 4:1)

When a child's basic security needs have been reasonably satisfied during his first years of life, he is more capable of coping with frustration, disappointment, and loss. A child learns self-control by seeing that his parents are in control of themselves, especially when they discipline him. Discipline is not an end, but rather a means of helping the child become more group-minded. He controls himself in order to show respect for the needs of others (e.g., for peace and quiet, orderliness, and thoughtfulness). He avoids laziness and selfishness by contributing his share to the cleanliness of the home. When he sees his parents devoted to the study of Torah and the joyous fulfillment of mitzvoth, he develops the same devotion, not out of fear but out of such great love for his parents that he wants to imitate them. He avoids hurting others, not so much out of fear of their reaction, but out of love for Hashem's creations. A child who has a close connection to his parents feels connected to Hashem and will want to serve Him with joy.

### GENERAL RULES FOR GOOD COMMUNICATION WITH CHILDREN

1. If you want cooperation:

   a. State what you want clearly *after* getting the child's attention. Stay in the present. If the child makes excuses, accuses you of not being fair in the past, or tries to otherwise avoid the issue, use the "broken record technique" in which you simply state your wish over and over, i.e., "Wash your hands now. Please wash your hands."

   b. Describe the problem without mentioning the person or what you want done, in order to give the other person the opportunity to come up with his own solution and to feel that he has some power in the situation. "I see that the dining room table is messy."

   c. Give information about the consequences. "If the table doesn't get cleaned up, I can't put out dinner."

   d. State rules: "There will be no sleep-overs on school nights." "There will be no hitting or screaming in this house." "Gifts won't be used until 'thank-you' notes have been written."

   e. Describe how the situation makes you feel: "When you make a lot of noise, I get so jittery that I lose my appetite."

   f. Write notes: "I did not find my scissors in the sewing box when I needed them. It is very upsetting to not be able to find my things."

   g. Have charts and schedules to apportion household chores.

2. Discipline children without vengefulness or hostility:

   a. Show the child how to do something right in the future, if he lacks skills. Have him redo the task in front of you, to make sure he knows how to do it.

   b. Give a choice: "Don't take between-meal snacks unless you are willing to wash your own dishes. Otherwise, wait until regular meal times."

   c. Take action: "I'm locking my sewing box." "Please go to your room until you can talk to me respectfully."

   d. Decide together on logical consequences. "If you lose your key again, you will have to do certain extra chores to pay for it." "If you don't let me know when you will be late, you'll be grounded for three days."

   e. Replay the scene. "Go out of the room, come back in, and talk to me nicely this time."

   f. Stop. "I'm going to stop the car until the noise stops."

   g.  Use fantasy. "Oh, your poor coat is on the floor. It looks so lonely. I bet it wants to be with its friends in the closet."

3.  To gain respect from children, show respect for their needs and feelings, especially when you must deny their desires.

> Who is honored? He who honors others.
>
>                        (*Avoth* 4:1)

4.  Use humor whenever possible. (Be careful to avoid sarcasm or ridicule.)

> "When you all make demands on me at the same time, I feel like a cat being chased by a pack of dogs. I don't know where to turn first."
>
> "I notice that you've been missing the garbage pail on those last few throws."
>
> "If people around here don't help, that makes this a restaurant, and I'll start charging good money for my excellent service and good food."

*Note*: Do all this with a pleasant tone of voice. In the long run, you will gain much more than if you yell and scream.

*Example*: My three year old was being *kvetchy*, *davka* at dinner time when I was trying to keep the house in order, cook the meal, tend to the baby, as well as help my six year old with his homework. I was ready to scream at him to go away. I thought about his need for warmth. I held him in my arms for five minutes and just stroked him, while I helped his older brother with his homework. That five minutes saved me from exploding. Afterwards, he went away happy.

*Example*: When I left for my EMETT night group, I instructed my twelve year old to clean up the kitchen. When I came back, it was messier than ever. I was ready to drag my daughter out of bed, even though she was already asleep, and make her clean up. Then I thought, "Look at me! I come home from an EMETT group and here I am in such a temper." I decided to give her the benefit of the doubt and clean up the kitchen myself. In the morning, I calmly asked her what had happened (I was hostile on the inside). She said that as soon as I had left for class, the baby had awakened screaming, and that she had walked back and forth with him for two hours, until they both had fallen asleep. Oy! When I thought of the damage I could have done if I had treated her roughly the night before! Here she had been working hard trying to calm a screaming baby for hours, and I was ready to accuse her of being lazy and inconsiderate.

*Example*: It was just before Shabbath and my husband said he wanted to go visit his parents. I was ready to say something nasty about him not helping me. Then I thought, "What kind of *middoth* am I demonstrating to my children if I criticize him in front of them?" I decided to let him go and talk about the incident when we were both calm.

## MAINTAIN SHALOM BAYITH WITH RESPECTFUL SPEECH: CULTIVATE A GENTLE VOICE

There is a hidden treasure which, when found, can support a home forever, a well whose clear waters are an eternal blessing, yielding happiness and *shalom bayith*. The name of that treasure is...respect. He who shows respect for his fellow man will, in turn, be treated with respect.

(*The Jew and His Home*, p. 82)

Love of God is love of man and vice versa.

(*Ha-yom Yom*, p. 81)

Take a few minutes to talk to your spouse and children about a firm decision that you have made: i.e., not to allow disrespectful talk in the home to anyone, by anyone. Then stick to it! If someone does something that bothers you, jot it down on a piece of paper taped to the refrigerator or another convenient place. Then talk to the person about it, when you are out of temper and can avoid shaming the person in front of others or arousing resistance. Train yourself to have a gentle voice.

Whenever possible, ignore nonharmful behavior. No one goes to the *chuppah* with a pacifier in his mouth. And it is not likely that your children will refuse to stand up for *kiddush* or will be whining by the time they are adults. Don't make an issue out of anything which is not worth a fight. Don't display poor character traits while training your children to have good ones. It won't work. If you have a good relationship, a stern look will usually keep them in line. And if you don't, all the beatings in the world will not instill in them your highest ideals. Whenever possible, demonstrate self-restraint to your children by illustrating that they do not automatically have to become unhappy or angry about some event.

*Example*: M (age 4) kept calling Y (age 6) a liar. Y told me that he wanted to bash M's head in. I called M over and told him that he should continue calling Y a liar, and that I would pay Y a quarter every time M called him that name. Suddenly the situation changed drastically in Y's mind. He said, "Yes, call me a liar" with a cheerful gleam in his eyes. Poor M. The fun had gone out of his cruelty. He half-heartedly said, "Liar" to Y, but Y was happy because he had earned a quarter. I told Y, "You see, just a minute ago the word 'liar' was making you angry. But now that your thoughts are focused on the money instead of on getting your brother's approval, it doesn't bother you anymore."

Use every opportunity to prove to yourself and those around you that it's not the people, places, and things around us which control our happiness, but rather our attitudes do. Be creative!

> *Example*: I told my four-and six-year-old boys that as soon as they got into bed, I would give them a very funny assignment. They quickly got undressed and into bed. Then I told them that they could have a contest to see who could keep his eyes open the longest. They weren't even allowed to blink. They got so tired, they begged to be able to close their eyes and go to sleep.

No technique works all the time. As long as the atmosphere in your home is generally loving, accepting, and secure, your children will turn out just fine despite moments of resentment and defiance.

Why should a parent go to all these extremes to find creative solutions to problems, instead of using force and threats? It is because the latter destroy the child's sense of self-worth, which is built on feeling loved and achieving mastery over his world. Because of his small size, lack of awareness, and skills, a child naturally feels insecure and inferior at times, even though he may not show it. Avoid reinforcing a negative self-image with constant criticism. Self-esteem is the foundation of mental health.

> Rabbi Yisroel Salanter advised educators that the way to reach people is to instill in them elevated feelings about themselves. Rabbi Noson Tzvi Finkel...praised his pupils profusely. A teacher who tends to lower the self-esteem and confidence of his students should either change this tendency or change professions. One of the most important lessons an educator can convey to students is that they have inherent worth and should strive to utilize their potential. To increase self-esteem...have them become aware of [their] strengths and resources.

> (*Gateway to Happiness*, p. 133)

If you do lose control or find it necessary to punish, reassure the child of your love at some point afterwards. Remember that immediately after Adam and Chavah were told of the punishments they were to receive for having sinned, Hashem clothed them (*Bereishith* 3:16-21). A child lacks the sophistication to recognize that he is loved even when his parents are angry with him. When he is expelled from the paradise of your love, clothe him with a word of kindness, a hug of reassurance, or some other gesture of concern as soon as you feel that he can be receptive. A one or two year old will welcome a hug almost immediately. With an older child, it may take longer and require setting aside time for a discussion of the incident. Understand that he may try to save face by attacking you at first. That shows the degree to which he feels wounded. Patiently rebuild trust.

## RECOGNIZE CHILDREN'S INSECURE THOUGHTS

Children often think insecurely:

"I can't do anything right!"
"I did something bad. That means I am bad."
"I didn't get what I wanted from my parents. That means that they don't love me."

Help children understand that they often need to challenge their attitudes. You might ask:

"Do you think that I don't love you because I don't give you everything you want?"
"Do you think that this problem will last forever?"
"What are you afraid will happen if you don't get your way?"

You can reassure your child that you love him, even if he doesn't see it — just as the sun exists at night. Reassure him that he will grow up to be big and strong and able to handle himself and the world. Protect him from neighborhood or family bullies if he's being victimized. He doesn't have the skills to fight someone who's bigger. But don't overprotect or he'll never develop those skills. Allow him to express himself. Show interest in him, especially if he is really in distress. Help him understand himself. Once you know how he interprets events, you can help him become a more secure, rational thinker.

## TEACH CHILDREN TO BE SOLUTION-ORIENTED, NOT FEELING-CENTERED

There are many ways to help children overcome bad habits. One is by telling a story which illustrates someone else overcoming that behavior.

*Example*: M, aged four, was going through a period of whining excessively. So I told him a story about a little boy his age, named Meir, who loved to have disappointments and frustrations because he looked at them as a challenge. For example, little Meir went with his family to Bnai Brak for Purim. Just after they had loaded the car and were on their way, they got a flat tire. Everybody else started to cry and fret, saying, "Oh no, we'll never get to the Megillah reading on time." But Meir stood up and said, "It doesn't help to whine and cry. We have to find solutions." And he did. He flagged down a taxi and they loaded everything on — all the suitcases, blankets, and food. After a few miles, the taxi ran out of gas. Again, everyone started moaning and 'oy veying' except Meir. He got out and said, "It doesn't help to whine and cry. We have to find a solution." And he did. He flagged down a car that was pulling a boat. The whole family got into the boat and went on their way. A few miles down the road stood a cow who wouldn't budge. Meir found a solution, and in the end everyone got to Bnai Brak on time. I repeated this story to my son each day. He loved it. Within a week, he himself was saying, "It won't help to whine and cry. I have to find a solution."

You can train even very young children to be solution-oriented by using everyday events to teach them self-trust and self-confidence. For example, if a child says, "I'm hungry," instead of giving him the solution, ask, "How can we solve that problem?" If he says he's thirsty, cold, or sleepy, don't give him your solutions. Ask him, "What can you do about that?" If there is something he doesn't like, empathize with him and then ask, "Do you want me to help you solve that problem? Let's look at the possible solutions. I'll give some and you give some, and then we'll pick the one that seems most likely to work."

## HELP THEM DEVELOP SENSITIVITY FOR ANOTHER'S NEEDS

When your children are being excessively noisy, demanding, uncooperative, or otherwise irritating, what you want most is for them to be sensitive to *your* need for peace and quiet, order, honesty, etc. You can help foster such sensitivity by role-playing, role-reversal, and play-acting. For example, you can act out stories from the lives of great *tzaddikim*. One rabbi remembers how, as a young child, his father asked the children to act out stories from the life of the Chofetz Chaim. This instilled in him a great appreciation for *chesed* throughout his life.

If a child does not want to do his homework, try role reversal. You play him and he plays you. Let him experience how difficult it is to get *you* to do your homework. (Don't give in too easily!)

*Example*: My oldest daughter was being very critical. I have learned that criticalness is a sign of lack of trust in the other person. Instead of taking offense at her remarks, I realized that we needed to do something for our relationship. It was hard to get through to her. She was very aloof and defensive when I approached her. But when I asked her to role-play me in a scene, I quickly understood how she felt. Even though I did not agree with her picture of me, it was how she was viewing things at the time. As I began to become more sensitive to how she was feeling, she became more understanding of me. It took time, but it was well worth the effort to avoid the buildup of an even greater wall of hostility between us.

## DEALING WITH THE HIGH NEED LEVEL CHILD

All children need attention, reassurance, and discipline. But some have greater needs than others. If you had a child with a physical handicap, you would not blame him for it, or ignore his needs with the excuse that, "He's just trying to get my attention." The same is true for the child with unusual sensitivities or emotional needs. Whether the problem is due to minimal brain damage, a tense home atmosphere, parental discord, or other traumas, these children require extra doses of patience and love. They are a tremendous test of one's *middoth*, because they can easily bring you to their level of negativity and aggression, or you might become completely unresponsive to them. There is a famous statement that, "A child needs love most when he is least lovable." The following suggestions may help you to keep that in mind when dealing with such children.

1. Do not use force unless danger is involved. You'll need to use more and more as time goes on.
2. Use indirect means of awakening positive *middoth*. Engineer situations so that he can experience himself in a positive way.
3. Hold him whenever possible to reassure him of your love.
4. Keep a "*Middoth* Notebook" and write down all the positive things the child does to remind you that there *are* good times as well as bad.
5. These children are very responsive to tangible rewards: money for small services builds self-esteem and a sense of power and responsibility; small prizes for good behavior prove to him that he is capable of self-control, etc. However, don't reward bad behavior by telling him, "If you don't hit, I'll buy you X." Rather, when you see that he has not hit anyone for a few minutes, tell him so.
6. Don't blame the child. If he knew of a better way to get the love, power, and pleasure he wants and craves, he would do it.
7. Don't blame yourself. You too were doing the best you knew how all along. And you are probably doing the best you can now. However, this does not mean that you can't do better. Read books, get counseling, and talk to peers about how they cope.
8. Try to spend as much time as possible communicating with this child alone. He needs explanations, stories, and time to awaken greater awareness of his own and others' feelings. Don't turn off to his needs or

he'll turn off to yours. Don't be cruel to him or he'll be cruel back. He needs proper attention. Give it to him and you will be richly rewarded later on. Check with an occupational therapist to see if he suffers from sensory integration dysfunction.

9. Celebrate the small victories. Watch for the little acts of kindness. Mention them. ALLOW YEARS TO HELP THE CHILD OVERCOME HIS HANDICAP.

10. BE PATIENT AND HAVE FAITH! If you are very patient, yet firm; if you set strict limits and enforce them consistently with love, you will see major changes by the age of six.

11. Avoid insecure thoughts such as: "I'll never be able to cope." "I'm a failure." "He'll never be normal." "It's hopeless."

12. Examine your motives when you are impatient or hostile toward him. Is it in the child's best interests to have you on his back all the time, making an issue out of every little thing he does? Or, is it your own sense of personal prestige which is at stake?

One of the greatest mistakes many parents make is that they think they are inferior and inadequate whenever their children misbehave. This occurs more often when parents have a high need child. Once you have learned to avoid the condemnations, you will find it easier to cope in a positive manner.

*Example*: My eight year old was becoming more and more hostile. I was at my wits' end. I felt so ashamed that I didn't want to admit it to anyone, even myself. Finally, I had the courage to be realistic and seek help. It was a great relief. The counselor helped me to see that I wasn't a failure. Even experts have difficulty reaching such children.

*Example*: Whenever we have one of those crisis moments in our house, I think to myself, "Look for the M & M's — the mitzvoth and *middoth*." It's like the distracting music that my dentist uses. I'm so busy thinking about creative solutions that I don't dwell on the anxiety-producing condemnations.

*Example*: My difficult child got worse when my last baby was born. The worst time was the morning. I just couldn't get all my kids off without at least one of them in tears. Finally, I decided to bathe the two and four year old at night and put on their clean clothes, so that they would be ready for school when they awoke, and only would need to eat. I did this until my baby was a few months of age, and I had the strength and patience to dress them properly. I'm glad I had the flexibility to put *shalom bayith* and my children's mental health first. With a good breakfast and a calmer mother, my oldest was far less hostile and remote.

Creative parents may seem to have more difficulties with their small children than excessively authoritarian parents. This is because they are sensitive to the individual needs of the children and are more willing to give of themselves. Yet by the age of five or six, these children usually have internalized a positive value system and are less problematical in the long run. Whatever kind of children you have, make character training a long range goal, one on which you are willing to spend years of effort.

## MAKE YOUR HOME A PLACE OF EMOTIONAL FREEDOM WITHOUT TEMPER

Tell your children that you appreciate the fact that they communicate with you, even if you don't like what they say.

*Example*: My teenage daughter, who happens to be quite critical, told me that she didn't want me to come to the parent-teachers' meeting because I didn't dress nicely and was overweight. She said she was embarrassed. I couldn't believe my response. I just said, "Thank you for being so honest. You're right. I need to take better care of myself and go on a diet." She couldn't believe me either. Suddenly, all her anger was gone and she actually cried and said she was sorry she had hurt my feelings."

*Example*: My four year old said he hated me. In the past, I would have slapped his face for disrespect. This time, I just said, "Wow, I can see that you're upset with me. I'm sorry. Tell me what's bothering you."

When you keep the lines of communication open, children will often respond. Children who have the most difficulty communicating their feelings are apt to be more aggressive or withdrawn. This is especially true of boys, who are encouraged in our society to suppress their feelings and pretend that they do not experience pain. If they grow insensitive to their own pain, they will be insensitive to the pain of others. Underneath their anger is hurt. Let them talk about what hurts them. It doesn't mean that you have to do what they want. Just listen. That is often enough.

*Example*: My daughter lost an expensive sweater on a camping trip to the mountains. When she told me, I had the impulse to tell her how careless she had been and rebuke her. Instead, I just sympathized with her. She was already feeling sad. Later, she came and thanked me for not getting angry. I knew she had learned her lesson because she asked me to order name tags for her to sew onto her clothing.

*Example*: Every few days, my son comes home and tells me about the fights he has with other boys at school. I listen to all the details of what happened and sympathize with his frustrations and hurts. Often, he starts off by saying, "I'm not going back there tomorrow." But after we've talked, he feels better. When I ask if he wants me to call the principal, he always tells me not to, that he can handle it himself.

Be there for your children. It helps them become emotionally self-aware, mature, and sensitive human beings who can care deeply about others.

# 10.

## Use Your Imagination
## to Promote Change and Creativity

Our actions and attitudes are determined, to a great extent, by our childhood conditioning and experiences. We tend to repeat these early response patterns without questioning their efficacy or appropriateness. For example, if we were forced to eat certain foods as children, the sight of those foods may still make us feel anxious or disgusted even though we are now adults. If our parents were indifferent to us or abused us, we may have no sense of our strengths, and we may feel weak and dependent. We may be overwhelmed easily, fear rejection, or desperately want approval but never believe that people care about us. Or we may be cold and critical in order to avoid close relationships which, we believe, only can bring pain.

Many people want to exercise more self-control, yet believe that they cannot restrain themselves. The goal may seem too difficult or unrealistic. It is important to understand two main internal barriers to change in order to identify when something can be changed and to know when there is a genuine limitation which cannot be overcome.

*The Belief Barrier.* Two forces are needed for voluntary change: will and imagination. If your beliefs (linked to the imagination) are in opposition to your will, then you will lose the battle. In other words, if you would like to be more self-confident, creative, communicative, or self-controlled, yet believe that you are irrevocably cowardly, dull, cold, or lazy, then your mind will reject your goal as being impossible. If you imagine that losing weight will be "absolute torture," or that calmness is only for the saintly, which you are not, then your imagination will win, one hundred percent of the time.

*The Experiential Barrier.* When your experiences contradict your desired goal, you may think that you are incapable of changing. For example, you decide that you want to feel more in control and competent, but you find yourself exploding angrily at your children; you are unable to grasp a difficult *gemarah*; or you are constantly procrastinating. You may think, "See, I want to change, but experience shows me that I can't." The very effort to improve seems to make things worse. Not only have you kept your old behavior, but you may have reinforced it with another experience of failure. No wonder so many people give up on diets and exercise programs, feeling that, "It's useless." Or, "I'm not meant to change."

Thankfully, there is a method which can cut through these barriers. It is called Positive Experiential Programming, or P.E.P., for short.

## THE IMAGINATION CAN CUT THROUGH ALL BARRIERS

> Reb Zushe used to say, "When I come to *olam ha-elyon* (the next world), no one will ask me why I wasn't like Moshe Rabbeinu. Instead, they will ask why wasn't I like Zushe — why didn't I live up to what I was capable of."
>
> (anecdote of unknown origin)

There is an inner power we can use to help us reach our potential — the imagination. If you imagine that you can overcome a bad habit, then the brain is more likely to accept this, almost as though you experienced it in actuality. This is done with a simple technique called Positive Experiential Programming (or P.E.P.). With this technique, you first define the *middah* which you want to improve, and then you imagine yourself succeeding in that area. In this way, you send new input to the brain (the bio-computer), which can challenge the old information. When the will and the imagination work in unison, they are very effective in helping you to change. Anger- or anxiety-producing thoughts attract thoughts of a similar nature unless we forcefully overcome them with positive actions or secure thoughts.

The first step in this exercise is to formulate your precise goal. Make it realistic and attainable. Do not make your goal dependent on someone else changing (e.g., "I'll be happy when I get married/have children/when my wife stops nagging/when my husband is more helpful, etc."). Do not make impossible goals for yourself. ("I want to always feel good, healthy, stable, loving, or competent.") Rather, have realistic, definite improvements in mind:

> "When I go to the wedding tonight, I will look at the sweets table and walk past it."
> "When my children come home from school and the atmosphere is frantic as usual, I will not get angry at their simultaneous demands and will stay calm."

Don't use the words, "I'll try ...." That presupposes that you're not sure. Give yourself firm orders. You know that when you tell someone, "I'll try and stop by," you're already thinking that you won't. The same with the mind. It accepts a goal if it is presented with confidence.

## USE THE P.E.P. EXERCISE TO EXPERIENCE YOURSELF IN A NEW LIGHT

The next barrier to break is the experiential one. With the following exercise, you will experience yourself thinking and behaving differently.

Allow your body to relax. Find a comfortable position. Now close your eyes. Imagine a relaxing scene from the past, a quiet place where you felt happy and calm. Allow your breathing to become deep and relaxed as you count backwards from ten to one. Ten...nine...you are becoming more relaxed...eight...seven...more deeply relaxed...six...five... four...three...more deeply relaxed. You have a pleasant floating sensation. Two...one....

[Optional, if there is time: Now we will count again and this time relax the body in progressive stages. Ten...relax the facial muscles, the muscles behind the eyes and around the mouth...nine...relax the muscles in your neck and shoulders. Let go of the tension. Eight...let go of the tension in your upper arms, lower arms, and fingers. Good. Breathe gently. Seven...let go of the tension in your chest and stomach.... Six...release the tension in the upper part of your back...five...in the middle of your back and now all the way down your spine so that your back feels relaxed and free of tension. Four...release the tension in your upper legs...three...in your knees...two...in your feet and toes...and now one...release any remaining tension in your body.]

Good. With each breath you take, feel yourself becoming more deeply relaxed. Breathe in relaxation, breathe out tension; breathe in hope, breathe out discouragement; breathe in love, breathe out judgments and demands; breathe in confidence, *emunah*, and *bitachon*, breathe out anxiety.... Feel your entire body bathed in a gentle feeling of relaxation.

Now we will begin P.E.P., Positive Experiential Programming. Think of a *middah* which you want to improve. Don't think of changing yourself as a whole. Only one small factor. Think of a situation which occurred recently, to which you reacted with negativity. From the safety and comfort of your position as a detached observer, watch yourself being anxious, angry, or discouraged. [Pause] Now, tune into the part of yourself which is creative, which has unlimited potential for change, and which wants to help you improve your *middoth*. That part of you knows what resources you need to apply in order to respond in a more Torah-like manner. [Pause] Now, using that new resource, actually imagine yourself thinking, talking, and acting differently. You may be responding in a dynamic, assertive manner. You may simply be experiencing serenity and acceptance. You may be walking away without hostility or resistance.

[The closing statement is essential. Otherwise the person will walk away feeling "spacy."] On the count of four, you will open your eyes. Your mind will be completely clear and you will be ready to face life with a renewed energy, confidence, and love. One...two...three...four.

P.E.P. can be used to practice visualizing your use of the variou temper-reducing tools listed in this book. It can also be used in helpin children to change.

## USE AN ABBREVIATED FORM OF P.E.P. FOR QUICK TEMPER REDUCTION

If you find yourself in a negative state, which you want to change quickly, you can use a simple, quick visualization technique. Start by closing your eyes and imagining yourself in your negative state (resentment, self-pity, anger, discouragement, etc.). See yourself in that state. Then see yourself in the opposite state by imagining yourself feeling calm, secure, happy, accepting, inspired, loving, enthusiastic, etc. By going back and forth between the negative and positive for about a minute each, you "unfix" the mind's grip on the negative state. If you cannot imagine yourself feeling better in the future, imagine a time when you had those pleasant feelings in the past. Always start with the negative state first, then go to the positive.

1. Imagine yourself getting very upset when this particular person criticizes you. See yourself tense and angry.
   Now, see yourself acting in a Torah-like manner, with calm detachment or polite assertiveness. Experience the calm feeling.
2. Imagine things falling apart and getting chaotic, and your feeling overwhelmed and incapable of coping.
   Now imagine that things are falling apart and getting chaotic. However, you are not condemning yourself or anyone around you. You are simply doing whatever you can do to keep things under control as best you can, recognizing that you can never be perfect or have total control.
3. Imagine that you are doing this particular thing which you have been afraid to do. Imagine being subject to various physical discomforts or disapproval.
   Imagine that things don't turn out as you want and that some people are actually disapproving. Experience the fact that disapproval can be painful, but that the painful feelings subside shortly. See yourself

bearing the physical and emotional discomforts with a feeling of inner trust and tranquility. See that it is not as awful as you had thought.

4. See yourself getting up in the morning feeling lethargic, blue, and "blah."

Now imagine yourself waking up, saying *modeh ani* with gratefulness and enthusiasm. See yourself doing five minutes of simple exercises to strengthen your back muscles and give you a feeling of energy and strength.

Bad habits start off "like a spider web and end up being like the cable of a ship."

(*Succah* 52a)

We have a Torah obligation to strive for moral excellence, no matter what our background was or the internal or external obstacles which are in our paths. It may look like an impossible task at times. Yet we are told,

Torah is close to you, in your mouth and your heart that you may do it.

(*Devarim* 30:14)

The hardest thing is that first step forward, the decision to make a change in the way you think, speak, or act. From then on, you will experience an automatic pull toward your goal.

If a man consecrates himself in a small measure down below, he is sanctified much more from above.

(*Yoma* 39a)

Self impulsion induces heavenly inspiration.

(*Zohar* II, 135b)

When a person takes upon himself the responsibility for an important project, he will have a special degree of divine assistance....

(*Me-archey Leiv*, vol. 1, p. 37)

Dynamic, vigorous, happy people are dynamic, vigorous, and happy because they have goals. It is erroneous to think, "If only I had more energy/skills/ organization/time, I could really do something with my life." Rather, it is in the striving for self-improvement and giving to others that you feel energized, competent, and loved. You will find that your life suddenly takes on a structure and order in which you will have time to do far more than you believed possible when you have worthwhile goals.

## OVERCOMING THE DIVIDED WILL

No army would last long if the general told his troops, "Well men, if you feel like getting up early, then there will be an exercise class at 5 A.M. If you're too tired, you don't have to come and we'll cancel the march we had scheduled." Halfhearted attempts to improve will not get you very far. Give yourself firm messages which carry a sense of resolute determination.

"No more name-calling here in the house. Not for *any* reason!"

"No more explosions over the monthly bills. We'll work it out with a financial counselor if necessary."

We all struggle to some extent with a "divided will." One part of us wants to be kindhearted and industrious, and the other finds it more convenient to be selfish and lazy. We want to be giving, but we're afraid of being taken advantage of. When we experience a divided will, we must think of our priorities, not our present desire for pleasure, domination, or prestige.

## USE P.E.P. TO STORE CREATIVE SOLUTIONS

When a crisis occurs, one tends to fall back on old, comfortable habit patterns. To prevent this, P.E.P. can be used to store "emergency rations" which can be drawn upon during stressful times. You know which situations tend to be "button pushers" for you. Anticipate that they will occur and prepare positive attitudes and actions in your imagination, so that your mind will not draw a blank when you need creative ideas.

# *11.*

## *Leaders' Guide: The EMETT Meeting\**

An EMETT meeting consists of:

1.  Fifteen to twenty minutes reading from the EMETT book, with each member reading a paragraph or two.
2.  Four to five examples given by class members, each approximately ten minutes. Each is followed by five minutes of "highlighting" comments.
3.  A fifteen-minute question and comment period about the examples given.
4.  Ten-minute optional P.E.P. visualization exercise at the end of the class.

Rules:

1.  No food, smoking, drinking, craft work or other distractions. Babies under two months can be allowed, at the discretion of the leader.
2.  Examples are to be given by members who have attended at least three meetings and are familiar with the book and EMETT terminology.
3.  Members do not talk unless called upon by the group leader.
4.  No examples are to be allowed about members who are present.
5.  Examples are to be confined to trivialities or non-overwhelming upsets. When EMETT first began, we confined examples to very minor stresses to build familiarity with the tools. However, we found that as the years went on, longtime members were able to talk about major events in a way which did not overwhelm them or the group. New members should not talk about major problems until they have *extensive* practice in applying EMETT tools on minor irritations.

---

\* Leadership Training Manuals are available from the author.

6. No examples should concern religious or legal transgressions. However, trivialities around these events may be given, such as forgetting to turn off the light in the refrigerator before Shabbath and the discomforts that that entailed, or the humiliation of getting a traffic ticket.

## FINANCES

Many leaders allow newcomers to attend the first session free of charge. After that, there is an initial fee for the eight-week class. Once the course has been completed, members can go anywhere in the world, attend any EMETT session, and feel right at home. Most leaders ask for $1 fee per session. The initial fee is very important. It is sometimes the only thing that makes members come back each week and bear the discomfort of something new. They may be thinking just before group, "There's so much to do at home and so many other activities. But I've paid my fee, so I'll go." Once they have experienced four to six weeks of EMETT, there is no need for outside incentives, because they'll see how much the sessions have helped in their daily lives. Also, people tend to value the class more if they have to pay for it.

## DISCIPLINE

It is very important for the leader to maintain discipline. We come to class to work on ourselves, not to talk aimlessly. It is important to stay focused on self-awareness. To do this, the leader must make sure that:

1. The member gives the four-step example thoroughly, yet quickly. The only flexibility can be in Step 2, where the member can list the emotions before the thoughts, if the former are very strong. If the member reverses the order of Step 2, don't contradict him.
2. Other members do not intrude with questions or comments during the four-step example, unless the example is totally incomprehensible without certain information. It is not usually necessary to know very much background unless it is essential to understand the example-giver's response. The leader must be strict about not allowing extraneous questions. Remember, the goal of Step 1 is simply to help the example-giver identify his pattern whenever events of this nature (a mistake, disappointment, insult, etc.) occur. The particular event is not that important.

## HOW TO LEAD AN EXAMPLE

The leader should always remember that he is a lay person, not a therapist. His job is to lead the example-giver through the four steps, not to diagnose, analyze, or solve problems. If he keeps this limitation in mind always, stays within the realm of trivialities, and keeps things simple, these disciplines will enable him to go through an example without problems.

*Giving the Example.* For Step 1, the leader will ask the member to mention the upsetting event and perhaps state what is universal about it. The leader must stop the example-giver when enough information has been given to make the example meaningful, but before it gets too complex and detailed. The leader can keep the example relevant to all by highlighting the universal aspects:

> "O.K., here we have an example of a negative response to an insult."
> "Yes, you made a mistake. What we can all relate to here is the initial discouragement and self-condemnation which often follow such an event."
> "You were obviously in a lot of pain. I'm sure we can all identify with that. What were your insecure thoughts?"

*Step 2a:* The leader will give a short time to allow the member to state his insecure thoughts. If he can't think of any, the leader should move on. By the end of the example, when the member has calmed down, he may be more in touch with what his insecure thoughts were.

If the example-giver has no insecure thoughts, then the leader should go on to *condemnations,* by asking, "In what way did you feel that you or anyone around you was inadequate or failing in any area?" Or, "Did any labeling (name-calling) pop into your mind?"

Next is *unfulfilled demands.* The leader asks, "What did you want that you weren't getting?" Or, "How would you have liked things to be?"

*Step 2b:* Next, the leader asks for the *harmful impulses.* Even if there was only two minutes of "processing," that is enough to count as a harmful impulse. If the person says, "I wanted to throttle that kid," that should be accepted as a very average response. Mention that one brings *kedushah* into the world by overcoming one's negative impulses. This statement helps people to accept their own impulses and to reveal themselves to others more easily.

*Step 2c:* Often, the member will say that he had no *physical sensations.* Yet, while giving the example, you may notice fist-clenching or other manifestations of stress. Point this out, or ask, "Think back to the event for a second. Where did you feel the stress in your body? This is important, because it is a clue to you that you are in temper. This may appear as a slight tightening in the back of the neck or tension around the mouth. It is important to be aware of these changes, because they alert us of the need to do some mental or physical work to get back to a state of inner harmony."

*Step 2d*: Next, give the member a minute to go through the list of emotions. Although many people feel the emotional impact first, and may be allowed to mention them before Step 2a if they are very strong in the present, the list is placed in juxtaposition to Step 3 for two reasons. First, the truth is that most of our emotions are produced by our thoughts, however fleeting those thoughts might be. We want members to get used to the fact that insecure thoughts produce unpleasant feelings, even though we do not usually think of this sequence as true. Secondly, by placing 2d next to 3a, members get used to the idea that no matter how negatively they may be feeling or how hurt they may be, a positive step is always available. Thus, people who are afraid to experience their feelings become more honest and aware of them. And those who tend to be too expressive can be gently pushed along to Step 3 by the leader at the appropriate time. For some, the proximity of Step 3 is like a life preserver, and it helps people feel more secure while they are recounting their pain.

*Step 3a*: The leader's task here is to teach and reinforce the tools used by the example-giver to overcome temper. The leader asks, "What tools did you use to keep from exploding angrily," or, "Look through the list and tell us how you kept yourself from sinking into a state of discouragement and self-pity." If the member has difficulty answering, the leader can "prompt" a bit. For example:

> "When you were told that there would be layoffs at work, you said that you were numb with shock, but that you somehow got yourself out of that state and started talking to people about other job possibilities. Look through the list and tell us what tools you intuitively used to get yourself moving. For example, you might have worn the mask of calmness and confidence in order to generate those feelings in yourself."

Sometimes a member will say, "I didn't use any tools. I failed miserably." In such a case, ask the member to think of what tools can be used the next time such an event occurs.

> "You said that whenever your daughter is disobedient, you get angry. Look at the list of tools and see what might be helpful the next time she doesn't do what you want, to help you deal with the conflict in a more constructive manner. Remember, if you're not thinking of yourself as a failure as a parent, you can be assertive without being hostile, and will be able to think more clearly. For example, perhaps you can stop comparing yourself to Mrs. Perfect, who always seems to be in total control. How else can you avoid the feelings of inadequacy which make you so angry?"

*Step 3b*: Ask the member what, if any, positive muscular acts he did to help him divert his attention from a situation over which he had no control, or to solve the problem assertively. If the member says he didn't do anything positive, let him know that even mundane acts can be considered in the category of PMA.

> "When you saw the mess, you controlled your speech muscles and remained silent. That's better than what you used to do."

Do not allow yourself as the leader, or the other group members, to provide answers or solutions for the example-giver during this step. By going through the steps, the example-giver exercises his own "spiritual muscles." He will lose that opportunity if others rush in with their own advice. Wait until the highlighting period to provide encouragement and additional insights.

*Step 4a*: Members are sometimes reluctant to mention their endorsements for fear of seeming proud. The leader should remind them that this step is essential because it increases their faith in their ability to improve further and gives them something positive on which to focus when the next crisis arises.

Usually the member will state that before EMETT, he would have responded more negatively, by withdrawing in fear or self-pity or reacting with hostility. In the rare instance in which the member says that he would not have reacted differently, the leader can ask, "Do you feel that, at least, you were more aware of what you were doing wrong, even though you reacted as you did in the past?" In most cases, the member will reply that, indeed, "Yes, I was aware that I should not be acting like this and that I do have control if I want to exert it. Before EMETT, I thought I had no choice in the matter." The leader should mention with enthusiasm that awareness is always endorsable and is the first step to change.

If a member keeps repeating in example after example that absolutely no progress is being made despite attendance at EMETT meetings, the leader should see this as a sign that the individual may have serious problems and is in need of a more intensive type of therapy than EMETT can provide. The leader should not play therapist. He might mention tactfully to the member after group that EMETT is not for everyone, and that professional guidance might be helpful.

*Step 4b*: Many people regard this as the most critical step in the entire process, for it is here that they realize what they have been doing to keep their temper alive. You can often see the very palpable relief on the member's face as he suddenly realizes:

> "Wow! That's it! I'm taking excessive responsibility for my in-laws' happiness."

"You know, when I drop all my condemnations of myself and those around me and just accept what is, I have such a sense of inner peace."
"Now I see! I'm so wrapped up in my gloomy extrapolations of possible future catastrophes that I'm not able to enjoy the present."
"Oy, what a relief. I see what I'm doing. I'm awfulizing Pesach cleaning so much when, in reality, it is simply extra work, much of which I can actually enjoy if I adopt the right attitude."

Some advanced members prefer to go through these "mental saboteurs" before Step 3a in order to gain insight into their insecure thoughts and relief from temper. Only then do they find that the temper-reducers in Step 3a are truly meaningful. An experienced leader can allow for such flexibility if he and the member so desire.

*Step 4c:* This is optional. It is an additional reinforcer which proves to the member that various *middoth* were, indeed, strengthened or that these *middoth* need to be worked on in further situations of this sort.

If the example is getting overly long (i.e., more than fifteen minutes) the leader should ask the member to identify only two or three items in each category.
If the member does not gain relief after going through these steps, the leader may state that it may take many months, even years, of using EMETT tools in order to scrape away the layers of negative conditioning which have accumulated over the course of a person's lifetime.
If the member seems greatly relieved, on the other hand, it may be appropriate for the leader to state that EMETT is like a "spiritual bath." The member is apt to feel refreshed and strengthened after a meeting. However, just as one physical cleansing does not keep a person permanently clean, so too must EMETT tools be used each and every day in order to keep a person elevated in the midst of the painful situations which everyone must face.

*Highlighting.* Once the example-giver has finished giving his example, he must then be silent and listen to the five-minute "highlighting" period. This is when five or six members make brief comments reinforcing the positive thoughts and/or actions of the example-giver, or add further insights or tools which could have been used in this particular situation. Unless a class member makes a comment which shows that he has totally misunderstood the example, the example-giver just listens during this time, in order to be able to think more objectively about what is being said, and to avoid giving more details about the example. Highlighting consists of one or two sentence phrases, taken from the EMETT manual. These can be of the following:

1.  Further insights and endorsements, using EMETT tools or Torah principles, which were used or could have been used to reduce temper.
    "It is very average to feel humiliated when you can't pay a bill on time."
    "She really did the thing she feared to do most when she spoke up."
    "She should be endorsed for not going for the empty, symbolic victory, but focusing on *shalom bayith* instead."
    "He should endorse himself for giving the benefit of the doubt."
    "She wore a mask while working her temper down and functioning with a lot of discomfort."
    "He controlled his speech, even though he was in hostile temper. That's an example of a true *gibor* — he who 'conquers his passions ' " (*Avoth* 4:1).

2.  If the example-giver used temperamental language, this can be pointed out tactfully. Temperamental language is called "self-sabotage."
    "She said that her daughter's behavior was exceptional. That was sabotage because her behavior was definitely within the normal range."
    "He said that he couldn't help but explode. But the Torah says that we have control over thought, speech, and deed. It's sabotage to think that we can't control ourselves. Better to say, 'I cared not to.' "
    [All this should be done very tactfully so as not to hurt the person's feelings. Before sabotage is pointed out, endorsements should be given — also afterwards.]

3.  Pointing out progress:
    "There's a lot less complaining and dramatizing in this example than he used to do."
    "It was difficult for her to give this example in such a disciplined way. She should really endorse herself."

4.  Additional points during the highlighting period:
    • Members do not talk about their own personal examples except perhaps to say, "I can vouch for the fact that her response was within the normal range, and that her children's behavior was average."
    • Highlighting should be kept to one or two sentences. No philosophizing or intellectualizing.
    • All questions should be jotted down and handled at the end of the meeting.
    • Avoid all communication roadblocks such as: advising, minimizing, moralizing, etc.

5. Members should refer to the example-giver as "he" or "she." This non-confrontational atmosphere has two important purposes. First, if the member is very talkative, then there is a constant temptation to engage in conversation if the member receives direct eye contact. Consequently, the highlighting period gets overly long and the member tends to give more and more details about the example. Second, the member may be very shy, and will feel uncomfortable if the entire group keeps looking at her. In either case, the example-giver will find it much easier to listen to the members' comments about the example if those comments are not directed at her specifically, but rather are directed toward the group leader. In this way, the example-giver can listen attentively and objectively.

6. An EMETT class can easily become a talk session focusing on theoretical discussions and philosophical debates. Do not let this happen. If someone says, "What would you do in such a situation?" say, "Please give a specific example illustrating your question." Do not allow members to debate the best course of action following an example. Get used to saying, "This is outside the scope of an EMETT meeting," or "I will check with Mrs. Adahan or a Rav and get back to you." Four or five examples should be given during each meeting.

*The Leader's Example.* The leader should give an example every two or three weeks to demonstrate that he is an equal member of the group, working on his own character traits. When this occurs, a veteran member should lead the example and the highlighting period.

### IMPORTANT REMINDERS FOR LEADERS TO MENTION

• Don't rush the process of change. It takes time. If you have a lifelong habit of being a complainer or a procrastinator, it won't go away in a week.

• Don't rush people past Step 2 by saying, "It's just a triviality." That is a misuse of EMETT tools. Be compassionate first.

• Keep the method simple. Too much probing and analyzing will defeat the purpose of the example. Do not get into intellectual discussions about the best possible course of action in any given situation. That can take place outside of the class.

### NO PRACTICAL ADVICE DURING EMETT MEETINGS

One thing which members may have difficulty accepting at first is that we do not give practical advice. Nor do we tell people:

"Why didn't you just walk out of there?"

"My goodness. I would have given him a good whack and sent him to bed without supper."

"You should have told him exactly how you felt!"

There are many reasons why we do not give advice. Foremost among these are:

1. The member may feel inferior for not thinking of it himself.
2. He may think that the advice-giver thinks he's stupid for not thinking of it himself.
3. The advice-giver may get angry at the person for not taking his advice.
4. When advice is given, it detracts from the EMETT goal, which is to help the individual develop his own inner resources for dealing with that universal problem. For example, if the example-giver is very sensitive to criticism, telling him "Walk away," or "Speak up for yourself," will make him feel bad. The problem is not in that specific example but rather a general problem of low self-esteem, judgmentalness, and an excessive need for other people's approval. We want to *focus on the member's general response pattern*, not on the specific details of this particular event. Indulging in self-pity or exploding in anger are general responses to frustration which are not tied only to this example.
5. You never know all the background of any example. The person may be discussing a close family member, which requires different tactics than when dealing with a more distant relative or a stranger.
6. Advice will switch the emphasis from uncovering the underlying condemnations and insecure thoughts to the application of temporary solutions which do not uproot the temper behind the problem.

Exceptions:

On the other hand, we might point out a general principle such as, "In such situations, we do have options such as to speak up respectfully, go to a therapist, or seek legal aid." Such comments should be kept general. In other words, simply point out options and alternatives. Also, a member can approach the example-giver after the meeting and say,

"I have a very similar problem. Here's my telephone number. Call me if you like."

"My neighbor had the same problem. Would you like to know how she handled it?"

Let the example-giver take the initiative in accepting the offer. Otherwise, your advice giving may be seen as an attempt to dominate.

## DO NOT MAKE DIAGNOSES OR ANALYSES

EMETT offers a protective and supportive environment. Do not say anything which would make the member feel wrong, sick, or stupid, such as,

"You say you're not angry. But I bet you are seething inside!"
"I know why you can't stand up for yourself. It's because you're such an approval-seeker."
"It's obvious that you're trying to buy their love with money."

### EXCEPTION

If the example-giver has done something totally out of keeping with EMETT principles, this should be pointed out. For example, "It may be common to hit children for minor infractions, but excessive force is totally against EMETT principles."

## EXPRESSING DEEP PAIN IN CLASS

Underlying temper is often deep pain about a significant loss or area of unfulfillment. Since temper can act as a suppressant to such pain, the leader can help members express their feelings when they are part of an example. Sometimes, it is like opening a Pandora's Box: the member starts off with a triviality and suddenly finds himself in tears or engulfed in a strong emotion. The leader must be disciplined about sticking to the four steps, but can spend a few minutes teaching members how to let their feelings rise and fall, and then move on to a place of greater acceptance. These examples are often as follows:

"A good friend is dying of a malignancy. I just can't bear the thought of how much she is suffering."
"We have no children after many years of marriage. This afternoon, all the other mothers in the neighborhood were out with their children. Many were pregnant with their next. I looked out the window and just sobbed. I felt devastated."
"My mother died a few months ago. I miss her terribly. I have trouble doing even ordinary tasks. I often don't want to get out of bed in the morning."

The leader should identify the pain and distinguish it from temper. He might say to the group: "This is not an example of temper, but rather very real pain over a deep loss." To the example-giver he can say, "Take a minute to be with the pain. Keep your mind clear of all thoughts. Simply experience the sadness, the emptiness, the longing....Close your eyes if it helps." To someone who has just lost a close friend or relative, he might say, "Experience the great love you

have for him (or her), combined with the pain of not being able to express it."
After two or three minutes of silence, the member will usually sigh, or the
tears will stop if she has been crying. This is a pause which signals that she is
ready to move on. At this point, the leader can say, "Let's look at Step 3 and
see what tools you can use to help deal with the pain."

If the member seems to be getting more deeply into his grief, even after the
two or three minutes of silence, the leader should tactfully say, "I'm going to
allow you the opportunity to be with your own pain and experience it as
deeply as you want, while we go on to another example." The leader may say,
"As we see, acceptance is a process. It often takes time for us to be at peace
with a loss, to internalize deeply within ourselves that everything Hashem
does has purpose and wisdom. We have to allow the healing process to take
place naturally, over the course of time."

Sometimes, the task of the leader is to help a member get over his temper
so that he can experience the pain beneath it:

> "My father is dying. We've had a very difficult relationship, ever since I
> can remember. I don't want to go into details because of the danger of
> *lashon hara*. I have so much anger and resentment that I can't even go
> and face him."
>
> "There is a close relative who is very cold and critical. I've never
> experienced being loved. This person has made it clear that that's how it
> always will be."

Here the leader can say, "Take a minute or two to be with your pain, the pain
of not having the unconditional acceptance and love of a close family
member, which is something we all want. Keep your mind clear while you
experience the pain of not being able to reach someone, of not being able to
share, of feeling so alone." Once that moment of emotional release has been
achieved, as evidenced by the person's face, or simply allowing a minute or
two to pass, then the leader can say, "In order to help you reach a place of
acceptance of the situation and compassion for the person, look at Step 3 and
mention the tools which can help you let go of your resentment."

As you can see, such examples can be overwhelming, if not handled
skillfully. If you think you lack the skills to handle such situations, remind
members that they will have to stick to trivialities. Don't get in the habit of
having such major examples in group, or you may find that you never hear
trivialities again!

## DEALING WITH SERIOUS MENTAL DISTRESS

Although EMETT is essentially for normal, functioning people, people with
serious mental disturbances have attended EMETT meetings and have found the

disciplines to be of tremendous help. They usually do not let other class members know about their illness. Instead, they focus on their own trivialities and work on becoming average participants. Once such a member wrote the following letter in the hope that it would give encouragement to others who suffer from despair, low self-esteem, and hypersensitivity:

I used to be depressed a lot of the time before I came to EMETT and once was hospitalized. Even though I had managed to come out of my depressions hundreds of times, each time I felt "down," I would think, "This is it. This is the one time that I won't come back up again." I lived with the constant fear of going crazy. When I first came to EMETT, I hated all those trivialities and trite sounding phrases. I was determined to prove that I was really hopeless and that this method, like everything else I had tried, was going to fail. But something pulled me back to class week after week. Almost in spite of myself, I began to practice the disciplines. I put up stickers around the house saying, "Distressing, not dangerous," and "Endorse for effort." Sometimes I had to endorse myself for just brushing my teeth or smiling. On the bathroom mirror, I wrote a note to myself saying, "You're worthwhile even though you're not perfect." I never thought I would believe it. Yet slowly but surely, I noticed changes.

I began to trust my basic strengths to pull me through stressful situations. I knew I had really made progress when, in the middle of a depression, I thought to myself, "It's dark now, but I trust that I will see the light again." I also began to form relationships with very healthy, functioning members from my EMETT class. This was a big step for me. I had been criticized and beaten so often as a child, that I didn't think anyone could ever like, let alone love me. Most important, I began to think securely, recognizing my choice of attitude toward each and every event in my life. This did not take days or weeks. It took months and years of practice. I encourage anyone with similar problems to stick to the EMETT method. Put forth maximum effort and you will see maximum change.

## HEALING THE WOUNDS OF THE PAST

EMETT is not only a method to deal with current distresses and heartaches. It is also a means for healing lingering wounds from the past. One way to do this is to treat others differently from the way we were treated. Positive acts in the present allow past hurts to fade:

My son said he didn't feel well and he didn't want to go to school. My first impulse was to jerk him out of his bed and tell him to stop this nonsense. Instead, I sat down and held him for a few minutes. I told him that I also used to feel that way when I was little. Then I held him. Sure, I wanted him out of the house so I could start my day. But he was my first priority. I felt that by holding him, I was healing the child within me who was so often slapped and ridiculed whenever I didn't do what I was supposed to be doing. In a few minutes, he said that he was ready to go. A couple of weeks later, the same thing occurred. Again, I took time to tune into him. It turned out that he had a slight fever which I would not have noticed if I had been in my usual hurry to get him out of the door.

Another technique can be used when images of past hurts arise in your mind. You can tell yourself over and over that the people involved were doing the best they could, given their level of awareness. You may have to do this thousands of times, but eventually you will find yourself being truly forgiving. You'll know that you have forgiven these people when you no longer feel an emotional "charge" when the memory arises.

Or, you can examine a traumatic event in the light of present knowledge, to see that it wasn't "awful" — it was merely uncomfortable.

Lastly, you can look to the past to uncover messages and fears which now need to be eliminated. Perhaps you became fastidious, stingy, passive, or mean in imitation of people whose love you hoped to gain by modeling yourself after them. Perhaps you are overreacting to certain essentially harmless traits in your children because they remind you of people in the past who were mentally ill or who abused you in some way. Perhaps you assumed that you were unlovable because the people around you were incapable of loving. Only by being aware of these messages can you begin to override the patterns which keep them alive.

When you have a wound, you place a bandage on it. When you are wounded emotionally, especially at a young age, you place a protective barrier around yourself, adopting behavior which is designed to keep people from getting close. You may play the phoney "nice girl," always submissive and available; or the tyrannical bully, pushing people away with criticism and indifference; or keep yourself outside the human community with depression, gloom, and bitterness. We are all at different points along the road to mental health. We all have wounds which can be healed. It is a lifelong journey.

# Appendix A

## Some Frequently Asked Questions about EMETT

1. "Why do I feel worse now, after being in EMETT for three months, than I did when I started?"

This is a common problem. First, you are now noticing habits and character traits which you may not have paid attention to before. Or, you may have thought it was acceptable to feel a great deal of resentment and self-pity or to yell and complain whenever you were upset. Now, you may be feeling more guilty about your behavior. You now recognize that you have responsibility for thought, speech, and deed. You now know that you have a choice in this matter. That leads to the second problem: perfectionism. You see the problem and you want to solve it — this morning, if possible! Some habits can be changed quickly. For example, you can decide that there will be no more name-calling in the house, and put that into practice right away, with yourself, at least. However, making those condemnations mentally will take more time to overcome. Change is often a slow process. Be demanding and at the same time, be gentle. If you don't experience success, you will become discouraged and stop working on yourself. Look for the success experiences.

Also, be aware of the tendency to negate or discount the good. You may display self-control for two or three days (or weeks) and then suddenly do something you regret. You may think, "See, EMETT isn't working." What you have forgotten are all the moments when you successfully used EMETT tools. To overcome this tendency, endorse for being aware of the need for improvement, even if you don't succeed every moment. Then endorse for all your efforts, if not the successes. Finally, endorse for the small gains. They are there!

2. "How long will I have to come to EMETT?"

You can learn the basic tools in two or three months, just as you could learn the basics of an instrument in that time. After that, you can become more expert at applying and refining what you have learned. Many members have been coming to classes for years. They may drop out for a while and then come back for a "refresher course." Others make it a discipline to attend each week, or twice a month.

3. "What can I do about a certain family member who doesn't want me to come to class?"

Very often, this is the case when the class member has been in a subordinate position in the home. The dominant one is afraid that he may not be able to maintain such rigid control. If you have been subjected to constant verbal abuse or other threatening tactics from such an authoritarian person, you need EMETT more than ever to build your self-respect. Remind such a person that EMETT has the *haskamah* (rabbinical approval) of many widely respected rabbis. People whose mental health is basically good are usually enthusiastic about EMETT. If you live with someone whose is not, you might consider the aid of an Orthodox counselor, who can work in conjunction with EMETT to help you avoid the role of victim, and will provide the support and understanding you need in order to be assertive about your right to be treated with respect.

4. "How do I handle people who think that now that I've come to EMETT, I should be perfect?"

Be empathetic: "I know I'm sometimes difficult to live with." Reassure them: "I am working on myself. You may not see it, but I do have better control." Challenge their beliefs about perfection: "Only God is perfect. I'm a human being. I deserve respect even if I'm not perfect. No one can practice EMETT 100% of the time. That is unrealistic. I'm striving for excellence, not perfection." If you do something which you regret, admit it. You might say, if true, "Look, I wanted to yell a lot longer and say a lot more, but I held myself back." Or, "I might have *schlepped* this resentment around for weeks. This time, it just lasted a few minutes."

5. "How can I get my family members to use EMETT, when they can't or won't come to classes?"

The best way is start using the terminology in a very natural way, when referring to yourself and your own reactions to events:

"When you made that mistake, I thought of the total view, which is very positive, and that kept me from speaking angrily."
"I angered myself just now by thinking insecure thoughts, but then I remembered to give the benefit of the doubt. I'm sure he didn't do it

*davka."*

"There's no right or wrong here. So let's solve the problem without any excessive emotionalism."

"Just because I didn't give you what you wanted, doesn't mean I don't love you. That's an insecure thought which you should check out before you jump to conclusions. Feelings don't aways reflect objective facts."

"I'm feeling a little down right now, but I'll wear the mask and go. On a scale of 0 to 10, this is only a 'three.' "

In addition, help family members get in touch with their insecure thoughts when they are upset. Try to do an example a day (a week?) with your husband or teenager.

6. "Aren't my problems too severe for EMETT?"

EMETT does not take the place of therapy. We encourage the latter, when necessary. Even so, EMETT principles are necessary for character development. That is something you can use, no matter what your problems are. True, it's more difficult to apply EMETT when you are under severe stress. However, you can find minor aspects of your problems on which to practice non-judgmentalness, forgiveness, assertiveness, and endorsements.

7. "How do I handle the guilt I feel for not having come to EMETT sooner? I feel that I've messed my kids up by my behavior."

Take the secure thought that your children will have EMETT classes to attend when they are older. Accept the *hashgachah pratith* of coming to EMETT at this time in your life. It was meant to happen now. If your children are still at home, they will see you working on your manners and *middoth* in order to overcome bad habits. That is an invaluable lesson for them. If you never had good communication with them, it will take time to build a foundation of trust. Don't try to change too fast, or you will confuse them and discourage yourself.

8. "How can I avoid feeling guilty for not being happy?"

It is impossible to always be completely happy. You can, even in the midst of pain, keep a part of yourself in a state of quiet joy, because of your faith in Hashem. But no one can maintain the same emotional state continuously. That would not be normal. We all have ups and downs. If you find yourself chronically depressed or resentful, you might need to make some major changes. Find out what needs to be done. If you generally feel good about yourself and life, don't get overly upset about the times when you don't feel that way. However, do use those times to examine your unrealistic demands and expectations of yourself, life, and people.

# Appendix B

# A Summary
# of Major Temper Reducers

How shall a man train himself in these dispositions [patience, kindness, and courage, etc.] so that they shall become ingrained? Let him practice again and again the actions prompted by these dispositions...and repeat them continually until they become easy and are no longer irksome to him, and so [they] will become a fixed part of his character.

*(Hilchoth Dei'oth, 1:7)*

## TEMPER

Take away the condemnations of yourself and others, and temper will fade.

Measure the discomfort on a scale of 0 to 10.

Look at the situation later, when you have calmed down, since temper blocks insight, love, and creativity.

Temper is a harmful substitute for constructive action. It makes you think you're doing something when you're not.

You don't have a choice over your initial response — only whether to work it up or down.

People, places, and things don't put you into temper. You do with your attitude toward them.

## FEELINGS

Report your feelings without temper or drama.

Feelings may not be based on objective facts. Assumptions are not facts.

It's not so much how you feel, but how you function that is most important.

Accept the feelings. Let them rise and fall. But challenge the temper behind them.

Having undesirable feelings doesn't make you a bad person.

Be solution-oriented, not emotion-centered.

## SECURE, REALISTIC THINKING

You can only have one thought at a time. Make it a secure, strengthening one.

Lower your standards to a realistic level, so that your performance can rise.

Don't look for perfection. It sets you up for certain failure. Be realistic, not romantic.

You cannot think rationally unless you avoid exaggeration, extrapolation, emergency-izing, excessive responsibility, excessive emotionalism, exceptionality, and unrealistic expectations.

Don't waste time fretting about situations over which you have absolutely no control.

## HUMILITY

"It is a mark of humility to be happy with what we have" (*Duties of the Heart*, p. 117, 6:10).

To know that you don't know is the greatest wisdom.

Avoid the attitude of inferiority or superiority. Both are a sign of arrogance.

"There is no man so wholly righteous on earth that he [always] does good and never sins " (*Koheleth* 7:20).

## FEAR AND ANXIETY

Identify your fear. Is the danger real or imaginary?

Calmness generates calmness. Do something — anything — that demonstrates control, and you will begin to feel more relaxed.

Objectivity terminates panic. Use the "mental helicopter," and then imagine yourself bearing the discomfort of the situation.

Make a firm decision and stick to it. Doubt is agony.

Keep doing positive muscular acts. Endorse for each one. Eventually, the muscles will teach the brain that there is no danger. Keep functioning and keep thoughts secure, even if you are anxious. You create anxiety with fearful predictions. "Minds are shaped by deeds" (*Sefer Hachinuch*, precept 16).

## WORRY

Worry is a bad habit. You can break it with secure thoughts, positive action, and by cultivating a spirit of gratefulness for all that you have in the present.

Ask yourself, "Are my present thoughts strengthening or weakening me?"

## FIRST AID FOR PANIC OR LOWERED FEELINGS

"This is distressing, not dangerous."

"Many people suffer from this. I can wait for it to pass. The situation is temporary. It is all within the normal range."

"I endorse for all my efforts, for my small victories in continuing to function, for my secure thoughts, for being patient, pleasant, and trusting in the midst of pain."

"I drop condemnations of myself and others for the sake of my mental health."

## JUDGMENTS

Drop judgments for the sake of inner peace. Remove the *davka*.

"Judge not thy fellowman until thou art come unto his place " (*Avoth* 2:5).

"Whoever forgives is forgiven in return " (Rabbi Moses of Couçy, 13th century).

Tell yourself, "They are doing the best they can with the tools they have."

Ask yourself, "Where is this thought getting me? Is it helping me or anyone else to have these judgments?"

## ANGER

"The whole world exists only in the merit of he who bridles his mouth during a quarrel " (*Chulin* 89a).

"Do not appease thy fellow in the hour of his anger " (*Avoth* 4:18).

"A soft answer turns away wrath " (*Mishley* 15:1).

Wear the mask of politeness and make the insincere, forced gesture to arouse a sincere gesture of compassion and love.

Be assertive, not aggressive.

Sandwich rebuke between love. "Good is open rebuke out of hidden love " (*Mishley* 27:5).

If you expect others to make you happy, you'll always be angry. Take responsibility for your own happiness.

Anger is designed to protect you from harm, and to get you to make constructive changes in your attitude or your life. Otherwise, it's useless.

"Do not despise any man " (*Avoth* 4:3).

## OUTER ENVIRONMENT

Everything outside of thought, speech, and action is outer environment (including many physical sensations and responses) and, therefore, not under our full control.

You can't change people. You can only model what you think is correct behavior.

During quiet moments, imagine yourself *not* handling your outer environment in a constructive manner. Imagine yourself angry, discouraged, confused, etc. Then imagine yourself relaxed, assertive, or confident in the same situation.

The past and future are outer environment. Do not review the past with guilt and blame or preview the future with anxiety.

## DISCOMFORT

Awfulizing is the source of most temper, especially the habit of awfulizing discomfort or telling yourself, "It's awful not to get what I want in life."

Tell yourself, "It's distressing, not dangerous. I can work up my willingness to bear this discomfort."

Everyone functions with some discomfort. The trick is not to attach anxiety-producing thoughts to the discomfort.

Comfort is a want, not a need. Comfort is not a supreme value, nor a sign of success in life.

Be assertive about the discomforts you can avoid, and divert attention from what you can't.

## TRIVIALITIES

"A man should separate himself from anything which is not essential " (*The Path of the Just*, p. 191 ).

The word "triviality" implies that the event is temporary, bearable, and not significant in comparison to our ultimate goals in life. Therefore, do not put your emotional energy into trivialities. Save it for priorities.

Money is a triviality in comparison to your mental health.

Change your time perspective when you're upset about a triviality. Think about how you'll feel toward the event twenty years from now.

## SELF-ESTEEM

Every act of self-discipline promotes self-respect. "To restrain oneself is to strengthen oneself" (see Rashi, *Bereishith* 43:31).

Be self-led, not symptom-led. That means doing what's right and healthy even if you don't feel like it. Don't get into temper over feelings of inadequacy. We all feel that way at times.

Don't let other people's judgments determine your worth.

"Who is mighty? He who subdues his passions " (*Avoth* 4:1).

We have worth even though we are not perfect, for "Man is created in the image of God" (*Bereishith* 1:27).

Build self-esteem by doing the difficult, and by doing the thing you most fear to do.

If you're busy endorsing, you can't be blaming or shaming.

Feelings of shame are likely to make you angry at others.

Givers tend to be happy people. That's what you need most to make you feel good.

## CHILDREN

Your children's judgments, moods, and behavior do not determine your worth.

You're not a failure — just inexperienced. All parents feel inadequate at times.

Character training is a long-range goal. It's not complete when children are three or four.

Model the behavior you want your children to have.

Never discipline out of anger. Discipline the child with the goal in mind that he become self-disciplined. That means you must be self-controlled.

Don't try to make children continuously happy. From their point of view, we can never do enough. Instead, focus on *middoth* — yours and theirs. In doing so, they will learn that Torah behavior makes them happy.

Children are natural antagonists of adult goals. That's how they establish a sense of independent identity. Don't be angry at them for doing so. Encourage mastery of themselves and their environment. But remember, a child cannot be truly independent until his dependency needs have been satisfied.

Like all discomforts, the discomfort of raising children should be borne with patience, courage, creativity, and humility.

Don't compete with or compare to other parents.

Focus on the total view, not the day-to-day conflicts and crises.

Love yourself and your family members as they are and you and they will become all you are capable of being.

# Bibliography

## HEBREW

*Aley Shur*, Bais Yaakov, 1968.

Attar, Rabbi Chaim ben Moshe, *Or Ha-chaim*, Biblical commentator, 1696-1743.

Bloch, Rabbi Yosef Leib, *Shi'urey Da'ath*, Cleveland, Telshe Yeshiva, 1964.

Bromberg, Rabbi A.I., *Mi-gedoley Ha-Torah Ve-ha-chasiduth*, Jerusalem, 1954.

Bruk, Rabbi Ben-Zion, *Hegyoney Mussar*, Jerusalem, 1969.

Chasman, Rabbi Yehudah Leib, *Or Yahaeil*, Jerusalem, 1960.

*Chasidim Misaprim*, 3rd Edition, Hotzaath Mosad Harim Levin, Jerusalem, 1979.

*Chayei Ha-mussar*, Hotzaoth Chochmah U-mussar, Bnai Brak, 1961.

Halevi, Rabbi Aharon, *Sefer Ha-chinuch*, New York, Century Press, 1962.

Karelitz, Rabbi Avraham Yeshayahu, *Chazon Ish, Emunah U-bitachon*, Jerusalem, 1954.

Klainman, Rabbi M.S., *Or Yesharim*, Pietrokov, 1924.

Levovitz, Rabbi Yeruchem, *Da'ath Chochmah U-mussar*, New York 1969.

Lipson, Rabbi M., *Midor Dor*, 1929.

Lopian, Rabbi Eliyahu, *Lev Eliyahu*, Jerusalem 1972.

Munk, Rabbi Meir, *Schar Ve-hanashah Be-chinuch*, Bnai Brak, 1982.

*Orach Chaim*, E. Romm, Vilna, 1911.

Rambam, Rabbi Moshe Ben Maimon, *Mishneh Torah*, Jerusalem, 1974.

Ramban, Rabbi Moshe ben Nachman, *Igereth Ha-Ramban*, 13th century.

Rokotz, Rabbi Yoetz Kayam Kaddish, *Siach Sarfey Kodesh*, Lodz, 1929.

Rosenstein, Rabbi Moshe, *Ahavath Meshorim*, New York, 1958.

Schwab, Rabbi Moshe, *Me-archey Leiv*, Bnai Brak, 1981.

Surasky, Rabbi Aharon, *Marbitzey Torah U-mussar*, Israel, 1976.

Yaakov Yosef of Polonoye, Rabbi, *Ben Porath Yosef*, Pietrokov, 1884.

Yona, Rabbenu, *Sha'arey 'Avodah*, Binyomin Yehoshua Silber, Bnai Brak, 1970.

Zalman of Liadi, Rabbi Schneur, *Likutey Amarim — Tanya*, London, Soncino Press, 1973.

## ENGLISH

Bachya, ibn Paquda, *Duties of the Heart,* translated by Moses Hyamson, Jerusalem-New York, Feldheim Publishers, 1970.

Dessler, Eliyahu E., *Strive for Truth!*, translated by Aryeh Carmell, Jerusalem-New York, Feldheim Publishers, 1978.

Hilsenrad, Zalman Aryeh, *My Soul Thirsts*, Jerusalem-New York, Feldheim Publishers, 1976.

Hirsch, Samson Raphael, *Horeb*, translated by Dayan I. Grunfeld, New York-London, Soncino Press, 1981 (4th ed.)

Kahan, Yisroel Meir, *Ahavath Chesed*, by the Chafetz Chaim, translated by Leonard Oschry, Jerusalem-New York, Feldheim Publishers, 1976.

Kitov, Eliyahu, *The Book of Our Heritage*, translated by Nathan Bulman, Jerusalem-New York, Feldheim Publishers, 1973.

Kitov, Eliyahu, *The Jew and His Home*, translated by Nathan Bulman, New York, Shengold Publishers, 1963.

*Kuntres Ahavath Yisrael*, New York, Kehot Publication Society, 1977.

Luzzatto, Moshe Chaim, *The Path of the Just*, translated by Shraga Silverstein, Jerusalem-New York, Feldheim Publishers, 1966.

*Orchot Tzadikkim*, anonymous 14th century author, English edition, Jerusalem-New York, Feldheim Publishers, 1974.

Pliskin, Zelig, *Gateway to Happiness*, New York, Aish HaTorah Publications, 1983.

Pliskin, Zelig, *Guard Your Tongue*, Jerusalem, Aish HaTorah Publications, 1975.

Pliskin, Zelig, *Love Your Neighbor*, New York, Aish HaTorah Publications, 1977.

Rambam, Moshe Ben Maimon, *The Book of Knowledge*, translated by Moses Hyamson, Jerusalem-New York, Feldheim Publishers, 1974.

Rambam, Moshe Ben Maimon, *Guide to the Perplexed*, New York, Dover Press, 1956.

Singer, Yaakov and Chaim David Ackerman, translators and annotators of *The Vilna Gaon Views Life, Even Shleimah, The Classic Collection of the Gaon of Vilna's Wisdom*, Jerusalem, 1974.

*Webster's New Collegiate Dictionary*, New Jersey, Prentice Hall Inc., 1973.

# Glossary

The terms that follow are defined as they are used in this book.

*agmath nefesh*: pain, heartache
*akshan*: stubborn person
*aliyah*: move to Israel to live
*avodah*: spiritual work
*Avoth*: *Ethics of our Forefathers*
*baal teshuvah*: an observant Jew who was previously non-observant of Torah
  commandments
*Bamidbar*: *Numbers*
*baruch Hashem*: thank God
*Beith Hamikdash Hakatan*: miniature Holy Temple
*Bereishith*: *Genesis*
*bitachon*: faith, trust
*brachah*: blessing
*chesed*: compassion
*chov*: to judge unfavorably
*chuppah*: wedding canopy
*davka*: intentionally
*Devarim*: *Deuteronomy*
*emunah*: belief
*gemarah*: explanation and elaboration of Mishnah
*gibor*: hero
*goral*: fate
*hachnasath orchim*: welcoming guests into one's home
*halachah*: Jewish law
*Hashem*: God
*hashgachah pratith*: personal supervision by God
*hashkafah*: proper Torah attitude
*hashlamah:*: feeling at peace
*haskamah*: rabbinical approval
*hester panim*: God's apparent non-involvement in an event
*hishtadluth*: efforts to accomplish something

*kaparah*: atonement

*kavod*: respect

*kedushah*: holiness

*kibbud av*: honoring one's father

*kiddush*: a special grace before Shabbath meals, usually said over a full cup of wine or grape juice

*kipah*: skullcap

*klutz*: clumsy person

*Koheleth*: *Ecclesiastes*

*kvetch*: a complainer

*lashon hara*: harmful talk about a person

*le-chaf zechuth*: to give someone the benefit of the doubt

*madreigah*: spiritual level

*mashlim*: at peace

*mechilah*: forgiveness

*middah/middoth*: desirable Torah character trait/s

*Mishley*: *Proverbs*

*mishnayoth*: the written Oral Law

*mitzvah/mitzvoth*: Torah commandments

*Modeh Ani*: prayer of thanks to God, recited upon arising in the morning

*motzaey Shabbath*: night after Sabbath ends

*nisayon*: a trying, but educational experience

*olam habah*: the afterworld

PMA: positive muscular act

*ratzon Hashem*: God's will

*reshaim*: evildoers

*shalom bayith*: harmonious home life

*Shemoneh Esreh*: eighteen blessings which constitute the main part of the prayers

*Shemoth*: *Exodus*

*shidduch*: date arranged by a matchmaker

*shiur*: class on Torah-related subject

*shleimuth*: moral perfection

*shmattah*: rag

*siddur*: prayerbook

*simchah*: religious celebration

*sinath chinam:* baseless hatred between people

*Tehillim*: *Psalms*

*teshuvah*: repentance for sins

*tikun*: correction

*timtum ha-lev*: hardening of the heart

*tzaddik/im*: righteous man/men
*tzeddakah*: charity
*Vayikra*: *Leviticus*
*Yesha'yahu*: *Isaiah*
*yetzer hara*: evil inclination
*yirah*: awe
*zechuth*: favorable

# Index

*personal notes and insights*

*personal notes and insights*

*personal notes and insights*

*personal notes and insights*

*personal notes and insights*

*personal notes and insights*

*personal notes and insights*

*personal notes and insights*

*personal notes and insights*

*personal notes and insights*